CW01653042

Brazil through Irish Eyes

a travelogue based on letters home

Catherine McClintock

Catherine McClintock

Copyright © 2011 Catherine McClintock
Cover Design © 2011 by Janet Angelo of IndieGo ePublishing LLC

Published by IndieGo ePublishing LLC in the United States of America. All rights reserved. No part of this book may be used or reproduced in any manner whatsoever without written permission of the publisher or the copyright owner except in the case of brief quotations in articles or reviews.

www.indiego-epublishing.com

Dedication

In loving memory of my mother, to whom all the letters were written about our daily life and travels throughout Brazil. These brought her much joy and delight. May she forever rest in peace.

Table of Contents

Page
No.
1 ... Prologue
5 ... We've got here!
13 ... Our Home in Brazil
17 ... Exploring Our Surroundings
Fazenda Santa Maria - Brotas - Soccorro
27 ... Our First Christmas and New Year in Brazil
Bara Bonita - Foz do Iguaçu - Hotel Bourbon das Cataratas - River Paraná - Parques das Aves
35 ... São Paulo, Brasilia and Guaruja
Campinas - Holambra - São Paulo Zoo - Museo Paulista - Cidade Universitária - Cathedral Brasilia - Guaruja Beach
47 ... Carnaval and Easter
Paixão do Cristo at Parque Engenho
51 ... Daily Life in Piracicaba
61 ... Rio de Janeiro
Cristo Redentor (Christ the Redeemer statue) - Prainha Beach Petropolis - Pão de Açúcar (Sugar Loaf) - Copacabana Beach - Barra Shopping
67 ... World Cup Fever!
71 ... P. E. T. A. R. - Parque Estadual Turistico do Alto Ribeira
Apiai - Caverna Santana - Caverna do Diabo near Eldorado - Piedade
76 ... June brings Festa Juninha
79 ... Springtime in September
87 ... Our First Brazilian style party - on Election Day!
89 ... Weekend at Poços de Caldas
Thermal Baths - Palace Hotel
92 ... Weekend at Caraça
Santuário do Caraça in Minas Gerais
102 ... The Amazon!
Natal - Rifoles Praia Hotel - Opera House, Manaus - meeting of the waters at the Rio Negro and Rio Solimoes - Ariau Jungle Towers Hotel

123 ... Passeio Ecologico
125 ... São Paulo, a Beach Trip and the Museums of Rio
Snorkelling at Anchieta - Museum of the Republic - Jardim Botânico do Rio de Janeiro - The Museo do Indio
132 ... Sueli's Sitio
136 ... Tropical Bounty
Penedo in Rio State - a calango andando - coffee and pinga production
149 ... Balloon Competition and a Calango Andando
154 ... Adventures in Ecotourism – Bonito and Pantanal
Bonito – Grotto Azul - Estancia Mimosa - Rio da Prata - Olho da agua - Buraco das Araras
Pantanal – Refugio da Ilha - River Salobra
165 ... A Nature Walk and an Air Show
169 ... Holambra and a Wedding
173 ... Curitiba and a Trip on its Railway
Botanic Gardens - Opera Arame - Parque Tanga - Curitiba-Paranagua Railway
180 ... Family News and Updates
182 ... Fernando de Noronha
Dolphin Bay - The TAMAR/IBAMA Centre
200 ... The River Paranense
202 ... Rio and the Carnaval Parade of Champions
208 ... Brazilian Living
216 ... A Trip to Minas Gerais
São João Del Rei – Tiradentes - Resende Costa – Congonhas – Mariana - Ouro Preto
223 ... July and the Festa do Divino
228 ... Our First Balloon Trip!
236 ... Discovering Peru
Lima: Museu de Ouro - Parque de Amor; *Machu Picchu:* Cusco - Aguas Calientes; *Lake Titicaca:* Puno - Hotel Sonesta Posada del Inca – Juliaca; *Nazca Lines*
260 ... Our Life in Brazil Comes to a Close
264 ... Epilogue

Brazil through Irish Eyes

Prologue

In October 2000, my husband, Alan, was summoned to the boss's office. After the usual polite interchange, he was asked, "How would you like an assignment abroad? It would be for about two years."

"Where?" Alan asked trying to maintain a calm demeanour, not wanting to give away the fact that his mind was already racing with the exciting adventures that living abroad would mean.

"Brazil or China."

The thought that flashed through Alan's mind was that he at least should appear to think about the proposal instead of immediately jumping at the opportunity, so his response was, "I'll go home and talk it over with my wife," knowing that I would jump at the chance too.

I got quite excited about the idea of China, being such a very different culture from anything we had ever known, to the extent that I bought some maps. It was not to be. Brazil was selected. I don't know by whom, but the decision was fine by us as it still meant living abroad. We didn't know much about Brazil, but it would be an exciting challenge: the Amazon ... coffee ... and rainforests!

We would be going to a town called Piracicaba.

"Pira ...what?" I exclaimed.

"Pi-ra-ci-ca-ba," my husband enunciated, then he told me that it was located about two hours' drive inland from São Paulo. Just knowing that we would be a few hours from São Paulo seemed a bit daunting, as the reports one hears of that city are never good - shanty towns, drug problems, murders, kidnappings - but we reminded ourselves that we would be far enough from all that to feel safe.

The company Alan worked for, which was owned by Caterpillar, made generators and wanted to set up a production line in Brazil. There was an existing Caterpillar plant, which made 'big machines' in Piracicaba, with plenty of space to allow a generator production facility to set up in a corner.

It was all happening at the right time for us. Alan was having a difficult time at work. I was trying to recover from chronic fatigue, and our daughter Sarah (aged seven at the time) was bored at school. A complete change would be good for all of us, so the wheels were set in motion for us to move to Brazil.

We were told that visas should take about six months to process. That would take us to May 2001, so we settled on July 2001 as the time to depart as that would give Sarah time to finish the school year, and moving in July would give her time to get acclimatised before starting school in Brazil. Meanwhile, we began taking Portuguese lessons (the language of Brazil) with a Portuguese postgraduate student from the local university.

Alan went out to Brazil for a week in January to see what he was letting himself in for. Most International Service Employees (foreigners like us), we were told, opted to live in secure condominiums (we weren't sure what that meant) in Campinas, a large town of about two million people some forty-five minutes from the Caterpillar plant. There was an American school, which we were told would be great for Sarah, as the teaching was in English, though Portuguese was spoken in the playground, as many of the pupils were Brazilian. There was also a large expat community, as there were a lot of foreign companies based in Campinas.

We decided we wanted to live in Piracicaba so Alan would only have a five-minute commute to work (he hates commuting); furthermore, we wanted to live among Brazilians and have Sarah attend a Brazilian school. Our reasoning was, why go all the way to Brazil to live amongst Americans, Scandinavians, French, Germans, when we already had that experience living in Europe? We wanted to have the complete experience of living like Brazilians.

During Alan's visit, he was shown a number of houses and apartments, and was taken to several schools and met all sorts of people. He came back with glowing reports about the place. In May, the two of us went to choose somewhere to live and a good school for Sarah. Our heads were reeling by the end of the week from having looked at so many places, but we finally settled on an apartment and chose a school we felt would be right for Sarah. Apparently, of all the I.S.E. families coming to the Piracicaba factory, we were the first to send our child to a local school.

Alan returned with a photo of our soon-to-be hometown, and it looked beautiful, intriguing and so very different from Ireland – just what we needed:

Once back home in the UK we just had to wait for our visas. July came and went, and still no visas. Our house was more or less packed up, and the tenants were ready to move in whenever we moved out. We had given 23rd August as the date for them to move in, allowing us some contingency if the visas were late coming through.

However, 23rd August arrived and still no visas. We moved in with the neighbours for a few days and then to my parents' house. We didn't know how long this arrangement would be in place. August became September, and Sarah went back to school. I had to retrieve her school uniform from the family I had given it to as a spare.

On the 11th September, Alan phoned from work and said, 'Go and turn the television on and watch the news.' I did, and there, unfolding as we watched in disbelief, were the horrific events taking place at the World Trade Center in New York City. Then came all the restrictions on flying, and we wondered if we would get to Brazil after all.

Monday, 24th September, our visas finally arrived, and Wednesday the 26th we were on the plane to Brazil. Heathrow airport was so quiet it was eerie. The flight was fairly empty too, but at last we were on our way to – well, we didn't know what, but it had to be good!

We've got here!

Sitting on my balcony - temperature a balmy 27°C - with a breeze and a fridge full of cooled drinks ... ah, yes, we made the right decision to move here! We are still in the hotel, which has its pluses and minuses. I don't have to think about buying food, but it is one of those hotels that doesn't provide lunch and dinner, so you have to go out foraging. They do offer a small selection of food in the evening, but it is not great. Breakfasts however, *are* delicious: there is an array of fresh pineapple, mango, papaya, guava, apples, oranges and grapes; a generous assortment of freshly squeezed fruit juices, including watermelon, orange, mango, papaya and orange and even pineapple and mint. All this is accompanied by cheese, ham, salami, bread rolls (though more brittle than we are used to) and various types of sweetish 'breads' served with lots of jams. Just when you think you're stuffed to the gills you realise there are various tiny cakes (occasionally crème caramel), not to mention cereal, toast, scrambled egg with ham or bacon mixed in, and you can even have frankfurters in tomato sauce if that's your preferred breakfast! Everything is self-service, so we start the day well.

Sarah has settled well into her school and is being spoiled rotten at present. The relevant person in Caterpillar had phoned the school to say we had arrived, and I assumed we would take her in on Monday (which would be Oct 1st) since we had arrived on Thursday.

Instead, we were told, "Bring her in on Friday. School starts at 12.45."

I assumed it was just to meet her teacher(s). Not one bit of it! They gave her a t-shirt (school uniform) and whisked her away to her classroom because everyone was longing to meet her.

"Come back at four o'clock," I was told, and that was that! I thought we might be picking up a weepy heap at four o'clock, but no - she was perfectly happy.

I think the school had set just the right tone by greeting Sarah with this colourful sign of welcome:

She doesn't seem in the least bit worried that she can't speak or understand much of the language yet. At seven years old, the brain is still like a sponge I guess, absorbing everything, and not cluttered with the distractions that occupy an adult's brain. She has Portuguese lessons twice a week. The first one was today at 8.30 – 10.30 a.m. Teacher says she is very smart! The school day for her starts at 12.45 and goes on 'til 5.45, so it will definitely be a case of 'Mum's taxi' today. I took her to school for 8.30, picked her up at 10.30, back again at 12.45 and so on.

It takes five to ten minutes by car depending on traffic. I've just about got the hang of changing gear with my right hand, but I still automatically reach for the seat belt on the wrong side. The central area of town is more or less laid out in a grid system, with most streets one way, alternating each block, but there are exceptions. I haven't worked out the parking system yet. There is something called *zona azul*, which involves obtaining some sort of ticket from the surrounding shops. Otherwise, I think you take potluck, and there may be someone sitting on the pavement who will expect to be paid for minding your car (usually one to two reais, which is 30 – 60p). At present, I am happy to use the hotel car park and explore from there. It is close enough to the town centre.

There is a nicely paved walk alongside the river called Parque Mirantes. It is not very long, but it starts beside a posh restaurant that overlooks the waterfalls. There are lots of big trees with a wonderful variety of foliage, and huge rubber trees with vast trunks and roots coming down everywhere. We came across a whole line of what appeared to be mobile flower petals and leaves; they were being carried along by ants! We also saw lots of long legged white egrets standing on rocks amongst the waterfalls, presumably waiting for lunch.

A bit further down the river is a sugar mill no longer in use. It is now called the Parque Engenho. It looks like nothing more than a number of old red brick buildings in varying states of disrepair, but is apparently safe. There seemed to be no attempt at repair. Maybe buildings don't decay as quickly in this climate. Apparently, it is a venue for all sorts of exhibitions and festivals.

We had a massive thunderstorm the other night, with lots of lightning and insufficient thunder to back it up! Now I know where all those spectacular photos of lightning come from. You'd only have to hang about for twenty minutes here to get some good shots. And there was plenty of rain to go with it; torrential downpour is putting it mildly! The river here is about 200 feet wide, and I would guess that the level rose about three feet with all that rain. Three days later it was still swollen.

We need to get tree/bird/flower identification books. There are banana trees with pink flowers, mango trees with mangoes hanging from long stems, avocado trees, hibiscus with pink flowers, poinsettia trees with the coloured leaves at the end of the stems and little foliage anywhere else. There are lots of flowers on the trees; in fact, it is mostly trees that are flowering. I have to remind myself that it is spring here (in as much as there are seasons here at all), which is hard to imagine considering that it's October, but then again, we're in the southern hemisphere.

The temperature so far has ranged from 34° C down to 17° C one night. Bruno (a French chap who works in Caterpillar and lives with his family on the top floor of the apartment block where our flat is) recommends that come the hot months, it is not worth trying to do anything in the middle of the day except stay inside or in the swimming pool. We will have our air-conditioned flat by then. There is air conditioning in our hotel room, but it is very noisy (and so is the traffic outside). But one gets used to it. I don't know when we will move into our flat. At present, it contains a freezer and a microwave. Before moving into our flat we will need beds (or at least mattresses), a cooker, a fridge, pans and so on. We can 'camp' for a while, but the difficulty lies in finding the time to do this.

Alan leaves for work about 7.30 a.m. Sarah finishes school at 5.45. Shops tend to be open late, but at present we still have to go out for food, though I asked for a microwave in our hotel room so we can heat things there (the room should have a microwave anyway, I think). There is a small swimming pool on the roof of the hotel, which is very pleasant, though we haven't used it much. It is great for a bit of wallowing and cooling down!

We went exploring in the car one afternoon, to the south of Piracicaba. The landscape is beautiful, with rolling green countryside punctuated by gashes of red soil. Whatever you see that is green and growing in farmland is almost entirely sugar cane in all stages of maturity, from just planted to just harvested. It is a quick growing crop, with two and sometimes even three crops planted and harvested each year.

They burn it before harvesting, so the air seems permanently full of charred sugar cane foliage. (I exaggerate. It happens several times a week, but the general impression becomes one of never ending black snow falling from the sky! Certainly, the swimming pool on the roof has lots of black bits in the bottom.) It is burnt to get rid of pests and to remove excess foliage, which facilitates cutting. It is cut by hand for the most part, using very sharp machetes. The workers are bussed in, and by the time they have finished they are black from head to toe because of the soot left from the burning.

Gradually however, the sugar cane farmers are changing over to mechanised harvesting, though that will be a blow to the cane cutters who will lose their jobs. The move is partly because of the hazardous nature of the work (numerous cutters have been seriously maimed over the years, working with the lethally sharp machetes), but also to reduce the carbon footprint of the industry. Mechanised harvesting does not require the cane to be burnt prior to cutting. This will also mean an end to the constant 'black snow' and less air pollution, which will be greatly welcomed by those with respiratory problems exacerbated by this process.

One of our first experiences in Brazil was to taste some sugar cane juice. They make a drink by squeezing several lengths of sugar cane and flavouring it with lime, pineapple and sometimes passion fruit. Several two-to-three-foot lengths of cane are passed through two revolving 'toothed' wheels, three or four times, with the last pass incorporating the flavouring fruit. The resulting juice strains into a jug filled with ice. The vendor then pours it into plastic cups. It is very refreshing and quite sweet. I found the lime flavoured one very nice, but the pineapple was too sweet. It has to be drunk almost immediately because it starts to go bitter fairly quickly. We bought the drink from a street vendor, who had set up shop with his portable press at a second hand car market! Every Sunday, this market is filled with cars of all ages; we saw one car that was thirty-four years old. There is hardly a speck of rust anywhere on them. What a difference climate makes (no salt on the roads in winter due to no snow).

The countryside is very sparsely populated, since most of the population live in villages and small towns. The road we were on was paved, though many of the smaller ones aren't. We met about two vehicles in a 20 to 30-kilometre stretch, and people sightings are just as rare; again, there's practically nobody anywhere except in the villages.

We saw coffee being grown, though very little. All I can say from what we have seen so far (which isn't much) is that given the proportion of coffee plants to sugar cane, the Brazilians must like extremely sweet coffee!

And lastly, we saw some cows – a very interesting variety with a shoulder hump and floppy ears. These cows are a breed called 'Nelore', and apparently they are descendants of the Indian Ongle breed. According to records, the first pair arrived in Brazil in 1868, with more brought over in later years. They can survive in much more rigorous conditions than other breeds; are resistant to all sorts of tropical hazards such as heat and insects; and are generally better suited to Brazilian conditions than European breeds.

Apparently, there was a massive increase in cattle in Brazil in the last 50 years, increasing from some 55 million in 1965 to about 160 million in 1995, with two thirds of them being these Nelore cows. Certainly, there are a lot of them about.

Humpy cow – or rather, a bull

Slightly further east, the hills are a bit more dramatic and the countryside more picturesque. We were taken to a small town one weekend, which specialises mainly in ceramics: pots, plates, cups – the lot, anything from chunky ceramic to fine porcelain and all stages in between. There must have been at least twenty shops of that sort and we didn't find anything we liked! Well, that is not entirely true. For some reason (which we couldn't understand because our Portuguese wasn't up to it), they were reluctant to sell us what we wanted but offered an almost identical substitute which was not as nice, so we came away empty handed. You can buy wind chimes made from agate slices for about £3.

We start Portuguese lessons today. We met our teacher last week, and I think she will be very good. The school she works with not only teaches languages, but they offer a backup service to the likes of us foreigners in case we get stuck trying to do something and can't cope because of the language: we simply call them and they will come to the rescue. Our teacher, Teresa, will go around a supermarket with us and explain some of the items available for purchase. She will also explain Brazilian customs and etiquette, and generally help us to find our feet here. The director of the language school has lived abroad (United States, I think) so he knows what it is like. Naturally, he speaks very good English.

One thing we find a bit daunting at present, but will no doubt welcome later on, is the service here. The minute you walk into a shop, you are pounced upon by shop assistants. I have managed to sort out a phrase along the lines of 'just looking', which seems to have the desired effect. It has its uses, though - being pounced upon - as it makes us use our Portuguese. There's nothing like being immersed in a culture where very few people speak English to propel you forward in learning their language. Nonetheless, we are getting better at communicating as the days go by.

Sarah has been invited to a birthday party, and apparently, fancy dress is the order of the day. We went for a wander and found some lovely rainbow fabric in very lightweight polyester. Using a sleeveless top as a base, I draped and swagged it into a pleated skirt of sorts, with wings attached to the back of the top and something to cover the front. I'm not sure whether she was a rainbow butterfly or a fairy, but it didn't matter much. Others came to the party wearing off the peg costumes; there was the usual assortment of sparkly princesses, a superwoman, superman, batman and the like. A good time was had by all.

There is certainly quite a fluctuation in temperature here. One day it can be 35°C and the next, down to 20°C. We are becoming acclimatised. Sarah says she doesn't notice the heat, and certainly, she never complains. The shops here tend not to have doors; in fact, they have no fronts at all - they are just open to the street. (This can be seen in the photo of the wind chime shop.) When the shopkeepers open for business in the morning, they simply unlock and roll up the security shutters, which at the end of the day are pulled down and locked for the night. Any shop selling small items, such as shoes or jewellery, have all their goods in display cases.

Another attractive feature of streets here is the pavements. Many are mosaics made with random shaped stones approximately two inches in size. Usual colours are black, white and a yellow ochre colour, though I have seen some red. They have simple patterns, such as a star at intervals, or waves or stylised flowers, and sometimes stripes. Some shops and businesses have their names done in mosaic on the pavement. There is a church near us, which has mosaic crosses on the pavement.

The day we arrived here, we went into work with Alan – and were greeted by a huge lizard! It was outside his window. Sarah has since made a drawing of a lizard just like it and has modelled three others, one out of pizza dough, which we were given one evening at a restaurant to amuse her while the adults talked. She made another one out of the rectangular block of foam rubber that came out of her pencil case, and yesterday, she made a clay one at school. At present for her, the best bit about Brazil is the lizards.

Sarah received her pencil case from one of the I.S.E. (International Service Employee) staff. There is a whole department (well, about half a dozen people) in Caterpillar whose function is to see to the needs of the foreigners (mostly Americans) working in the plant. We were picked up from the hotel at 8.00 a.m. one morning to go to Campinas, a large town about an hour away, to organise getting our identity cards. The I.S.E. lady came with us. We were taken to a police station, which deals with such issues, and after waiting for about an hour, we were taken in, handed over the copious numbers of photographs which had been taken the day before, had our finger prints taken (Sarah as well, though they only took her thumb print), and finally we were allowed to go home. Cards would be through in about a week, we were told. On the return journey, the I.S.E. lady handed Sarah a package of all the stuff she needed for school, which included various exercise books, a file and a pencil case in the shape of a dog, which was filled with pencils, a ruler, a sharpener, and so on. Sarah promptly started drawing in one of the books much to the amusement of the good lady.

I've been exploring supermarkets again – no fresh milk, but plenty of long life stuff. Alan may have to change his breakfast habits!

Our Home in Brazil

We still have no computer yet. Buying things like a cooker, fridge and cars has taken priority. We are now installed in our flat, and all our boxes of stuff have arrived and been unpacked. It is two months since we last saw all this stuff, and we looked at some of it and thought, *Now why on earth did we bring that?!* Certainly, the token sweater that was put in for each of us seems totally out of place when night time temperatures here at present exceed 'hot' daytime summer temperatures in Ireland. Maximum temperature these last two days has been 40°C and we're not in the hottest months yet. (January and February are the hottest months.) We are surviving. I'm having to turn my usual way of thinking back to front; for instance, here we close the windows to keep the heat out - not the cold!

One advantage of the hot weather is that the burning of the sugar cane comes to a halt. (Hot season also means wet season, and this is why the harvesting - and thus the burning of the cane - stops.) Harvesting is carried out from the beginning of March to the end of October, so it is always a relief when harvesting is done.

We have a large L-shaped living room, with a passage running behind it with bedrooms and bathrooms, and yes, there is a bedroom and bathroom for the maid. The kitchen and bathrooms (and utility) all have granite floors. The living room floor is wooden, and unusually, the bedroom area is carpeted. All the other flats we looked at had wooden floors in the bedrooms. The lift opens on to our mini hall. There is no common hallway for the two flats on each floor as there was in most other apartment blocks we looked at. Each side has its own lift. The service lift at the back is shared.

I've made an interesting observation: cold water as we know it in Ireland doesn't exist here. What comes out of the cold tap is almost tepid because the climate is so much warmer. Many wash-hand basins have provision for just one tap (most houses/flats have a guest bathroom with toilet and wash-hand basin adjacent to the living area), and there is no hot water plumbed into the utility room in our flat. The first time I washed my hands under the cold tap, I braced myself for the blast of ice-cold water that I'm used to back home, but here it is not an uncomfortable experience to wash your hands under the cold tap!

We have acquired a sofa from the French family who lived three floors up because they just went to Japan. We also acquired their washing machine and dishwasher, so we are getting settled in with all the comforts of home. We need a dining table and chairs, and have seen a set that we like at a cost of about £800 - 900 made of good Brazilian hardwood. There is a table and chairs three floors up, but I don't particularly like it. It is very Brazilian with a glass top set into a wooden surround. I don't like seeing my knees when I I'm dining! (I have since discovered that Brazilians always use a tablecloth, so knees would not be an issue.)

Our maid (whom we also inherited from three floors up) will probably start on Monday but will not be living in. She has her own family anyway. I'm not quite sure what there is to keep her occupied five days a week, but received wisdom is that it is easier to have a maid full time than to try and negotiate part time! I might as well enjoy a spotless house while I can.

Our flat is in a 'nice' area and full of wealthy people. There are useful shops close by, such as a fruit and vegetable market, a laundry, chemist and bakery; shops selling meat, fish and water (drinking water comes in 10 or 20 litre containers); clothing shops, and a small supermarket.

We have a lovely park about five minutes' walk from our flat. It is not a park as such, but an agricultural university (of international repute, apparently). There is a large old building surrounded by lots of other more modern buildings which house the various departments of the university, all set in huge grounds.

The Agricultural University, better known as the Agronomia, or E.S.A.L.Q. (Escola Superior de Agronomia de Luiz Queiroz)

About 100 years ago, Luiz Quieroz, the man who owned the house and land, bequeathed it all to the state on the condition that it should become an agricultural university. The grounds are open for anyone to enjoy, and you can always find people walking, picnicking and just enjoying being out of doors in a beautiful setting. Dogs and bicycles are not allowed.

There are several supermarkets in the town, which sell more or less everything from car tyres, washing machines and computers to wine/beer, as well as food. I have arranged to go round a supermarket with our Portuguese teacher here so that she can tell us what is what – which are the good brands, what the cuts of meat are, what the various kinds of fish are, the uses of the different cleaning lotions and potions, and so on. Recipes from home don't quite work here, and the basic ingredients are slightly different, so maybe our maid (Paula) can teach me some basic Brazilian recipes and I can get a recipe book as well.

Alan and I have two Portuguese lessons a week and Sarah has three. Ours consist of a one-hour language lab session followed by an hour of instruction with the teacher, all fairly formal and all conducted in Portuguese (though Teresa usually teaches English!). I think we are progressing and our ears are getting attuned to the language, but it will be awhile before we will truly be fluent.

I have found a craft class and am learning to do mosaics – or at least I am covering a tray with broken tiles. My ambitions as usual are much bigger than a tray. I fancy a tabletop! I go to the class more to listen to Portuguese than to learn a craft. I have also found a yoga class. The postures bit is fine because I can watch the teacher and the others in the class, but I haven't a clue what he says in the relaxation bit of the class – but I relax anyway. I *will* understand eventually!

I think Sarah is beginning to join in her class at school instead of sitting drawing all the time (with her teacher's permission, I may add.) They had a Halloween party today, and Sarah went dressed as a bat. Everyone else was a witch or a vampire, I think. Halloween is big here because of the American influence, and also because it's another excuse for a party. At the weekend, there were parties everywhere, and people dressed as witches (or whatever) were all over the place, but no fireworks. I think those are reserved for New Year and carnival time.

We have met various residents of the apartment block (the swimming pool is quite good for that), and they are all very welcoming. My Portuguese at least extends to being able to tell everyone where we are from, what we are doing here and for how long!

The wind is blowing a howling gale at present. That seems to be the pattern: hot, hot, hot during the day, and about two hours after sunset, the wind gets up for several hours and then dies down. Quite welcome to cool the place down before going to bed. It is currently 10.00 p.m. and the temperature inside is 28°C. Outside is much the same. The advantage of living this high up is that we get the full benefit of the breeze.

It is time for bed - though if I were Brazilian, I would just be in the middle of my dinner!

Exploring Our Surroundings

Practically every small town seems to have a small zoo, including Piracicaba, but it is under refurbishment. We visited the nearest zoo, in a town called Americana, about half an hour's drive away. It was small and attractively laid out with lots of trees and plants. It had a lake with islands for monkeys. Lots of people were visiting this lovely setting to see many different kinds of animals in their natural environment.

The next day, we did even more exploring. This time we headed north, looking for something called an *eco parque* in São Carlos, and a fazenda nearby. We didn't find the eco parque, but we did find the fazenda. In this instance, fazenda equates to what at one time was a large estate with an expansive house known as Fazenda Santa Maria. It was about two kilometres down a dirt track, and just as we were beginning to wonder whether we had been wise in heading down an unknown dirt track, we came upon a somewhat dilapidated pink mansion, though it still managed to retain an air of grandeur.

Fazenda Santa Maria

It dates from about 1888. There was a sign with the word 'museum' written on it with an arrow pointing towards the house, but it all looked very closed up. We decided to wander about a bit when a lady came walking towards us and politely asked if we were looking for the museum. Our fervent nods told her ‘yes’, and so she directed us back to the house. She disappeared, and soon we heard the sounds of shutters and doors being opened, and then the same lady opened the front door, this time with a purse strapped round her middle. The entry fee was four reais each (roughly equivalent to a little over a pound, with Sarah’s admission free.) Her husband then gave us a guided tour of the three rooms open to the public.

It was all very interesting. What we could understand (which I hasten to add was quite a lot) was that his grandfather had emigrated from Italy, and had built the place. Lots of Italians came to Brazil around that time. Jersey cows and Appaloosa horses seem to have been an abiding interest of the owners. There were lots of trophies for Jersey cows over the years, and there was a Jersey herd in the fields outside. The idea of trophies for cattle I’m sure came with the immigrants. As with all such houses, they are trying to make ends meet by opening the house to tourists and visitors. There is no longer an army of workers to run the plantations, which must have thrived at one time. Coffee, sugar and oranges were mentioned.

Our journey home was interesting too. We went cross-country instead of along the dual carriageway. Generally, there seem to be main trunk roads and then small side roads, which are quite often just dirt roads. We passed a vast eucalyptus forest grown for commercial purposes – oil and paper mainly.

I have discovered what cashew juice is! I had thought when I saw cartons of it on the supermarket shelves that it was some sort of nut milk. Not one bit of it! It is fruity and tangy! Cashew nuts come attached to a red and yellow pepper-shaped fruit, and this is squeezed for juice.

We went exploring again the following weekend. We found a sort of forest park near Piracicaba with a small lake and walks through the trees. It is nothing quite as organised as forest parks in Britain, but a pleasant haven away from the cityscape nonetheless. We came across some noisy cicadas with fat little bodies nearly two inches long with black-veined wings that stick out at least an inch longer. We also saw some clumps of huge bamboo growing there.

We then headed north going cross-country once again, but this time we discovered nothing wildly exciting: sugar cane, cows and scrub! We managed to find our way into a small town but couldn’t find our way out again – or at least couldn’t find the road we wanted. We eventually found a link road to the dual carriageway we had been trying to avoid. We arrived at our destination about two hours later than we intended. Carlos had recommended an open-air restaurant beside a waterfall at a place called

Analãndia. It was very pleasant and the food was excellent. We were ready for it, and were so glad they were still serving lunch.

Our next stop, about 50 kilometres further, was a small town called Brotas, which has about half a dozen waterfalls in the surrounding area and has various water-related activities on offer. We went to visit a couple of the larger waterfalls, and this entailed driving eleven kilometres along a dirt road, which was more sand than dirt.

As we drove along, we could see flat-topped hills in the distance. From what I understand, Brazil was formed from two ancient plates during Precambrian times, and is roughly divided by the Amazon River. These two plates consist of a Precambrian igneous basement rock overlain by Precambrian sediments, both of which are well eroded. Both regions of Brazil are noted for their distinctive, tabletop mountains. The southern region, the Brazilian shield, is less eroded than the northern region, and the tabletop mountains can rise as high as 1000 metres.

Also interesting to note is that the Central Amazonian region was once a large inland sea that drained into the Pacific. When the Andes were formed, it became a large inland lake, which eventually found its way to the Atlantic via a narrow gap between the northern and southern plates. The whole Amazon basin is very low lying, and Iquitos, in Peru, is only 110 metres above sea level, yet 3000 kilometres from the Atlantic. It is a mere 800 kilometres from the Pacific, but there are a lot of mountains in the way!

The road just went on and on past fields of humpy cows and vast orange plantations. I noticed that the fencing posts were mahogany – to us, good quality, expensive wood, but here it's just the local timber!

We were beginning to think that maybe we were on a wild goose chase when we rounded a bend and saw several buildings and the shimmering blue surface of a swimming pool, seemingly in the middle of nowhere! This was the tourist trap for the waterfalls - the place to park, get food and drink, swim and generally have a good time. Brazilians like sitting and talking, especially out of doors surrounded by the beauty of greenery, flowers and abundant sunshine.

We parked, had a drink, and set off to walk to the waterfalls on a path that took us through a meadow full of floppy-eared cows, which looked as us curiously. From what I can gather, they seem to be a cross breed between a Gir and a Holanda, with the Holanda being similar to the black and white Holsteins we are familiar with, thus making this a hardy and good milking strain.

After gazing at this bucolic scene for a moment, we headed off into some woods. At some points, the narrow path led us meandering round trees and scrambling over rocks, all the while accompanied by the sounds of birds and insects. After about ten minutes of this scrambling, we found a 55-metre high cascade splashing onto the rocks below. The second waterfall was much the same as the first: wider and not so high, but with the same peaceful attraction.

On the way back to where we had parked the car, we had a bit of excitement: a flash of yellow accompanied by a black body flew past us – a toucan! It's a wonder they can fly with such a vast beak, but it is mainly hollow. The toucan flew high above our heads and perched at the top of a tree, its beak a glorious splash of yellow in the midst of the greenery. We also saw several parrots flying overhead, but we could hear their screeches long before we spotted them.

After this full day of exploring far afield, we were ready to head for home, which meant driving eleven kilometres along the dirt track once more, but this time the sun was setting behind us creating spectacular back-lighting to the scenery.

Just as the sun was setting we decided that the main roads were probably a better option, as there was no point in going a scenic route after dark. Our trip home, however, was enlivened by a lightning storm in the distance ahead of us, which kept us entertained with dramatic displays that lit up the entire sky at times.

The following Sunday, we went for a brief walk in the agronomia and drank in the exotic beauty of the brilliantly coloured blooms on the trees. Blossom is too mild a word to describe the riot of colour found in Brazil. Here there are vivid shades of red, orange, yellow and purple. The highlight of our walk was finding lots of huge, brightly coloured caterpillars. They were about 3-4 inches long with pink/orange heads and tails, either end of a black body with yellow stripes. (I have since learned they are of the *Sphingidae* family, genus

Isognathus.) They also had something like a short aerial just above their tails (or maybe 'bottom/backside' would be a better description). If that is the size of the caterpillars, one can only imagine the size of the cocoons they encase themselves in – and the moths or butterflies that emerge from them!

There has been a definite change in the weather this week. Rain! It is the wet season, and we are assured that there will be a lot of rain between now and Christmas, with two, sometimes three torrential downpours a day. When it rains here, it's not just a light sprinkling or a shower. The sky delivers torrential downpours that last for up to twenty minutes, and the roads turn into rivers, but the drains work efficiently.

There was a holiday November 15th, so we decided to go away for the weekend. Not very far away, but we had no idea what to expect, whether we should book accommodation, and so forth. We had decided to head slightly east and north of Piracicaba to a hotel called Campo do Sonhos (Field of Dreams) in a place called Soccorro, and spend a couple of days there. This gave us a chance to see another aspect of Brazil's diverse geography, as Soccorro is definitely alpine in character, but less dramatic than the European version. Nonetheless, it is beautiful country.

Soccorro

We reached our destination in about three hours including a lunch stop. The hotel consists of about fourteen apartments with a swimming pool outside. There was one apartment left (spacious enough for five people), which we took after inspection. The setting was very pleasant, with hammocks slung between the posts of the inviting veranda, beckoning one to take full advantage of this perfect spot for relaxing while looking out over the swimming pool.

The main theme of Campo do Sonhos is being close to nature and de-stressing. They have lots of farm animals on the property. They also have a wormery and a vegetable garden. It reminded me of a sort of 'Butlins' with organised activities, such as yoga, tai chi and reflexology, as well as various other activities such as ping-pong, snooker, chess and a fitness room, but there is no pressure to participate if one's version of total relaxation involves lolling about the pool and swinging in the hammock!

We went to dinner at about 8.30, and on our way to the restaurant the frogs were in full chorus, masses of them, all croaking by the river. After dinner, we took a torch and went to find one of these singers. Judging by the noise, we decided that they must be quite large. We eventually followed some noise to its source and found a small green frog about an inch long (if even that) known as the Perereca frog. We watched it croaking, swelling out a sac in its throat and letting rip! What a noise from one so small! We also met a firefly on our trek!

Next day I opted to go for a ride through the mountains. Here they use ponies, not horses, and a fairly motley selection of tack, functional rather than pristine. The bridle on my mount was fabric with a rope for reins. The stirrup 'leathers' were webbing, but the saddle was of tooled leather with two pommels (to wind my lariat round after lassoing a steer, I guess!). Riding is western style. One can't do a rising trot, but the ponies have a gait that is somewhere between walking and trotting, which is reasonably comfortable. I got the hang of neck reining, but couldn't find the 'go' button! Heels had no effect.

Eventually, we were off, and it was a lovely ride along dirt tracks between fields with superb views of the countryside.

After lunch we lazed about, and later visited a small cave nearby, the highlight of which was a tiny hummingbird's nest suspended from a fern at the top of the arch at the entrance. The bird was in residence!

Our excitement after dinner was a large (by our standards) bat swooping past, and then, to my complete surprise, a small owl (about eight inches in height) landed at my feet just milliseconds after a large crunchy beetle had landed nearby. There was no beetle when the owl took off again, so I think the owl had its dinner as well! And of course, the fireflies (or *vagalume* as they are called here) were out in full force, weaving erratically around a tree. It was utterly fascinating watching them.

The hotel has an annual programme of educating schoolchildren about the indigenous Indian population. For thirty days each year, Indians come to the hotel where they live and carry out their traditional activities, and children from all sorts of schools come and participate. The decimation of the local indigenous population with the arrival of Europeans reads much the same as the North American equivalent and the Europeans.

Next day we explored the countryside, but due to the vagaries of the map didn't find half of what we were looking for, but it was a pleasant way to spend the day. Such beautiful countryside, and horseback is definitely the way to explore it. We did find a small *pinga* distillery – the local 'hooch', distilled from sugar cane. The distillery was very small and very scruffy. We didn't get the advertised tour, but we did get a taste of the stuff. Let's just say it's rocket fuel!

The name given to the local hooch varies from region to region. It is called *cachaça* or *pinga* in this area, with pinga being a nickname. The word pinga actually comes from the verb *pingar* meaning 'to drip', which alludes to how the liquid drips from the top of the tower during the distillation process.

Back at the hotel, we explored the land that rises above and behind the buildings and found sugar cane, coffee and banana trees, all growing and thriving. The coffee bushes were about ten feet tall with shiny green leaves reminiscent of Portugal laurel. Flowers were along the stems, whitish and small, and green berries were forming at the base of the stems.

The owl was waiting for us again after dinner. It must be his regular perch, just sitting there waiting for a tasty morsel to come by.

Next day, home again!

We went to a motorbike show in São Paulo at the weekend. Alan had done a thorough route plan. The traffic in São Paulo is a nightmare at the best of times. The show was in a large exhibition hall surrounded by ample parking space, which on Sunday morning was home to a second-hand car mart. The bike show itself was a sea of bikes and bike accoutrements, and outside there were stunt displays, which drew a crowd despite the heat. The journey to and from the show didn't take too long (a couple of hours), though it was Sunday and the traffic was light. We have proved to ourselves that with good planning, São Paulo traffic needn't be a nightmare, though we haven't tried a rainy rush hour. Rain tends to bring everything to a standstill.

The temperature is getting quite hot now, but at least we get a bit of a breeze at night. I've found Orion in the night sky, but he is upside down! Practically every town of any size has a small observatory, but we haven't been to our local one yet. It is open to the public on Saturday evenings.

Santa arrived at the shopping mall a week ago on November 23, and we forgot all about it. At least we could see the fireworks display from our kitchen window, but it was not as good as actually being there. There are Christmas trees going up everywhere, all artificial of course. I can't begin to think of Christmas in this tropical climate. It is too hot. Christmas should be cold! But Sarah is talking about Christmas decorations, so she at least is on the ball.

We went for a longish walk, first to the Parque Engenho, the disused sugar mill, where there was an exhibition of all things pertaining to the leisurely lifestyle: fishing (which seems to be a national pastime ranking alongside football), boating, jeep clubs, model aircraft/car clubs, canoeing, massage and so on. Next we crossed the river via the Ponte Pensil, a suspension bridge.

Ponte Pensil Bridge

This is a favourite place for 'chilling out' on a Sunday afternoon. There were lots of people sitting, chatting and making use of the various food and drink stalls around. We stopped for a reviving cup of caldo-de-cana (sugar cane juice) followed by a cob of sweet corn, all from street vendors. The sweet corn is somewhat tasteless and chewy, but they use the husks to wrap round the hot cob so that you can hold it without burning your hands, and they also make brushes from the husks to apply salt and butter to your cob.

The shopping mall seems to be another place to 'hang out' at weekends. We went there for our lunch one Sunday, and it was hiving, with people having lunch and waiting for the shops to open, or just sitting chatting. Talking seems to be another national pastime, along with fishing and football.

We were back at the shopping mall later that day to see the latest Harry Potter film and nearly couldn't get parked. Harry Potter is showing on three screens, such is the anticipated demand for the long awaited film. Two screens are in English with sub-titles and the third is dubbed! It was great for us having the film in English, and the film provided a welcome bit of escapism. When we came out of the cinema, having been immersed in the English language for a couple of hours, it seemed a bit strange to hear everyone around us speaking a foreign language. Must get our ears re-attuned to Portuguese once again!

Our First Christmas and New Year in Brazil

Christmas has been and gone, but it just didn't seem like Christmas, probably because it is hot this time of year. Blazing sunshine and temperatures around 35°C just don't add up to Christmas for expats from Ireland, in spite of all the Christmas trees, Christmas decorations and Santas everywhere.

The Christmas traditions here are European, having come with the immigrants, who in this area were mainly Italian. The highlight of the Christmas decorations are nativity figures placed at strategic points in the town, primarily at main road intersections, and also in parks. These often consist of conical forms about four feet high, with conical arms made from what appeared to be white polypropylene sacking supported on wire frames. The heads were white globes. Generally, there are just three figures in the grouping, two large and one small, but in some places, there were more figures, some with wings. The globes were lit up at night! They were very effective in their simplicity. You were in no doubt as to what they represented.

A Christmas activity, in which we participated, was a *passeio vagalume* - literally a glowworm walk. It was not as Alan assumed, some sort of nature walk, but a walk through a park (after several of the school choirs had sung and bands had played music in an outdoor bandstand), with lots of other children and mums and dads carrying candles or torches. It was lovely meandering through the park after dark with all the candles.

We were invited to spend the Christmas festivities with Carlos' and Carmen's families in Barra Bonita, a small town about an hour and a half drive away. On Christmas Eve, we went on a three-hour boat trip on the lake there (lunch on board was included though it wasn't great), and went through a huge lock at one side of the hydroelectric dam, up to the upper lake.

The highlight of the trip was the lock, which has a rise (or fall) of about seventy feet. It is quite impressive, with huge gates - not manual I may add, and no winding up the sluices! The gate at the lower lake was operated vertically, going up and down, rather than opening like conventional gates.

The boat trip kept us out from under everyone's feet as they prepared meals. We were staying in a hotel, rather than in someone's house, and the hotel was full enough already with relatives coming 'from all airts and parts'. We kept ourselves out of mischief, exploring the lakeside area, very touristy, and trying to get Sarah to have a wee sleep before the festivities began.

Festivities began around 9.30 p.m. at Carlos's sister's house. Lots of people, at least fifty I guess, lots of alcohol, lots of food (which we tried to eat as little of as possible, as food was planned for us at Carmen's mother's house.) All this took place outside by the swimming pool. The meal was precipitated (probably at least an hour earlier than scheduled) by Sarah announcing that she was hungry, so out came all the food and I think everyone was quite happy to see it. Drinks offered were whiskey, beer or soft drinks. It didn't seem right not having wine with the meal, but the wine here in Brazil is not good. One guidebook says that the best that can be said about Brazilian wine is that it is not poisonous!

We left about 10.30-ish to go to our next party at Carmen's mother's house where we would have Christmas dinner (but Alan and Sarah had already had a nibble at the earlier party). We didn't have turkey, though that is traditional here, but we had something called 'chester', which is in fact an extremely large chicken. It has been specially bred to produce a larger quantity of breast meat. The name 'chester' is a play on the English word 'chest'. Accompanying this was ham, a fruit sauce made from prunes, figs, pineapple and raisins (very good too), rice (no potatoes), and also farofa, which I think is mainly *mandioca* flour with vegetables and bits of bacon in it. Mandioca is a root vegetable which, when young, is often made into very tasty chips. However, as it matures it apparently becomes poisonous and takes a lot of processing to make it edible. At this stage, it is usually made into flour.

Another traditional dish at Christmas is whole roast suckling pig complete with head, though we didn't meet that until the next day when we stopped for lunch at a restaurant on our way home.

We actually sat down to eat (after grace was said) at about 11.00 p.m. (or a bit later). Come midnight, which couldn't arrive soon enough for the children, everyone hugged and kissed each other, with wishes of Feliz Natal (Happy Christmas) all around, and now that Christmas Day had actually arrived, the impatient children could at last start opening presents. There were seventeen of us in all, ten adults and seven children, the youngest being three or thereabouts.

I don't know whether Santa brings stockings in Brazil, but he managed to find Sarah in the hotel, and brought her, amongst other things, glitter glue, gold paint and such like (now where did he find that?) and also various Brazilian commodities. Carlos invited us to go to another party (at another relative's house) in a town about 50 kilometres away, but as we were setting off on our travels early the next day, we declined. We were going to see 'Foz do Iguaçu', Brazil's equivalent to the Niagara Falls.

We drove home via a scenic route, which involved about twelve kilometres of dirt road, not the six kilometres marked on the map, and it came out about five kilometres nearer the town we were heading for than was marked on the map! That gives you some idea of the accuracy of Brazilian maps. One has a vague idea of where the roads might be, but that is about it! We haven't managed to get lost yet, but we have invested in a compass to help with decision-making, assuming that north indicated on the maps is more or less magnetic north!

Arriving home again, it was time to shift gear once more and unpack the party clothes, pack the holiday clothes, and at 8.00 a.m. the next day, head for São Paulo airport (about two hours drive) and on to a plane for Foz do Iguaçu, a one-and-a-half-hour flight. A driver met us at the airport and took us to the hotel where we would be staying, the Hotel Bourbon das Cataratas, named for its proximity to the waterfalls.

This had been arranged beforehand. Having ascertained how long we were staying, he then offered to show us what trips were available and helped us plan our stay, if that was what we wanted. It certainly made life a lot easier, and what was more, he would be our driver the entire time. We would have wasted so much time trying to find out what was available and how to get there without his knowledgeable help. He offered us exactly what we had been planning and wanting. Ah, the joys of five-star hotels! The company he works for has offices in most of the major hotels in the area, and there are a lot of them, as it is a big tourist destination. The main attraction – other than the series of waterfalls – is cheap shopping of imported goods and a casino in Paraguay (no gambling in Brazil).

The River Paraná forms a border between Brazil on one side, and Argentina and Paraguay on the other. The river is vast, and it splits up into smaller channels that flow round islands. The major surge is about an 80-metres drop, so it is quite powerful.

We decided to fill our day with experiencing the waterfalls. We first saw them from the Brazilian side, and then from the Argentinean side from a boat and from the air. Our driver arranged all the necessary paperwork for us to cross the border into Argentina for a day. The waterfalls are truly magnificent, spectacular, and a camera doesn't do them justice. You can't hear the noise and feel the spray in a photo! The total width is about 2.5 km, with nearly two kilometres of that inside the Argentinean border. It is not one continuous fall, but has several major falls and many lesser falls combining to make up the whole (275 falls is the figure the guidebooks trot out).

River Paraná waterfalls

We made a boat trip in a large inflatable craft with two powerful engines – very necessary given the current coming down the river. We couldn't get up to the main falls – that would have been too dangerous. It was nail biting enough as it was, bouncing over large rapids at speed.

The highlight of the rafting excursion (of which we were unaware) was being taken under one of the lesser falls and getting thoroughly soaked – all part and parcel of the fun. We had wondered why some of the participants were doing the boat trip in bikinis, and now we knew why! In this climate you dry out quickly in the warmth of the sun. We returned by jeep to where our faithful driver, Iraci, was waiting for us, and we climbed out and dripped our way to his minibus. He was prepared and produced bits of plastic for us to sit on. Here is a look at the waterfalls we had just been under – exhilarating!

After lunch we took a helicopter flight over the falls. Yes, it is expensive, and the flight only lasts about ten minutes, but it is totally worth it if you ever have the chance to see the falls from this vantage point. Looking down at this vast river snaking its way through endless forest, only to tumble over a huge escarpment and continue on its way, was spectacular from a birds-eye view.

Garguantua do Diablo – The Devil's Throat

If you go, keep in mind that the Argentineans don't approve of these helicopter rides because they can cause a disturbance to the animals, so flights only originate from the Brazilian side of the waterfalls and are kept carefully within Brazilian airspace.

Our next stop was a bird park, the Parques das Aves, filled with an abundance of native species: toucans, macaws and parrots to name the obvious ones, and several others. The tourist literature cites that there are over 150 species of birds, and certainly we saw plenty. One that stood out was the 'bell bird', named thus not because of its plumage but because of the call it utters at intervals – a single bell-like sound that carries for miles. We could hear it all through the park.

One section was devoted to humming birds. It was wonderful being able to see these tiny birds easily, with their jewel like colours, flitting from flower to flower and hovering as they collected the nectar.

There were lots of butterflies as well, though you can find plenty of those in natural settings everywhere in Brazil. Their wingspans range from half an inch to six inches, and they come in a variety of the most wonderful vivid colours. Apparently, the park breeds them and releases them into the wild. Just before exiting this park, we were met by a man with a tame macaw and a parrot. He invited us to let them sit on our shoulders or perch on our arms. The macaw stepped off Sarah's arm, walked up one of my (bare) arms, went round the back of my neck, and was starting down the other arm when the owner removed him and set him on Alan's head, at which point the macaw hopped down and settled happily on Alan's shoulder.

Day Two was a trip to the Argentinean side of the river. You need to view the falls from both sides to get the full picture. You can't appreciate the sheer volume of the falls on the Brazilian side from Brazil, and you can't appreciate the magic of the laciness of the lesser falls in Argentina when you're standing on the Argentinean side. You have to look across at them from the Brazilian side.

We captured a perfect rainbow when we took this photo of the Argentinean waterfalls:

After lunch we went to visit the Itaipu hydroelectric dam, the world's largest such power station, and it certainly is big - eight kilometres long and the height of a 65 storey building. It is impressive in its sheer vastness and the huge scale of the planning, from building villages and associated structures to house the construction workers, to setting up rescue squads for the animals trapped by the rising waters. Itaipu has been operating now for about ten years and supplies 25% of Brazil's needs and 75% of Paraguay's needs. That is a lot of electricity.

I think they are still trying to justify their existence for such huge scale flooding. They finance various tourist projects, generating income for the locals round the edge of the lake. They don't charge an entrance fee to visitors to the dam, and there were at least ten busloads of us for the 3.30 p.m. slot, one of four tours that run each day.

The hotel is very plush, with two swimming pools, a health/fitness suite, a beauty parlour, and masses of waiters and bellhops waiting to do your bidding. Pricewise, for us with UK salaries it was not that expensive - somewhere in the region of £350 for three adults (our friend Geraldine had come along with us), which included everything: very nice rooms for three nights, drinks, breakfast and dinner, two massages, and ferrying to and from the airport. (I don't think they charged for Sarah.) The cost of trips and flights were in addition to this. If we can get day-trips arranged so easily by staying in a five-star hotel, we might consider doing so again. It just made everything so much easier.

We didn't do much for New Year as we decided that a bit of quiet after all the running round Iguaçu was in order. All day on New Year's Eve there were sporadic noises of firecrackers being set off. We had our tea on the balcony listening to all this. The frequency increased as night fell and midnight approached. Come midnight, the whole place erupted with fireworks everywhere, organised displays, but private parties. Living on the twelfth floor comes in handy for some things! We could see everyone's fireworks. It was amazing to be in the midst of it all and watch fireworks going off literally all around us. This went on for about a half hour before dying down, but there were still some being set off when we went to bed around 1.00 a.m.

New Year's Day is totally dead here. We tried to go for a swim at the sports club (which has three pools, all outdoor and bigger than the one at the apartment here), which usually stays open all the time. No luck. We tried the shopping mall (Sarah needs some shoes), again, usually open all the time. The only thing that was functioning was the cinema and we didn't really want to go there, so we went back home for a swim. The only other thing we found open was an ice cream parlour, or a *sorvetaria* as it's called here, with *sorvete* being the word for ice cream. New Year's Day seems to be more family oriented, with most people hosting private parties rather than going out on the town for the evening. Maybe everyone is recovering from the night before.

I gather Rio de Janeiro is the place to be for New Year's Eve with a huge organised firework display over the lake. It is also the place to be for Carnival, but I don't think we feel up to coping with the crowds with a child in tow. There will be something closer to here, but that's over a month away.

São Paulo, Brasilia and Guaruja

Lately we have been exploring more locally. On Sarah's birthday, we went to Campinas, about an hour away. It rained heavily and never let up all day, which is not the norm here, but it does happen occasionally. Our aim had been to browse a large craft market and then visit one of the parks, which has a mini zoo. We didn't find the craft market we were looking for (too many one way systems), but we did find a mini craft mart in one of the squares we passed, so we dashed through the rain and looked round the stalls of the brave souls who had come to sell their wares this soggy day. That was where I found the amethyst egg.

We had lunch inside, watching the raindrops. We have a workable system for eating out here. Generally, one doesn't order a separate dish each, but as a group or family, you decide amongst yourselves what type of meat/fish you want. Alan, Sarah and I always share one portion, which is usually more than sufficient. It comes with salad, rice and farofa. Alan and Sarah eat the steak and I eat the salad, and we are all happy. Farofa is a tasty mixture of mandioca flour, bits of vegetables and other flavourings. Generally, one buys farofa ready made in packets, and each brand has its own unique flavours, but you can make it yourself. The mandioca flour is fried in a vegetable oil with chopped garlic and onion as standard additions. You can add whatever takes your fancy, be it a variety of chopped vegetables, or chopped bacon or other meat, but it is mainly mandioca flour, and it is very good for sopping up juice.

Another common type of restaurant here is the *por kilo*. There is usually a wide selection of veg/salad type foods laid out buffet style, with several hot dishes and usually a man somewhere along the line carving off whatever portion of barbecued meat you want from his varied selection, from large lumps of beef or pork, to chicken hearts. You load up your plate with as much as you want. Your plate of food is then weighed, and you pay by weight - thus the term *por kilo*! It works very well, as everyone gets what he or she wants.

But I digress from my story of our damp trip to Campinas. With lunch over, we sallied forth into the raindrops again to find Jequibita Bosque, the park with a natural history museum, an aquarium and a mini zoo. It was just round the corner from the restaurant, and we found the entrance by luck rather than judgment. The museum was very small, devoted almost entirely to stuffed animals. It was quite interesting for us, not being locals, seeing what kinds of animals live here and learning their Portuguese names. There was also a small section with about half a dozen stuffed animals with strange mutations - the kind you read about but have a difficult time believing really exists: a calf with two heads; a duck with three legs; a goat with five legs; and a calf with one eye, Cyclops style, and so on.

From there we dodged the raindrops to the aquarium to see what sort of fish live around here – the smaller varieties. (You should see the size of some of the lumps of fish served in restaurants here, never mind the size of the bones!) Again, this was interesting to us as non-locals. All those tropical fish that cost a fortune in pet shops at home are indigenous to Brazil, along with various other oddities.

I think Alan was almost more excited by the vast quantity of large spiders in the toilet block!

Rain was easing so we ventured out towards the zoo; not bad for a small concern. Practically every town of any size has a small zoo. There were *Capivaras* (Capybaras) running loose around the place, which made things more interesting.

The following weekend, we visited Holambra, which is where a lot of Dutch immigrants settled. It is a very small town with very Dutch looking facades along the main street! They push their Dutchness for tourist purposes, but this was obviously low season. The place was practically deserted. We found a restaurant called Old Dutch and had a Brazilian/Dutch meal! I thought it was quite good, but Alan wasn't impressed: chicken stuffed with cheese in a cheese sauce. I admit that the sauce was lumpy, but the lumps were cheese, not flour. There is no equivalent to good old cheddar for making sauces. The everyday cheese here is a bit rubbery and reluctant to melt!

After lunch, we found a place called Parque Lindenhof, which boasted parrots, butterflies, a mini farm, loads of plants and of course, lots of Dutch themed decor. It too was deserted. We wandered round it in the increasing heat and decided that an ice-lolly and home was the best option. They did have a largish tortoise wandering freely, which Sarah talked to for awhile.

Holambra has a huge plant fest in September. Fest is about the best word to describe it. There are plants, plants and more plants. I'm not sure what the aim is, apart from selling plants. The town apparently supplies over 75% of all houseplants in South America – and that must mean a lot of plants from one small community. Maybe the Fest is simply their way of celebrating and promoting all things Dutch.

São Paulo was our next destination the following weekend. We chose Sunday because the traffic is quietest. Weekday traffic in São Paulo makes Belfast rush hour look calm and peaceful. Unless you have a special permit - e.g. taxi drivers - non-residents are excluded from driving into São Paulo on certain days depending on what digit your number plate ends in!

So with it being Sunday, we were off to the city, and where did we go? A safari park and the zoo! These are next to each other, on the far side of São Paulo from us, so we headed round the ring road 'til we found the place. The safari park was small but well laid out. We drove along the track through the park and it felt like we were going for miles (four kilometres in fact). The driving track actually meanders back and forth within quite a small area, but we saw all the usual animals - giraffes, zebras, deer, eland, camels, llamas, tapirs and ostriches, but they were not behind bars, which was great (though the carnivores are behind bars). The monkeys climbed all over the car leaving muddy footprints!

And then it was on to the zoo. I looked at the map and decided on the shortest route and off we went. The right turn I wanted to take was cordoned off with a sign saying one-way traffic only on Sundays and holidays, so we had to back track and go the long way round. (You need your wits about you when driving here.) We discovered why it was one way: The entire world and his wife seem to go to São Paulo Zoo on Sunday. There were people everywhere, but it is a big zoo so it didn't seem too crowded. Outside the zoo are masses of snack lunch places all trying to entice you, along with an assortment of souvenir stalls selling zoo-themed merchandise such as plastic animals, blow up animals, safari hats, and so on.

The zoo claims to be one of the best in the world. Certainly, it was good, but then Belfast Zoo is also one of the best. It was the first time I had seen a rhinoceros in the flesh. I knew they were big, but this made me realise just how big. I can now understand how a charging rhino could easily overturn a car!

Also, I don't think I had seen hippos in the flesh before I came to Brazil. They are interesting to watch, especially as they emerge to the surface of their pools, a gradual process that is capped off by a great blowing-out of air from their huge nostrils! Another first was seeing an anteater. They really are extraordinary animals. They appear to be walking on their knuckles and seem fairly oblivious to what is going on round them - which is understandable given that their sight and hearing are very poor - but their sense of smell is sixty times better than ours. Maybe if we smelled like ants, they might get more excited.

The zoo also has lots of parrots and macaws all screeching and letting you know of their presence. Sarah likes the scarlet macaw - red with yellow tummy. I like the Hyacinth macaw - all blue - and endangered.

We've sorted out the task of fetching and depositing people at the airport. Flights from Europe tend to arrive here early morning and leave late at night, so we book into a hotel nearby for the night. As our recent guest was leaving on Saturday night, we decided to stay over (rather than drive the two hours back to Piracicaba late at night) and explore some of São Paulo the next day.

Alan's secretary booked us into a plush hotel near the airport called the Caesar Park Hotel. On arriving there, we discovered that the hotel has a shuttle service to and from the airport every twenty minutes. Beats the hassle of airport parking any day, and you are dropped at the door instead of having to find your way from the car park. An added bonus of this hotel is that they do a special rate for Caterpillar employees, which turned out to be a quarter of the usual rate. This made a four-star hotel very affordable, especially at Brazilian prices. So if you're staying in Brazil and anyone is flying in to visit you, please have them arrive on a Sunday morning and depart on a Saturday evening. It will make things so much simpler!

After our breakfast, we set off into deepest São Paulo. First we visited the Museu Paulista.

The Museo Paulista has a large display of sedan chairs, hats, fire engines, pictures and furniture, all pertaining to the history of São Paulo The building is a large, deep yellow stately mansion with colonnaded wings extending from the upper floors, all set in a formal terraced garden with lots of steps taking you to different levels of garden. It is built on a hill, so not all the steps are cosmetic. It is a vigorous garden stroll rather than a leisurely one!

Next stop, central São Paulo where there was an antiques market on one side of the main central street, and a craft/art market on the other side. Now we know where to bring visitors for their shopping! These two markets offer the best of both worlds, antique and new: cameras, jewellery, porcelain/ceramics/glass, photographs, silver, toys, magazines, ethnographic bits and pieces, and fossils. We bought a trilobite, which came from Bolivia! We didn't linger in the craft mart as time was marching on.

Next stop was a large park called Cidade Universitária, situated beside the ring road, which seems to house lots of university departments, among them a research centre that conducts studies in snake venom and its antidotes. They had what was termed a museum, but it was full of all sorts of snakes of varying shapes and sizes, with interesting information about them. In addition to the usual information, such as species, family, food and habitat, it included teeth type, whether venomous (which is indicated by the teeth), what antidote is needed for the venom, whether the snake is aggressive, and so on. We only had half an hour there before it closed, but I think it needs another visit.

There is so much to see in São Paulo, and from a traffic point of view, weekends are the only realistic time to go, otherwise the traffic is horrific – hence my suggested arrival and departure days for visitors to Brazil: so we can have the excuse to play in São Paulo for a day!

Another weekend (it was actually Carnival weekend, but more of that later), we went to Brasilia to stay with our friend Susie, who is originally from Ballycastle in Northern Ireland. She's married to a Brazilian named Roberto. We had to fly out of São Paulo, and decided that leaving home at 4.00 a.m. on Saturday morning was preferable to braving the hazards of São Paulo traffic at rush hour on a holiday weekend, with the possibility of missing the plane. Even at 5.30 a.m. on a Saturday morning, the road leading into São Paulo and the ring road were busier than you would expect (people leaving early to go to the beach).

We arrived at the airport with no problem and reached Brasilia by 9.00 a.m. after a one-and-a-half-hour flight. Susie met us. She has two small children,

Mariana and Luciana. They live about twenty-five minutes' drive out of Brasilia in a house they built themselves on about six acres of land. They have been there six years now and started with a bare plot. The garden is now quite mature, and Susie tries to keep to native species. She has planted about every sort of fruit bush/tree that grows in Brazil: mangoes, limes, papaya, pomegranates, grapefruit, oranges, avocado and guava, to name some familiar ones, and pitanga, amora and jabuticaba to name some of the unfamiliar ones. The latter are all small berry fruits rather than the larger lumps of fruit like the former. Susie has made delicious jams and chutneys from various combinations of these fruits. They also grow soya beans and mandioca, and keep a vegetable plot and hens, with a gardener to look after it all, whose wife helps in the house. They live on the property in a house provided by Roberto and Susie.

The house is at an elevation of about 4,000 feet, which is quite high for Brazil, and they have a superb view over the *cerrado* – the Brazilian equivalent of the African savannah – a seemingly never ending plateau landscape dissected by numerous streams and rivers. The cerrado is covered with scrubby trees and bushes, which tend to catch fire during the dry season. These are interspersed with grassland, used for raising cattle.

Cerrado near Brasilia

Roberto took us for a short walk through the cerrado, from the house to the edge of the drop that takes you down into the valley. He showed us various medicinal plants. Certainly as we walked, I could smell something akin to eucalyptus, though there were no eucalyptus trees in the vicinity. We must have crushed some plant as we walked along. Indeed, the smell was still clinging to my trousers when I washed them the next day. We saw a variety of insects, including a praying mantis.

We had a brief guided tour of the capital, Brasilia, in the rain. It's different from so much else you see in Brazil with its 60s architecture and no high-rise blocks. We visited the cathedral, which is the picture one sees on all tourist literature about Brasilia. The pictures usually show a cone of concrete pillars, but that gives you no indication of the interior.

Cathedral, Brasilia

You can only get the 'wow' factor on the first visit. To get into it, you go down a short dark ramp through a small tunnel, and when you step into the interior, your first impression is just that - Wow! It is so bright and spacious. The ceiling/roof is white stained glass with a blue and green swirl through it, and the walls (about six feet high) and floor are white marble. There are three large angels suspended from the centre of the ceiling.

There is an interesting church in Brasilia called Dom Bosco, a rather box-shaped church, with walls made entirely of stained glass in varying shades of blue supported by concrete pillars. It was much more peaceful than the stark whiteness of the cathedral.

All the government departments are situated along a wide central avenue in Brasilia. Residential areas are in two wings on either side of this avenue. These are divided into *quadras.* A 'quadra' consists of about four, long, four-storey blocks, with each 'quadra' having shops, medical facilities, a school, and so on, the idea being that they should be more or less self-contained. This is fine in theory, but human nature being what it is, the grass on the other side is always greener. These do not have street names, just numbers, north or south, depending on which side of the central avenue you live. It has the same soulless feeling as Craigavon. We decided that we would not like to live there. All the embassies and up market housing were further out with large gardens and were generally more livable looking. Susie said that when she went out for her first visit before she married Roberto, she felt that there was no way she could live in the city. Roberto had been looking for somewhere else to live, and so he was able to show her the plot of land he had in mind. She decided that she could cope with that. As it was, she had to live with Roberto's mum for awhile before their house was habitable.

The presidential palace is very modernistic, looking for all the world like a glorified green house. Who wants a green house in Brazil! Heaven knows what it must be like to live in! The presidential guard (ceremonial) wears a white uniform with long black thigh boots and a helmet with a long tassel of presumably horsehair. The white is embellished with red and gold.

We were assured that Brasilia would be hot - very hot - so we didn't pack any warmer clothes. The temperature hardly reached 20°C apart from the day we left there, and Alan had to borrow a jumper (sweater). The day we arrived was also misty - you could hardly see to the end of the garden, but it cleared, and then everything was damp - the beds, the lot. Susie says there are times when she cannot get anything dried. I never thought damp would be a problem in Brazil, but I guess it is usually short lived. Brasilia has a very definite dry season, in winter, (July/August) with no rain for weeks on end. As you get nearer the coast, this is less pronounced.

This weekend just past, we went to the beach. I now understand the Brazilian preoccupation with going to the beach for every holiday. The beaches are fabulous - and we've only seen one and not a spectacular one at that. It really is all that you see in the pictures of tropical beaches, and more. There are miles and miles of white sand with palm trees, and rolling waves, and lots of sunshine, and beach umbrellas (essential). On the downside, masses of people and urbanisation right up to the edge of the beach, but the latter two don't seem to impinge - it is all part of the beach culture.

Beach life, Guaruja: 1-2 hours' drive south of São Paulo

I had by this stage bought a bikini. At first I didn't feel comfortable with the idea of a bikini so I bought a one-piece bathing suit. I soon learned from spending time around the pool at our flat that bikinis were the norm, and I began to feel overdressed! Only the over-80s seem to sport a full one-piece! We also resisted buying Sarah a bikini as it seemed fairly pointless at her age, but bikinis are the norm.

Carlos and Carmen have a mini apartment just down a street about 500 yards from the beach. It has only one bedroom, so their two boys sleep on the floor in the living area. We stayed in a hotel about four blocks away, but we were also close to the beach.

We drove down after dark on Friday evening, the journey taking about five hours instead of the usual three because the traffic in São Paulo was bad. It is usually fairly clear after 8.00 p.m., but Carlos reckons there must have been heavy rain earlier, which always seems to make the place grind to a halt, and we must have hit the aftermath of that. In heavy rain, visibility is almost nil, so you have to slow down, and on that São Paulo ring road, it must be almost suicidal driving in that sort of rain.

The beach we went to is about an hour south of São Paulo, and about a half hour beyond São Paulo we started to go downhill - down, down, down, along sweeping curves, through tunnels, and we could catch glimpses of lights way below us. It was dark, so we had no idea what was below. I knew Brazil had a narrow (in relative terms) coastal strip and a plateau-like interior, but I hadn't really considered what the reality would be like. We must have descended steadily for about twenty minutes. This is definitely a trip to be done in daylight! At least we would have a chance to see this view on the return trip, as we would be returning home during the daylight hours.

We skirted round the edge of Santos, Brazil's major port, where all the parts for Alan's generators arrive from Larne. (One of his jobs here is to source the parts locally.) Santos, as you can guess, is heavily industrialised, with oil refineries and heaven knows what else. In the dark we could see the columns of smoke (from where they were burning off the gas) from miles away. We reached our destination and had something to eat at about 11.00 p.m., and soon thereafter, we went to bed.

On Saturday morning, we just had to have a glimpse of the beach before having breakfast. All I can say is wow ... brilliant! ... and people were already heading for it at 8.00 a.m. But we had breakfast first and then walked to Carlos' apartment, gathered up all the beach paraphernalia (umbrellas, chairs, a cool box of drinks, all packed onto a trolley) and trundled down to the beach. It was 10.00 a.m. and already hot. I had covered us with sun cream before leaving the hotel. We were assured the beach would be fairly empty, but there were beach umbrellas spaced about two to three metres apart, and our looks conveyed what we were all thinking: This was empty? Apparently, on holiday weekends, the umbrellas are literally touching, making a sort of umbrella roof that extends along the beach. Finding your own space is almost impossible. As I said before, hordes of people are part of the beach scene, and a deserted beach would not seem right, though I don't think I would like my neighbours on top of me (as they would be on busy weekends).

We set up camp, and Alan, Sarah and I just had to find out what the sea was like. Answer – warm! I think the others thought us crazy, but it looked so inviting. Maybe one waits until one is overheated, and then heads to the sea to cool off. But with water this warm, some cooling off that would be – more like a soak in tepid bathwater! We didn't expect the water to be freezing cold, but we didn't think it would be this warm! Okay, so it was an incoming tide over hot sand, but Alan measured the temperature at 31°C! At least the waves were just right for playing in, not massive, but enough surf to be fun. We must have played for at least half an hour until we decided that a break from the sun would be a good idea. We headed back toward the umbrella where we had a sit down and a cool drink under its shade. After a bit, we decided it was time for a walk along the beach, followed by another sit down and relax followed by more playing in the sea. There are no shells of any interest other than the long pointed spirally ones, which were small, but occupied.

Lunch consisted of a series of snacks from a variety of food vendors along the beach, some with stationary stands, others walking along the beach selling their wares. Besides food and drink for sale, there were beach clothes carried around on clothing racks supported on the shoulder of the vendor: hats, sandals, baskets, temporary tattoos, kites, jewellery, and just about anything else you could want for your day at the beach. I didn't see umbrellas and chairs for sale. Too bulky to carry round the beach, I suppose, or more probably, too much initial outlay for the itinerant vendors. No doubt there was a shop nearby where such items could be purchased.

We left the beach around 3.00 p.m. Carlos and family headed back to their apartment and we went to visit an aquarium. It was very impressive, filled not just with small fish, but several species of large fish as well as alligators, turtles, sharks, rays and crabs. They also had frogs/toads, about six inches long, lizards/iguanas, snakes, and a case/cage/tank of penguins. It was all very well done, with display boards about what was in the tanks, the ecology of certain ecosystems (such as mangrove swamps), and people on hand to answer your questions (and no doubt make sure you behaved yourself), and of course the obligatory gift shop that you walk through to get out. By Brazilian standards, it was very smart (and very expensive), but very well done.

Later Carlos took us to a craft market, where Carmen, Sarah and I wandered along the stalls of jewellery, beach clothes, and ornaments, while the boys sat and had a beer. I bought a Kanga with a hand painted dolphin on the back. Carmen was determined that I was going to have one. A Kanga is an almost obligatory part of beachwear for ladies, or rather 'going to and from the beach' wear. It is a length of coloured fabric about 2' x 6' which you wrap round your waist and tie or fasten in some manner at the front or side. Bikinis are OK for on the beach, but off the beach, one wears a Kanga over the bikini. As you can guess, the variety of colours and designs is limited only by the imagination. Sarah went from one jewellery stall to the next, and we eventually bought her a bracelet with a ring attached to it by a chain. Apparently, they are all the rage at school, having been popularised by some TV presenter/personality, I gather.

Next stop, dinner and then bed. It was Carmen's birthday, so Carlos took us to a good seafood restaurant and we had an excellent meal.

Before we knew it, Sunday dawned and it was time to head home again. We left at 11.00 a.m., well before the majority of weekenders leave the beach, to avoid the queues of traffic. We saw what we had come down on Friday night! No dramatic hairpins as you might find in the Alps, but nevertheless, quite a feat of engineering to get a road there at all. The coastline has a backdrop of steep, tree covered hills, the *mata Atlantica* or Atlantic forest. Apparently, this is a valuable and diverse ecosystem that they are trying to preserve. The hills are too steep to build on economically, and I suppose that in the past, farmland was easily available elsewhere without the need for terracing, which is why the forested areas have survived. It certainly makes for a beautiful backdrop: a wide variety of trees, all flowering at different times, which add vivid splashes of colour to the green.

We had to get to the top of those hills – in reality, the edge of a plateau – to get home. As on Friday night, this entailed navigating a series of sweeping curves and tunnels, climbing steadily all the time, but this time we could see that the sections of road between the tunnels were viaducts with huge concrete stilts supporting the road.

On the way to the climb we passed roadside stall after roadside stall selling bananas – just bananas!

The coast is certainly hot – though I think we managed to pick a hot weekend. São Paulo is usually about 5°C cooler than Piracicaba, being nearer the coast, but when you drop down 2,500 feet, it gets hotter still!

One of the disadvantages of this hot climate is that is takes a long time for things to cool down. For instance, the car can still be hot (engine and interior) five to six hours after you last used it, even if it has been parked in the shady garage all that time and out of the sun. Also I made a Dundee Cake as a birthday present for Carmen, and it took more than five hours to cool!

In all, though, it was a thoroughly enjoyable weekend. I think we will be exploring more beaches, and there are plenty to choose from. Brazil is not a major tourist destination – yet, but I think that will come. They are beginning to market themselves as such. I think years of unstable governments have kept Brazil off the tourist map, as well as the personal safety aspect, but all that is changing gradually.

We went to a barbeque with Isadora's family recently, which was fun. Next week we are invited to lunch at someone's fazenda. Life is becoming a social whirl! But we will still keep on exploring this amazing and beautiful country.

Carnaval and Easter

Carnival (or *Carnaval* as it is spelled and pronounced in Portuguese) happens usually in February, depending on when Easter falls. It is Brazil's equivalent to our Shrove Tuesday! It's a massive street party before the start of Lent. The word comes from the Latin: *Carne* - meat, *Vale* - goodbye, though there is some discrepancy over the Vale bit. I haven't noticed many Brazilians giving up meat for Lent! Monday and Tuesday, and in many cases Wednesday are holidays, so everyone heads for the beach for a long weekend.

Sarah's school had their own mini Carnaval on the Thursday preceding the holiday weekend. She had to take a costume to school (thank goodness I had one in stock from the birthday party she went to shortly after we arrived), and at 6.30, the parade left the school, led by a brass ensemble (dads and teachers, I think) on the back of an open truck.

The schoolchildren walked/danced about ten blocks throwing streamers, confetti and spray foam all over the place. Sarah was a bit overwhelmed by it all, mainly because I think she was hungry. She seemed to perk up a bit after finishing someone else's large packet of crisps. The ultimate destination of the parade was a small square where there were several very tall puppet type figures supported by some unfortunate person inside the bottom of the long garment. It was all fun. I joined in some of the dancing at the square. A passer-by along the route joined in and danced along with the schoolchildren, but it is the adults that seem to do all the dancing. The children just walked and fooled about, and when we reached the square, they spent the time running round and bursting the balloons on the truck.

We arrived back from Brasilia on the Tuesday, which is the actual day of Carnaval. Piracicaba does have a carnaval but it's fairly modest. We didn't go and watch. The big Carnaval in Rio is put on for tourists, and nowhere else has such a spectacular show. The groups in Rio that build the floats and costumes all get massive grants towards the cost - some floats costing as much as 2,000,000 reis (approximately 3½ reis to the pound) - and they are *huge*. Maybe next year we will go to Rio for Carnaval.

Moving on to Easter, Alan's mum came to stay with us for the holiday. We went with her to see Paixão do Cristo, Brazil's answer to Oberammergau, except that Piracicaba puts on its Passion Play every year, not every ten years like the German one, and it is certainly spectacular! I think this was the twelfth or thirteenth year. It started out as a small performance put on by students at the agricultural university. It is performed outside in the grounds of the old sugar mill, the Parque Engenho, using the different levels of natural terracing for varying stage elevations. There are 8,500 square metres of space with, I quote, 'exuberant vegetation' and a cast in excess of 800 people, plus 57 horses, a donkey and foal, a sheep and a dove.

The play (which is just under three hours in duration) begins with the birth of Jesus, and then it portrays various excerpts from his life to his death and beyond. Half the Roman army was mounted, which is where the horses came in. The set consisted of various key buildings – Herod's palace, the temple, Pilate's house, a tomb, the Sea of Galilee (yes, they had made an artificial lake), and these were all dotted about the terraces. Amazing light effects, combined with suitable sound effects made it a stunning experience. It didn't matter that you couldn't understand the dialogue, because if you've grown up with a Christian background, you know the stories anyway. When John the Baptist baptised Jesus – with all the cast members paddling in the 'Sea of Galilee' – an artfully concealed dove was released from somewhere amongst Jesus' clothing. He fasted in the wilderness and was tempted by the devil (with lots of red lighting during that part for effect); he collected his disciples, the 'fishers of men'; he fed the 5000; he held discourse in the temple; he raised Lazarus from the dead; healed the centurion's servant; calmed the sea of Galilee; suffered the little children to come unto him; rode into Jerusalem on a donkey (the same one that Mary and Joseph had fled on earlier); washed the disciples' feet, and lots more. Salome danced and got her reward. Judas did his bit.

The whole thing was incredible. The horses were amazing in that they were so well behaved amidst all the noise and light effects. The only time they were startled was at the thunderclaps when Jesus died – tropical thunderclaps, not the tame rumblings you get in Ireland. They were held in for two thunderclaps, then given rein and allowed to disappear rapidly – in an orderly fashion I might add – behind the scenes. The donkey foal (not a very young one) was a bit bemused by the light at one stage, and went for a drink from his mummy, but it added to the whole performance.

The grand finale was the whole cast (minus horses) coming out in the dark onto the various levels of the set, all with candles, and then Jesus ascending into heaven with angels all around. To create this effect they had four fifty-metre-high scaffolding towers rising out of the trees, with the angels dressed in white on top of the towers, all lit up with white light. It was utterly amazing. As Alan's mother pointed out, it is worth coming to Brazil just to see this, if nothing else!

Though safety precautions are taken, the production is not without hazard to the performers. They have to find their way to their place on stage in the dark or with spotlights in their eyes; then find their way back stage in the dark as they traverse over rough ground and through the trees with the benefit of very little light; and finally, those angels have to climb the scaffolding towers in the dark!

We heard that a Roman soldier fell off his horse, but we didn't see it happen.

Seating for the audience is comprised of tiers of benches on scaffolding, but Alan had been allocated a box (Caterpillar is a major sponsor), which meant we had plastic seats on a platform at the top under an awning in case of rain. Before the performance began, we were each served a plastic cup of water by a waiter in a white jacket and bow tie. Those with box seating were not frisked as they came in and were personally escorted to their places. Alan didn't ask for a box; it is what we got, and actually, I think we would have had a better view of the play from the top tiers of the regular seating area! Maybe next year we'll try for a seat in the 'thrupennies.'

The daughter of one of Alan's work colleagues was part of the cast as one of the people of Jerusalem. Her mother was saying she had been frantically sewing costumes, so yours truly has volunteered to help with this project next year.

Easter is very much a religious festival only. Good Friday is a general holiday, and that is all Sarah got for Easter holidays. Apparently, there was a procession in the town on Friday evening, from one church to the cathedral in the centre. We found out about it after the event, but the local church in our area had a parade (if that is the right word), which came past our flat, so we watched it from the elevation of our balcony. They had the body of Christ on a bier carried by four worthy persons, and towards the back, a statue of the Virgin Mary carried by four women. They also had a truck with speakers and a P.A. system for the priest. They would walk for a bit, singing, then they would stop and the priest would say a bit, then move on, then further down the street, stop once again and say a few prayers before continuing. There must have been at least a hundred people in the procession.

I was awakened by the sound of singing at 6.00 a.m. on Sunday morning. I went to the window to see this latest diversion, and there was a dawn parade – I assume the same church, following the same route. This one was comprised of all women carrying a statue of the Virgin Mary as before, but this time the singing was accompanied by two women with guitars. As they passed our flat, I went to look out the back and saw the menfolk coming the other way to meet them at the crossroads. They had the priest and the P.A. system with them, and after a brief oration by the priest, they continued on their way together back towards the church. The truly devout eat only fish on Good Friday, and certainly, one restaurant was advertising a wide variety of fish dishes to tempt the hungry. We ate fish that day at a well-known fish restaurant here, and boy was it busy, but they were doing well at getting through all the people waiting.

Daily Life in Piracicaba

On the last Saturday of February, we joined a group calling themselves Calango Andando, literally translated as 'lizard walking'. It is a Caterpillar company-based group, and once a month they organise a long walk. This one was 21.8 kilometres. We started at 6.00 a.m. walking first through Piracicaba, then on to a dirt road and on to an even smaller track, which led to a disused railway track. It took us along routes that we would never have found otherwise. We ended up on a dirt road through the inevitable sugar cane, and finally came to a small town called Rio das Pedras (River of Stones). Someone cut down some sugar cane, peeled the skin off and Sarah and I chewed our way the last two to three kilometres into Rio das Pedras. Raw sugar cane is very tough and fibrous, but the juice that comes out as you chew it is lovely. You don't eat the fibrous bits. Maybe it sustained us those last kilometres!

Lunch was organised at a small *peixeria* (peixe is Portuguese for fish) - a place with ponds where you can fish, and where you can also get drinks, snacks and lunch - fish of course. I think fishing is just as much a national pastime as football. Sarah wants to have a go at fishing.

I thoroughly enjoyed the walk, getting out of Piracicaba into the countryside proper (even if it was with about sixty other people!). Alan took his motorbike with ten litres of water on the back, and Sarah walked some and rode some. The water became very popular as people realised that it was there for all, not just us. I was a bit stiff the next day, but nothing drastic. It must be 20 years since I did a walk of that distance.

We had a very pleasant trip the weekend before last to yet another zoo, this time in Sorocaba about 100 kilometres south. We went in the company of Sarah's best friend Isadora and her family. It was my idea to go and I invited Isadora and her sister, and the parents decided it would be fun too, so we all went - in two cars of course. The children chose which car they wanted to travel in at whatever point. It was interesting to hear Sarah speaking Portuguese. She has the nasal quality of many of the words just perfect, which is more than can be said for her struggling parents. After the zoo, we headed back towards Piracicaba, and turned off the road to visit another town called Itu, having had lunch on the way. Itu's claim to fame is giant everyday objects around the town: a three-foot-high telephone; a set of traffic lights, with the lights section being about six feet high; a telephone kiosk twelve feet high, and so on. And of course there are tourist shops selling outsize goods, which is all great fun. The outing was also very good for our Portuguese, though both Isadora's parents speak English.

We still have two Portuguese classes a week (in theory, but Alan has to cancel frequently because of meetings). I'm getting better at understanding what is said to me and less frequently have to ask people to repeat themselves. Our teacher says that understanding comes first when learning a new language, then speaking, then reading, then writing.

I'm back to my weekly Yoga class, and I have also joined one of Sarah's school choirs. There is a group for parents, teachers and employees, and we number about thirty, females dominating of course. I'm very impressed with the teacher who runs the choir, just as I was very impressed with the standard of their singing when I heard them perform before Christmas. Now I'm doubly impressed. Generally in the past, music was not taught in schools, so the majority of the adults who join the choir can't sing. However, after a little prompting from Tânia, they can sing the note being played and sustain it. It never occurred to me that singing was something you could learn to do. I thought either you could sing or you couldn't. She also teaches mostly by ear. I don't know how many can read music. Not many I guess. Certainly at the performances I saw, no-one had any music. It made me realise just how much music I was taught at school.

As well as choir, I have enrolled on a *curso basico* of cooking, which, apart from teaching basic cooking skills (I do know how to cook vegetables and potatoes), will teach me day-to-day Brazilian cooking and, as an added bonus for me - Portuguese. I've already learned how to make some tasty salad dressings. Salad is very much a part of Brazilian cuisine, served with every meal and consisting of not only the usual variations on lettuce, tomato and cucumber, but also including cold cooked vegetables. Many puddings tend to be variations on condensed milk, and as testimony to this, the supermarkets are full of shelf after shelf of tins of condensed milk! Somewhere along the line, I hope to learn to make *feijão* and rice - a Brazilian staple of beans and rice. A pressure cooker seems to be an important part of every Brazilian kitchen. Maybe it is cooking all those beans!

I shall just have to keep a look out for a basic recipe book now that I can cope with recipe book language. We learnt about rice & beans, meat, chicken, fish, sauces, pies (savoury pies; in other words, pastry), and I can't remember what else, but I did take time to ask about various basic ingredients which were alien to me, such as, how long do you soak salt cod? What do you do with mandioca root? My success with fish here has not been great. The basic fish is much meatier than I am used to cooking, as the fish are much larger and thus cooking times need to be longer.

I shall have to look for another course/class to keep me out of mischief. Painting, embroidery, beads ... lots of choices. I would like to do something a bit more serious, but it would have to fit in round school. There are about four universities here so I should be able to find something. So far all the courses I've found at the Agricultural University last four or five years, though I must admit, the five-year agricultural engineer course looks very interesting

Sarah and I had our first experience of the theatre here. They had a children's show on, and all the schools were doing bits about this particular author, as it was his birthday. I would not be keen to repeat the experience. Firstly, I think the sound system broke down after the first ten minutes, and secondly, the children wouldn't stop talking. I don't know whether this was because they couldn't hear and were bored or because it is normal behaviour for children at the theatre in Brazil, but they talked incessantly, and most of them ended up leaning against the platform at the front, with some of them even climbing on stage. I couldn't hear any of the lines spoken by the actors, and as a result, just 'switched off'. It is bad enough having to concentrate to understand what someone is saying in another language without all the extra noise! Maybe I'll try something more adult next time.

In contrast, we went to a circus on Saturday night. It was a small family concern with clowns, juggling, acrobats, tight-rope walking, cracking of whips, performing poodles and a 'bullfight' with a Brazilian bull. He doesn't get killed or gored, as they need him for the next performance, but they rode him and somersaulted between his horns and harassed him with red cloaks. There must have been about seventy to eighty people watching - but the circus had been there for at least a week. We only discovered it by driving past and then circling back. They had a huge 'big top' with seating for roughly a thousand or more, I would say, and including the performers and attendant staff, about twenty people to do all the work. All seemed to juggle and whip, including a small girl of about six. The tightrope artiste also trained the poodles. The smallest clown must have been about three years old. The whole family was involved, and they put on a good show, but I couldn't help thinking what a hard life they lead! They have to put up and take down the seating and tents as well as drive the lorries between shows when they are not performing.

We went to a kite making session in a park yesterday morning sponsored by the town council, with all materials provided. We didn't arrive at 8.00 a.m., which is when it started, the inference being that you could turn up at any time, with the finish time being 11.00 a.m. It might have been better if we had arrived early, because when we did arrive, everything was a bit chaotic, but we got our bits and produced a passable kite, which we still have to test properly. None of us knows anything about kite making, and we weren't quite sure who the 'helpers' were, but it was all fun, and there were prizes for various categories - not that we fell into any of them! And they provided *lanche*, which is not lunch, but a snack - usually a sandwich or a roll of some sort. They do have *sanduiches* here, but they're not common.

We haven't had any rain here for a month, and the river is looking very peaceful compared to six weeks ago when the level had risen about two metres. Keep in mind, this river is quite wide. Every day, clouds build up with the heat during the afternoon, and as the temperature drops, they disappear. They're always very promising cumulo-nimbus clouds, but they don't like getting cold. Sugar cane burning has also started again, producing its gentle black snow as someone described it, though not in earnest yet. It is all very controlled, and you can read in the paper which day a particular area is going to be burnt.

We had a fun evening last night. Caterpillar is sponsoring an exhibition to do with preserving the rainforests, and so about thirty Caterpillar personnel went along to the opening night. We arranged for Sarah to be collected from school and to stay the night with her little friend, and at 4.30 p.m., Alan and I, along with the rest of the Caterpillar contingent, climbed on to a plushy bus and were driven in comfort to São Paulo. The exhibition was in a leisure complex housed in an old factory. Alan and I didn't rate the exhibition very highly, but others thought it good - maybe because they understood more of the commentary. It was aimed mainly at schoolchildren. By the time everyone had drunk their fill and nibbled the nibbles, speeches were made and exhibition visited, it was about 10.30, one-and-a-half hours before the bus was due to pick us up and return us to the Caterpillar home office. As none of us had eaten much since about midday - apart from nibbles - we all went for pizza in São Paulo. We caused a stir, all thirty of us descending at short notice on the restaurant! But soon they had a table ready for us, and once we were seated, the hilarity began. If you think the Irish know how to enjoy themselves, you should see the Brazilians. It is a long time since I laughed so much. It does help if you have at least one 'eejut' in the party, and we certainly had that.

As I have said before, the people here are great. They will include you in everything. I think that one asset we have (apart from Sarah) is the fact that we are not American (Americans are not very popular here) - and we have chosen to live among Brazilians instead of in the international community with other expats. The President of the Caterpillar office here, a delightful American named Bill, would prefer to live in Piracicaba as well (as would his wife), instead of with the international lot, but they are installed and settled in a very smart house with all the relevant security measures deemed necessary for someone of his position. He is a wonderful boss: he has a gentle disposition, is prepared to listen, and doesn't talk at top volume all the time. We all like him and his wife, a lot.

It's May now, and it's cold for this part of Brazil. We are into trousers and jumpers. The term 'cold' is relative of course. The temperature tends to be between 20° C and 25°C during the day dropping to 12°ish at night, but we are finding it a bit on the cool side. How will we ever survive an Irish winter again!

Sarah had a midterm report, which she came through with flying colours! Lowest marks – eight out of ten for Portuguese and P.E. Highest – 10 out of 10 for art, philosophy and English! Instead of her one-to-one Portuguese class, she has now joined a group of her (less able) classmates who have difficulty with their language, but she is a great help to me with the amount of Portuguese she has acquired. When we go into a shop and I ask for something in error, and Sarah realises it is not what we want, she takes over and sorts things out. I don't get a look in.

I have at last found an authentic Brazilian rug! Everything I had looked at previously was imported. I say Brazilian, but these rugs are handmade here (and the price reflects that) using a technique that came from Portugal with the immigrants. The designs are what I would call traditional – nothing too modern or desperately different. These rugs are made with wool on Hessian using a long armed cross-stitch, and the result is very attractive. You can buy kits, but they are expensive because the design is painted on by hand. The mother of Sarah's friend Isadora has a half-finished rug and says she will show me how to make one. Maybe I can finish hers for her! We bought a couple of round ones: one about five feet diameter for the living room and a little one for Sarah's room. Common sense suggested that we buy, instead of waiting for me to make one! I have enough unfinished projects without adding to them.

A few weeks ago, we spent a weekend with some of the members of the choir, up in the hills about an hour from here. It was a do-it-yourself weekend, the sort where you bring your own bedding, food and entertainment, but it was all very pleasant. I did learn to play the Brazilian equivalent of bowls, called Bocche. It's the same idea as rolling balls to hit a smaller one, but this is done on levelled sand and has few rules.

Bocche

The Brazilians certainly know how to enjoy themselves! We had a barbeque on the Sunday – someone had a guitar, and the three 'chefs' were providing a percussion accompaniment to the music with whatever they had in their hands at the time, be it huge knives and forks, large skewers, saucepan lids and so on. It really was very funny. They also managed to look after the meat at the same time!

Talking of the choir, Sarah and I had our first performances the weekend before last. I was singing at a shopping centre about a forty-five-minute drive away, at what I can only describe as a 'letting the people know about singing' sort of event. My performance was in the evening. Sarah and Alan stayed at home and I got a lift with fellow choir members. All went well and it was fun. There were two other choirs involved.

Sarah's performance was part of a youth choir get together at the theatre of one of the universities here. There were at least ten choirs, with each singing at least three songs. Some of them were very good. Sarah's lot were about fourth on, and I'm afraid we left once she had done her bit. She had a birthday party to go back to anyway! It was Isadora's birthday and the party started at 11.00 a.m., but as all her guests (all five of them, apart from her relatives) were involved in the choir, the party continued after the concert. Isadora is also in the choir, but because her grandparents were staying, she didn't go. It was a good cake too. Alan and I were invited to join them after the concert.

Last weekend was extremely busy! I was invited to a birthday party (a small celebration). It was my Yoga teacher's birthday on the Friday, and his wife along with one of the students arranged a surprise party to coincide with the end of one of his classes. He knew nothing about it. I stayed there for about 45 minutes, then it was home again, pick up Alan and Sarah and go to the Festa das Nações – the Festival of Nations. It is a charity fund-raising event. Each charity sets up a stand selling various foods and goods of another nation or a different region of Brazil, and there are costumed parades, a jazz band, rock bands – any excuse for a bit of noise and partying. We had our tea that evening in 'Japan', with a bit of sushi and yakisoba. The festival wasn't that exciting, but then I guess we went too early. We were there by 7.45 p.m., and as we were leaving at 9.30-ish the crowds were beginning to flood in, but that is Brazil for you. Partying starts late here (–well, late by our standards!).

Saturday morning, we had an early start for another *calango andando* with our walking group, up at 5.00 a.m. to start walking at 6.00. This time we trekked 31.2 kilometres through another stretch of lovely, undulating countryside. As the final destination was completely on the other side of Piracicaba from the starting point, at least a quarter of the walk was getting out to the other side of the town. It simplifies matters if they always start from the same point (which is conveniently close to us). We traversed up hill and down dale, across a stream where the road bridge had fallen down, but there was a plank across it in the neighbouring field. No problem for Alan on the bike, though several of the group were a bit skeptical. They obviously knew nothing about trails riding. As Alan put it, he had to concentrate for all of two seconds, and that was getting up the steep slope on the far side. Along the way, I was offered a freshly picked orange, Sarah was given a freshly picked avocado, and someone else picked a passion fruit.

There was a reception committee waiting for us at the final destination in the shape of a small boy and his horse. He directed us across a field to the *sítio* (a small holding) we were aiming for because it was a shorter distance than going by road. He didn't mention the soggy bit in the middle of the field, but nothing daunted, some walked through it with their shoes on, some, including me, with shoes off, and some took vast detours round the edge. At the foot of the final hill, on the far side of the field there was a small river with a little waterfall, and what did we all do – we bathed our weary (and filthy, for those who had paddled across the soggy bit) feet in it. With it being such a hot day, sun blazing down relentlessly, of course some ended up swimming – Sarah included. What a lovely way to finish the walk. After we were sufficiently cooled off, a BBQ was waiting for us, and then we got a lift home. Sarah was supposed to go to yet another birthday party, but as she fell asleep in the car on the way home, we decided that maybe she could give it a miss. It was one of the boys in her class, and boys' birthday parties tend to be all about football, football or football!

Poinsettias are in flower now, and the flowers really are the most bizarre things. The plants themselves have long straggly stems, growing to ten feet or more in height, bearing little resemblance to the small ones so popular at Christmastime in Europe and the US.

Poinsettia tree

The flowers start out as a cluster of round green buds, about a third of an inch across, in the middle of the red bracts that we all think of as the flowers. Each bud has a horizontal slit in one side. As the bud opens, short red stamens appear on the top of it. The bit with the slit separates from the rest of the bud and turns into what I can only describe as a pair of yellow lips that lie alongside the red bit. I guess it is like the male and female bits of the flower.

They look like little mouths!

Last weekend was quiet. Sarah had flu, so she and I stayed indoors doing very little. Alan went exploring on his bike. Sunday morning we went to see a theatrical production of *Puss in Boots*. It was aimed at children and was very good, all done with a cast of only about five on a limited budget. It wouldn't take much to push it into a full-blown pantomime.

In the afternoon, we went lizard spotting, which isn't very difficult to do here. It is a rarity to spot one as large as Alan's metre-long monster because people hunt them for food, but small ones are everywhere. I counted twenty-six one morning sunning themselves on about 200 metres of wall in the park where I go for a walk once a week while Sarah has her Portuguese lesson. These smaller ones range from three to nine inches long and are brown or sometimes a bit greenish. In the evenings, we can find small (three inches or less) almost translucent lizards on the walls of houses where the sun has been shining during the day. Indeed, one of these found its way into our bathroom about a month ago!

I said that I go for a walk in the park, but it is more a bit of brisk exercise, and everybody is at it. Many people go at 6 a.m. before they start work, all walking briskly round the park several times dressed in shorts or tracksuits and tennis shoes. It is taken very seriously, all doing warm up stretches before starting and after finishing. One lap is two kilometres, so it is easy to keep track of the distance walked if you have a daily goal. I tend to stop and look at things – like lizards. I do two or three laps before going back to pick up Sarah.

Thursday is a holiday here and Sarah gets Friday off as well. We are going to Rio de Janeiro, and will be staying with someone Alan knows through work. It will be good to have someone who knows the lie of the land to escort us round Rio.

Rio de Janeiro

Thursday was a holiday, so like most Brazilians, we took Friday off as well and headed to Rio de Janeiro.

Rio is some place, and the approach by air, is, as we were told, dramatic. Apart from the scenery, which is spectacular, the domestic airport is on a spit of reclaimed land so the sea was getting uncomfortably close before we actually touched down.

I can't say much about the city itself, as we didn't spend any time just wandering and absorbing the atmosphere of the place. We were met at the airport and ferried round from pillar to post by Omar, a business colleague of Alan's. Seeing a city this way for the first time has its advantages. It was great having someone who knew the city very well to lift and lay us, and Omar has known Rio de Janeiro since childhood. He has his own business, and his wife is a vet specialising in exotic animals, including lions and tigers (we didn't get to meet any). She works at the zoo. They have a lovely seven-month-old daughter who came everywhere with us. They also brought along with them a ten-year-old niece for Sarah to play with, which was very thoughtful of them. It would have been nice to have leisure time to just wander aimlessly and get to know the flavour of the city by gradual immersion, exploring its hidden delights by making discoveries on our own.

The setting of Rio is certainly dramatic, with a backdrop of mountains reaching about 2000 feet in elevation (some of the mountains have strayed into the city itself), and a fringe of fabulous beaches round the seaward edge as bits of the city jut out into the sea. The beaches are dotted with palm trees, adding to the exotic feel of it all.

Our first tourist stop was the vast statue of Christ at the top of a tall, narrow, steep sided mountain overlooking the city from about 2000 feet.

Cristo Redentor (Christ the Redeemer)

From this vantage point, one can take in spectacular views of the surrounding area, though it can be a bit hazy.

Taking in the view from this height gave us a general idea of the layout of the city, but the car certainly got a workout climbing the steep winding road to get us up to the park where the statue is located. Omar has a large black pickup type van, for towing generators. This park is a big tourist trap with about three tourist shops, a snack place, a small car park for workers, a tram station and nowhere for visitors to park. There just isn't any more room at the top to make a car park. Visitors are supposed to come up on the tram.

We went back down again to look for lunch, and found the perfect spot in a restaurant overlooking a beach. We drove by several beaches, and on one, we saw hang gliders landing – with two people on board! They do tandem flights – pilot and passenger, or novice and instructor – on short flights, launching from the top of one of the sheer mountains in the city (the peak next to the mountaintop Cristo). We were tempted.

We looked at Rio's biggest *favela* (shantytown) – one million plus people all living more or less on top of each other in a very small area. The houses (dwellings might be a better description) are so closely packed and the land so steep that they look as if they are built in stacks. They are not the make shift cardboard and tin dwellings that one hears about, though there are some of those. These are made from brick. One wonders about the availability of necessities such as water, power, and sewage, something that most of us take for granted. We did not drive into the favela – that would have been asking to be robbed. I gather that the favelas are very close-knit communities but are totally run by the drugs gangs.

Next we went up again, this time to the other side of the peak that Christ perches on top of, and went for a walk in the park there. Alan saw a monkey in the trees. I say monkey, but these are small creatures – more marmoset like. It was a very pleasant walk, though dodging the high speed skate boarders was not quite so peaceful.

We had barbecue for tea (everyone barbecues here in Brazil), and then fell into bed completely exhausted. It was a long day, especially since it had begun with a 4.00 a.m. start.

We had decided that Friday would be our beach day. We drove about 30 kilometres out of Rio to a beach called Prainha where the local Cariocas (those who live in Rio) go. It's a lovely little beach on one side of a narrow spit of land. Small maybe, but it had all the amenities – snack bar, toilets, and it even boasted showers. The waves were quite strong, so children had to be watched carefully (we had a three-year-old nephew in tow as well today).

It is a surfers' beach, and there seemed to be hundreds of surfers floating with their surfboards waiting to catch just the right wave. From the shoreline they look like tiny brown specks in a sea of deep emerald green. I don't know whether there is some sort of etiquette amongst surfers, waiting your turn and all that, but it seemed that very few of them actually rode the waves. Maybe they were indulging in that well-known Brazilian pastime – talking.

Soon it was time to move on, and everyone showered and washed sand out of their knickers after waiting in the queue while surfers washed themselves and their surfboards. Then it was on to a lunch stop with some friendly people we had met on the beach. We enjoyed eating and talking while the children played in the playground attached to the restaurant. Afterward, we went back to base to wash the salt off properly and relax for awhile before going out to sample the delights at one of Rio's Indian restaurants.

Saturday was a trip to Petropolis. The drive there was fantastic. Brazil has a narrow coastal strip, but then the road climbs, winding ever upwards through magnificent scenery until you get to Petropolis at the top. This is where the emperor once lived, and I can understand why. It is cooler for a start. We visited an historic sort of house, which was full of empty rooms, but some were fairly impressive.

The town grew up around the private estate of the emperor, Dom Pedro I, and was mainly populated by German immigrants. Some of the architecture is distinctly Germanic, and there was a restaurant/snack place selling German foods and mementos. The town became the summer residence of successive emperors and is now the summer residence of the president.

The aim of the day was to have lunch with a man named Nelson who also sells generators. He lives in Rio but has a weekend place in the mountains. What a beautiful location! The house is modest, but it is literally perched on the side of a mountain, complete with Jacuzzi (outdoor) and swimming pool, surrounded by breathtaking scenery.

We didn't actually have lunch at his house - rather, drinks and nibbles and then out to a local restaurant at about 4.00 p.m. Here, it was a buffet style arrangement. You got your plate and filled it, but it was not cold food. There was a vast wood-fired stove in the middle with a huge shallow tank full of hot water on top, which kept the constantly replenished pans of food hot.

It was getting dark by the time we left, so the descent to Rio was not as breathtaking as the ascent had been.

Sunday arrived, and Sarah wanted to see more tourist places. We visited Pão de Açúcar, which translated literally means Sugar Loaf. It's a high, steep-sided mountain overlooking the bay, the top of which can be reached by cable car. Those of you who have seen the James Bond movie *Moonraker* will remember the sights to behold from this vantage point. The cable cars were closed for maintenance, unfortunately, so we couldn't follow in the footsteps of James Bond, but there was a very pleasant walk round the base of it, with the sea on one side and the steep rocks of the pinnacle (covered with climbers) on the other. It was here that we met more of those small monkeys chittering away in the trees.

Next stop, Copacabana Beach, where all the rich and famous hang out. Frankly, the beach was not clean, but there was the usual Brazilian beach scene, with people playing volleyball, football, sunbathing, paddling, though not many swimming. It is almost winter now, and the water is too cold (but this is all relative, of course). We were stopped by a policeman on a motorbike on our way to the beach, because the two girls (Sarah and the niece) were sitting in the back of the pickup, and that is not permitted. This resulted in a penalty of 1000 R$ (about £300) and seven points on Omar's license, but a bit of chat and 20R$ into the policeman's hand sorted out the problem.

There are three police forces here. I'm not quite sure what each is responsible for policing, but one is 100% corrupt, another is 60% corrupt and the third is 30% corrupt. Omar admitted that he didn't really approve of what he had just done, but faced with the difference between 1000R$ and 20R$, I know which would get my vote, especially if it is allowed by the police themselves.

Lunch was in an expensive Italian restaurant called La Tratoria - and very good it was. After lunch, Omar took us up to see where the hang gliders launch (the ones we saw landing on the beach). This side trip is not for the faint of heart or those who are afraid of heights! The road winds steeply up and up; you feel as though you will climb upwards forever. When we saw the launch site, we weren't quite so keen to take a trip (not that we were really planning to). The hang gliders are launched from a 2000-foot sheer drop, with nothing but air between you and the Atlantic forest. You literally just run off the edge of the roof of a shelter and the next thing you know, your feet are dangling in the air and you're being held up by the hang glider's wings, soaring like a bird.

We watched three brave souls with their mentors, all strapped into the hand gliders, hurling themselves off the edge. One girl screamed as she left terra firma and then continued to scream every time the hang glider banked. They have cameras attached to the hang gliders so you can photograph yourself in mid flight. I wouldn't mind the flight, but I don't know that I could fling myself off that edge. Maybe if there was only a 500-foot drop...

Next stop was a shopping mall called Barra Shopping. It is huge – well, it seemed that way to us. It is full of a vast selection of clothes, shoes, and accessories as well as a book/record store and various sports type stores.

After a leisurely browse through the mall, we went back to base for a hasty pack and then off to the airport! Flight left on time, landed at about 11.00 p.m. and we were back home by 12.15 – or I should say 00.15! Sarah was asleep in the back of the car before we even left the airport, and this one was a small airport. She slept until 11.00 the next morning! We did carry her up to bed rather than leave the poor child in the car.

Alan dragged himself out of bed the next morning to go into work at his usual start time of 7.30, only to find four other cars in the huge and usually packed car park. Why? Football! World cup mania!

World Cup Fever!

They're football crazy here in Brazil; absolutely football mad! Every conversation starts and finishes with football. Nothing else matters during the World Cup. It is useful to know results pertinent to you (in our case, how close Ireland came to beating Spain).

We live four blocks away from the 'place to be' on a Friday and Saturday night, but the noise and the music and the flags being waved and traffic being disrupted by revelers - not to mention the firecrackers being set off (they are very fond of their firecrackers here) - seemed like a lot of celebrating just for a team win. The same team won something else a week later with the match ending at 11.30 p.m., and the world just erupted with firecrackers going off everywhere. Even as early as 6.30 the next morning, someone was either still awake or got up early to let off more firecrackers in celebration.

World cup fever is hitting the shops, with Brazilian flags all over the place, and yellow and green drapery everywhere. T-shirts in various combinations of yellow and green are in every shop. (Can you guess what the Brazilian team colours are?!) Employees in some of the larger supermarkets are clad in yellow and green t-shirts. Bikinis and knickers in said colours are also available for purchase. There is a fixture list on the notice board next to the elevator in the garage under this apartment complex, so while you are waiting to get to your flat you can plan your football viewing.

World cup fever is a highly infectious disease, and in Brazil, it reaches epidemic proportions with millions of working hours lost as a result. The symptoms of this fever are as follows: a yellow and green rash; television sets appearing in unusual places with hoards of the infected clustered about them in rapt attention; absenteeism from work; extreme, wild-eyed enthusiasm; excessive garrulousness; euphoria at team wins and deep depression at losses; insomnia; and a compulsion to make lots of noise, particularly through the excessive use of firecrackers.

Some companies anticipate this outbreak and take preventive steps to offset the loss of working hours. For instance, Caterpillar has been planning for the World Cup well in advance. Everyone has been working an extra hour a day since Christmas up until a few weeks ago so that they can have time off to watch the matches live on TV during working hours! They even have large rooms set aside with TV sets installed.

But the television does not need to be turned on to know when Brazil has scored a goal. The cheers erupting from the surrounding area, shortly followed by firecrackers, proclaim their victory. The outcome of the Brazil/England match was predictable, just from the celebrations outside.

As mentioned at the end of the last chapter, the Monday morning of June 3, when Alan was still so exhausted from our trip to Rio, he arrived for work at his usual start time of 7.30 to find the car park deserted. He had completely forgotten! Matches are relayed live on TV in Brazil, and the match on this particular day was with Korea, which is literally on the opposite side of the world from Brazil. Then, on the Monday morning of June 17, Alan, along with the president of Caterpillar and various senior managers, sat and watched the Brazil/Belgium match. No work was done anywhere in Caterpillar that day either, at least not while the match was on!

Some matches start as early as 3.30 a.m. because they are aired live. The time of day does not moderate the noise level of the celebrations, however. We were awakened at 4.19 a.m. one morning by the sounds of cheering and firecrackers, all because Brazil had just scored their first goal in the match against England. When the match finished somewhere towards 5.30 a.m., with Brazil triumphant, the view of firecrackers lighting up the sky all over the city was a sight to behold, and the noise of cheering and car horns continued unabated until about 6.30 a.m. If Brazil wins the cup, there will be partying in the streets for weeks. Hopefully we will have recovered by the time we return home in July!

One Saturday morning, Brazil's start time was 8.30 a.m. I went to the supermarket thinking I could shop in peace since I knew everyone would be at home watching football. It certainly *was* quiet. There were televisions at strategic points around the store, each with a small group of chairs clustered around it so that customers and staff alike could keep abreast of what was going on.

Then, a couple of days later, for the first time in my life, I sat through a complete football match! Brazil woke up holding its breath that morning. We had been invited for breakfast at Isadora's house to watch the final match (against Germany) on television, which had an 8.00 a.m. kick off time. It was actually more interesting watching the people watching the match on television (at least it was for me who knows nothing about football!). Their eyes and concentration were riveted as they sat totally immersed in the game, with someone leaping to his feet every time Brazil did something worthy of note, and everyone shouting 'Go-o-o-o-o-o-al!' whenever Brazil scored. When the match ended with Brazil victorious, the city, needless to say, just exploded. After breakfast we took to the streets along with all the rest of Piracicaba and made our way to Carlos Botelho (the road just up from our apartment) where we knew all the action would be.

The street was a sea of yellow and green. Another essential is noise. Anything that makes a noise will do – and you thought beating saucepan lids was confined to small children! Okay, so I guess we were all probably behaving like small children, but that's the fun of it.

ADVOCACIA
BODY SHOP
NUTRIÇÃO ESPORTIVA
VITAMINAS IMPORTADAS
CAMPEÃO

P. E. T. A. R. – The Parque Estadual Turistico do Alto Ribeira

We set out to do more exploring this weekend – this time to the south of the state of São Paulo. Piracicaba has a holiday on the Thursday, and Caterpillar and Sarah's school have added in the Friday, making for a long weekend. We had a leisurely start on Thursday morning, leaving at 10.30. We took the BR 166 road, also called the Raposa Tavares, on the route west from São Paulo. We had lunch in a very new churrascuria, which must be part of the improvement scheme – or maybe it was just that there is not much traffic on a Thursday. Whatever the reason, it was very empty. The food was good, though.

As we progressed southwards, the character of the landscape changed. Gone were the rolling slopes and vast acres of sugar cane. This was more cattle country, and as it became ever hillier, grass gave way to trees and forest. As we journeyed on, it also became more and more remote, and the hills became bigger and more afforested. We eventually reached Apiai, a small town where we had to turn left along a dirt road for about 25 kilometres to get to a B & B type place, which we had seen advertised on the Internet. It was about 4.30 in the afternoon. It starts getting dark about 5.30 this time of year, and sunset here doesn't linger. Within half an hour, you go from daylight to dark (none of this dusk business, like what we're used to in Ireland).

As we drove along the dirt road, we saw very little habitation. We were encouraged by the occasional car that passed us on the road. At least there must be something down there. Yes, the road was sloping ever downwards now. I looked up what information we had about this area. Apiai is at an elevation of about 3000 feet, and Iporanga, which is 40 kilometres along the dirt road, is at about 250 feet above sea level. That's quite a drop, and the 40 kilometres drive is not in a straight line! It would be a shorter distance as the crow flies (except that they don't have crows here).

We couldn't find the advertised *pousada* (Bed & Breakfast) immediately, so we tried another one who said they had no food in store to feed us. If we had booked a room with them, they would have been out doing some food shopping prior to our arrival! They directed us back up the road, and eventually we found the B & B we had been looking for, but as we hadn't booked, it was the same story; they had no food to offer us. They directed us to another place where the owner had a large family so would probably have food enough for us. Their hunch was correct. Not only did she have a large family, she had a busload of school children (teenagers) booked in and they were from Piracicaba as well! This settlement, called Furnas, consisted mainly of B & Bs, about fifteen of them. It is in the middle of nowhere, very remote, has about three small bars, no shops of any size (if any) and exists solely because the area is full of caves. In tourist season and holidays, it is probably quite busy, full of budding speleologists and sightseers.

The family who ran this B & B also ran the bar across the road and the small caving/souvenir shop at the entrance to the pousada. I reckon they could have taken about fifty people in their various chalets set in tiers up the mountainside amongst the trees and vegetation. It was basic but quite adequate. The meal was typical Brazilian fare, and about the best I have tasted so far: salad, which always includes cold cooked vegetables as well as lettuce and tomato; hot rice and beans; and then, almost as an afterthought, bits of chicken arrived in another dish. As is so often the case with simple food, it was very good. How do they cook vast quantities of rice without it turning into a lump?

After dinner, we went to explore the settlement - at least as far as the streetlights extended. It was such a wonderful experience walking in the near darkness amidst various jungle sounds, but otherwise so quiet, away from all traffic noise. We heard something at the edge of the road, and went to investigate. Was it an insect or a frog? We pinpointed the source of the sound in a trickle of water, but in spite of shifting a few stones and poking with bits of twig, we could not find anything. What we did find a bit later was a huge moth the size of a small bird, and it was doing what moths do best, fluttering around a lamppost.

The next day, we planned to visit one of the caves. The lady of the house came over to us at breakfast (again, typical Brazilian fare – fruit, bread rolls, ham, cheese, jam, hot milk, very strong coffee, and powdered chocolate – or whatever mix it is – for hot chocolate) and asked would we like a guide for the caves. At this stage, we politely declined, as we were unaware of the vast number of caves in the area. We said we would pick up a guide in the park as we were only going to Caverna Santana. We should have done our homework better.

To get to the caves, we had to go back up the road we had come down the previous day, but only about three kilometres. It was all fairly quiet. We managed to get in ahead of the school bus group, and then we found a guide. He gave us each a helmet. He had an acetylene lamp on his, and he brought a torch (flashlight) to light the way as well. We followed him to the cave and regretted not bringing any torches of our own to use. Ah well, that gives us a good reason to say, *Next time...*

We followed our guide through all sorts of nooks and crannies and along ledges and up ladders. Because it's a tourist attraction, they had put ladders where necessary and bridged streams/wet areas with single planks with a bamboo handrail lashed to something at each end.

The cave was amazing. I've explored caves in Ireland, but they don't compare with this. It was as close to serious caving as you can get without going with a group of speleologists.

Certainly wouldn't pass safety regulations in the U.K., but the simplicity of it was brilliant: just the guide and the three of us and all those weird and wonderful formations created by the passage of time and water. It was totally silent except for the continual drip, drip, drip of water – and totally black when all lights were extinguished. I didn't know that the rock formations known as 'curtains', formed by trickling water, were musical! Our guide tapped several and it sounded like bells ringing.

The next day we visited another cave, which was much more dramatic and open, and about 100 kilometres from the previous one. It is called Caverna do Diabo, and is located near a small town called Eldorado! It was a series of huge caverns with equally huge formations. This one was floodlit, but done quite tastefully with the lights partially concealed so that it retained its air of mystery.

Caverna do Diabo

Both caves were fascinating, but very different in character - one smaller scale and more intimate and the other huge and dramatic. In a word: magical!

We travelled on to Iguape, booked into a small hotel and braved the rain in search of supper. We had hoped to spend the next day at the beach, but the rain never let up, so we decided to return home a day earlier than planned.

We travelled along a very interesting road home through a banana-growing region. (In fact, the road we took from Iguape to Sorrocaba is sometimes called the Estrada das Bananas.) I think bananas like rain! Ripening clumps of bananas were covered with blue plastic bags to protect them from pests. This road was another example of leaving the coastal strip and winding ever upwards. This time, however, the coastal strip was fairly wide so we had quite a bit of driving on flat terrain before starting to climb. We had lunch in Piedade, a small town at the top of the hill. Apparently, this area is known for its pure air and is popular as a weekend destination for people from São Paulo, being within an easy driving distance from the city.

We followed the old road to Sorrocaba out of the town to rejoin the main one. It was of course a dirt road. There is a real maze of these dirt roads, and practically none of them are marked on the maps, so we were following our noses! It took us past small, well-kept farms as well as country residences looking smart and well cared for. Alan and I both noted the absence of any obvious security measures; for instance, there were no imposing fences, large gates, and other structures that typically send the unspoken message of Keep Out! It was quite refreshing to see. All too soon, we joined the main road again, and we were back to asphalt and traffic and cities. We arrived home mid/late afternoon feeling well driven, but it was a memorable trip and one not to be missed.

June brings Festa Juninha

In Brazil, the month of June brings the Festa Juninha, a celebration of São Joao. There are three saints' days in June (Peter, Anthony and John), and practically every organisation and school has a Festa Juninha to celebrate. There is no set date on the calendar; organisations hold their Festas at any time of their choosing within the month of June (and occasionally in July), Sarah's school included.

The tradition of Festas Juninhas was brought to Brazil by the Portuguese, but its origins lie in the much older celebrations of pagan Europe. A large bonfire is traditionally the centrepiece, representing protection against demons that might spoil your crops, cause a drought, and so on. Dancing in circles about the fire ensured a good harvest. With the seasons reversed here in the southern hemisphere as opposed to what the original European settlers were used to, the reasons behind the original northern hemisphere customs gradually changed. In Europe, these were early summer festivals; nowadays in Brazil, the Festas Juninhas are just another excuse for a good party!

Dress for the Festa is country, which means that men (and some women) wear jeans and a check shirt and a straw or cowboy hat. Women wear frilly dresses of floral fabric trimmed with lace, and many of the children put their hair in bunches and paint rosy red splodges of makeup on their cheeks, with freckles painted on as well. Some of the older teen boys dress in drag – something you don't see too often in Ireland (if at all!).

The road outside the school was closed off and we had a party in the street, with various food stalls and side shows (like what you'd find at a church fête). Various groups did their bit. The classes in the lower school (four groups) all sang and/or danced.

The choir I sing in ran the *doce* stall and made all the goods. (Doce literally means 'sweet' rather than 'a sweet'.) Doces are more or less the equivalent of buns and traybakes in Ireland, so when it came to my turn during a choir rehearsal to say what I would make, every eye and ear was turned in my direction, curious to hear what I planned to bring to the festival. I decided that caramel squares would fit the bill; *quadros de caramelo* would be the Portuguese translation, being very sweet and sticky, but of course I had to call mine Doces Irlandes! They went down a treat. Brazilians have a very sweet tooth. The recipe was much in demand.

We also went to a Festa Juninha at Tupi, which is about fifteen minutes from Piracicaba. This Festa was a bit more rural. It all took place round a large grassy central square, in the middle of which was the church. This one had a large bonfire outside the church.

Festa Juninha bonfire outside the church at Tupi

Stalls were set up selling various foodstuffs. We tried *Vinho Quente* (mulled wine for want of a better description), and *Quentão*, which is also hot but is made from *pinga* (distilled sugar cane juice) with a lot of ginger in it and I don't know what else. We decided that the wine was better. I tried a coconut doce, which seemed to consist of fresh grated coconut in caramel (very sweet), and I also tried strawberries coated in syrup – all delicious. There were about six strawberries on a wooden skewer, and then this was coated in chocolate or red syrup that hardened. The tartness of the strawberries offsets the sweetness of the coating, and it was very nice. They also do the same thing with grapes. *Pamonha* seems to be another typical food. It is sweet corn puree with sugar added, so it is *very* sweet, and is served in 'bags' made from the husks, which surround the cob. (You can also get sweet corn ice cream in Brazil, which I find very tasty.)

The entertainment here was on a stage of sorts, and several different groups were doing their bit, from school groups singing, to line dancing, to semi-professional bands – all very noisy in true Brazilian style.

The culmination of this particular Festa Juninha is walking across the hot embers of the bonfire. This practice stems from an old European tradition, when it was done to ensure good luck in the coming months of growing and harvesting crops. At 11.00 p.m. or thereabouts, the hot coals are raked out and some brave souls actually walk across them! We didn't stay to see the fire walking. Maybe we'll do that next year!

Springtime in September

September ushers in spring in Brazil, which is always an adjustment after leaving late summer/early autumn behind in Ireland when we return from summer holidays there. We had just got back to Brazil when Sarah came home with flu after being at school only three days. I got it three days later and Alan two days after that, but he wasn't hit so badly and shrugged it off in about five days. Sarah and I had to resort to the medical profession and tried homeopathy. It seems to have worked. The doctor has started us on preventive treatment with the goal being to strengthen our immune systems. You wouldn't get that in allopathic medicine, and this chap is an allopathic doctor as well as homeopathic, and he knows Chinese medicine and acupuncture, not to mention pediatrics as well. There is quite a choice here.

I think winter must be the season for repainting houses and buildings here, which makes sense considering it's the dry season. When we arrived back here at the beginning of August (when the brief Brazilian winter is turning into spring), we noticed that lots of buildings had changed colour or at least had a fresh look about them. Maybe the paint dries too quickly if it is hot, and then there is the rain to contend with during the summer. It is certainly hot today, as hot as the hottest day we had during the summer. What a climate. Last week, the temperature barely exceeded 20°C, and now we have 33°C on the balcony. The dry season is over now, too. We had some rain at last, having had practically none since March.

Alan went out for a drink with a friend from work a couple of weekends ago and got 'stormbound' in the bar – at two o'clock in the morning. Brazilians tend not to go out until about 11.00 p.m., and when you're here, you do as they do. Alan said the wind came up suddenly and literally blew the plastic tables and chairs to one end of the seating area outside the bar. Most eating and drinking takes place outside. The occupants of those chairs had been driven inside by rain earlier, which means it must have been fairly crowded inside, because most places have limited indoor seating. As Alan was walking home at 3.00 a.m., he came a across a squad of workmen cutting up a fallen tree. We had never experienced storm damage at 3.00 a.m. in Ireland, let alone repair of said damage, but as I find myself saying frequently while living here – what a country!

I saw another interesting sight recently, also rain related. Normal motorcycling attire here is a T-shirt and shorts, and the girls quite often can be seen riding their bikes wearing high-heeled strappy sandals and often not much else. (A lot of girls ride bikes here.) When it rains, those who earn their living with their bikes (the equivalent of despatch riders, except that you can get almost anything delivered by bike here) don lightweight waterproofs and put plastic bags on their feet. I saw one chap who had gone a step further and was riding his bike through the rain with bare feet! Ah, well, it takes all sorts.

The temperatures have been 30°C on average (and this is winter!), though this week it is positively cold at a little above 20°C. It got down to 7.4° last night, which is the kind of early winter cold I'm used to! I brought my hygrometer with me from Ireland, and the lowest we have recorded so far is 23% humidity. We have also recorded 90%, but that was in the middle of a downpour last week, the first we have had since we got back. There isn't too much rain this time of year, as winter is the dry season.

Being winter, not only do people put coats on (and there are always those who run around in skimpy attire, too), but they also put coats on their dogs! I saw two poodles groomed to within an inch of their lives, with – wait for it – their claws painted with nail varnish and matching bows on their heads. One had pink and the other purple! Most dogs, I am happy to say, don't have to suffer this indignity.

But yes, spring is certainly in the air, and its vibrant, colourful beauty is creeping across the landscape.

When we first arrived back from Ireland, I noticed a definite lack of green in our vista across the trees of the Agricultural University, which surprised me because I had always been told that tropical trees don't drop their leaves all at once. I suppose they gradually lose the exuberant deep green of summertime even if they don't have a traditional autumn season.

And now, in September, the dullness of winter greenery is being replaced with that lovely pale yellow-green of new young foliage, and there are splashes of brilliant colour dotting the landscape as various trees come into bloom with large showy blossoms.

The colors are extreme in their bold beauty – bright yellows, reds and pinks, and various hues of purple and fuchsia. Ipé is the national tree of Brazil because it grows in every state. There is a variety with mauve-tinted blossoms as well.

Yellow Ipé and Pink Ipé

Frangipani with pink and sunrise coloured blossoms.

Jacaranda

This is a Couroupita Guinensis, with its unique combination of lavender and coral pink blossoms.

We have noticed that some of the fruit here seems to be very shy! It doesn't hang about on the ends of branches like apples and oranges. For instance, the yellow star fruit hides in the tree amongst the leaves. To see it you have to get under the canopy of branches and look up. These star fruit trees are about ten feet tall, and often they are planted in the street for decoration. There is also jaboticaba, which is a small black berry about the size of a sloe, and the way the berries grow along the branches of the tree looks as though little balls have been stuck on!

Jaboticaba berries waiting to ripen, and three days later – ripe. The spots of whitish colour, which look like snow along the branches, are the flowers.

Each year during this season there is a month-long exhibition of humorous pictures at the Engenho. I don't understand a lot of them, as some of them are political themes, and others are caricatures of persons unknown to us, but I do understand the humour in depicting Spiderman climbing the wall because he is afraid of a spider; Jesus being presented with a bill at the Last Supper; and George W. Bush portrayed backwards on a bucking bronco. This is not confined to Brazilian artists. It is very international, with some artists coming from as far away as the Czech Republic and Iran. We stayed as long as Sarah's attention span lasted, and I think she appreciated quite a lot of the pictures. I'll have to go back at my leisure when she is at school.

I am at last back to my usual activities – Yoga class, Portuguese class and choir each week, and I also seem to be starting another weekly activity of walking at the weekends, with Carlos and his wife (the Carlos whom I invited to tea in July when we were home). This is serious walking – an hour of brisk activity, not just a gentle stroll; very Brazilian. You see people going to the park (or wherever) for their *caminhada* at 5.30 in the morning so they can get their exercise, then still have time for a shower and breakfast and be at work by 7.00. We start walking at 7.30, not 5.30. It is very good for my Portuguese, too, as Carlos' wife doesn't speak English. I spent a very pleasant afternoon with her last week, chatting. They were worried about my flu taking so long to clear up and wanted to help. They thought it might have turned to pneumonia. As I have said before, there are such nice, caring people here.

My choir had a performance last weekend at a town three hours' coach ride away. Talk about a long night. We left Piracicaba at 5.15 p.m. and were driven to Sertãozinho, north of here, with our conductor, Tânia, busy rehearsing us as we went. We were going to her hometown. We arrived at the theatre, had a warm up, waited while various choirs sang, did our bit - we were the last to perform - and then went to Tania's mother's house for a supper. By this time it was 10.45 p.m.! There were nearly thirty of us to feed, and the house seemed to be full of all the sisters, cousins and aunts, not to mention brothers and uncles as well. It was a big house by Brazilian standards, and we had our supper round the swimming pool. If a house has a swimming pool - and many do - the patio surrounding the pool usually has some sort of bar and often barbeque facilities adjacent. It wasn't a huge supper, but it was a lovely gesture, and she had produced some sort of delicious pavlova type confection. Usually I don't like soggy meringue, but this stuff was so soft it just melted in the mouth. Brazilians seem to use the same word here for meringue and marshmallow, and I'm not quite sure where the dividing line is.

Tânia had to throw us out because the bus was waiting - and had been since 11.00 p.m.! I reached my bed at about 3.15 a.m., but it was a fun evening, even if most of it was spent on a bus. They seem to have a network of choirs who have little meetings every now and then. I think Tânia's mission in life is to teach the world to sing. She firmly believes that everyone should be given the opportunity to sing, whether they think they can or not. So long as they want to sing, that is enough for her - and certainly she has done wonders with some of our choir members. I was in the minority starting out, in that I could sing and also read music - and I think Tânia was very happy to have me because of this.

Sarah seems to be enjoying her piano lessons. They last an hour, and she gets written homework as well. We have bought a second-hand keyboard for her to practise on. Prior to that, I had to take her to the school of music several times a week to practise, which was hard work, and really left Sarah very little time to herself. Now at least she can do a bit here and there instead of having to pour all her practise time into one concentrated session, all in one go. She takes after her Auntie Lu and prefers to play by ear. I try not to play what she is supposed to be doing in an effort to get her to read the notes.

Sarah made her solo stage debut last week, playing the piano. She has sung with her choir on stage before now, but this was her first piano recital. The school of music has concerts every now and again for all its little pupils, and they get up on stage one by one to perform (or two if they are playing a duet), whether their musical selection is thirty seconds or five minutes.

I think there were about forty performers that night. Sarah did very well, and two of the boys were outstanding. Most played as was to be expected, and as you can imagine, the violins at times were fairly excruciating.

Our First Brazilian style party – on Election Day!

Alan and I decided to host a party and invite all our friends in celebration of our tenth wedding anniversary and our first full year of living in Brazil. (If we were truly Brazilian, we would have had a party for each event!) We booked the use of the barbecue and adjoining area here in the apartment complex. Alan organised someone to come in and do the catering, which meant he (the caterer) would do the barbecuing and provide the salad, vegetables, bread, rice, and drinks – in other words, everything that we specified. We decided that we would provide pudding, as we are not awfully enamoured of Brazilian mass produced puds. I made chocolate mousse, cheesecake and fruit salad, which all went down very well.

We had about thirty-five adults and twelve children. The children swam and played football and whatever else took their fancy, and the adults talked (and voted, as the party was held on Election Day, and then came back and talked some more!).

We had a mix of Caterpillar employees (American, Lebanese and Brazilian) and school parents. We started the party at 12.30 – lunchtime – and the last guests left about 6.30 p.m. (not a.m., though I'm sure that would not be unheard of). We received lots of presents, half of which were pot plants and three of which were orchids.

Now I will have to learn how to look after orchids, which need a lot of care and attention. I get along better with plants that thrive on neglect!

Something we discovered at the party is that wine is not a Brazilian drink. Alan bought twelve bottles of wine and only two were drunk! Beer and soft drinks are the order of the day.

We had put together an album of photographs of our (first) ten years together, which everyone enjoyed. Alan had bought some firecrackers to cap off the party in true Brazilian style, and when he brought them out to set them off, he was met with proclamations of 'Ele é um Brasiliero!' – 'He is a Brazilian!' We had no cleaning up to do afterwards, which was great. The maintenance staff here at the apartment complex took care of all that. If we hadn't opted to do the puds, we could have sat back and let everything be organised for us! I made an ice bowl to serve ice cream from, with flower petals frozen into it. It looked very pretty and festive. It is something I've always meant to try, and this seemed like as good a time as any. It certainly kept the ice cream from melting so quickly, and it lasted long enough to get everything served – and it was a very hot day.

Since our party was held on Election Day, I'll digress to tell you a bit about Brazilian elections, as they are quite different from what I'm used to in the UK.

Election fever really got going in early September. Three times a day there were 50-minute political broadcasts on television. Just to add to the chaos, these elections are for MPs and the president, all at the same time. It is all computerised, and underneath each candidate's name on all the posters is a number in large digits. This is what the voters will key in to a computer on Election Day. (None of this sitting counting scraps of paper afterwards.) By the time the elections actually arrive, I think everybody must be so confused that they key in whatever number comes to mind first!

Election Day is on a Sunday, and voting is obligatory – unless you are prepared to fill in a form explaining why you are not voting. Schools are used as polling stations. On the Friday, the schools being used are closed to clear the place up and organise the rooms. Saturday is spent bringing in and setting up the electronic voting machines, and Sunday is polling day. The staff at the schools are expected to work in whatever capacity required for two hours on polling day.

Apparently, the average queue was about one and a half hours at peak voting time. Brazilians are very fond of queuing. If you are pregnant, disabled, elderly or holding a child in your arms, you can jump to the head of the queue. Reports were coming back via those who left our party to go vote that there were some quite large babes in arms! There are no campaigners and party supporters handing out leaflets outside the polling stations, simply because it is not allowed. In an effort to get around this rule, however, the campaigners just dump vast quantities of election propaganda on the ground outside the polling stations the night before – also not allowed – which means that plenty of street sweepers are required to clean up the mess!

The voters will have to return to the polls in fifteen days' time, however, because even though the most popular presidential candidate gained 47% of the vote, a simple majority is not good enough according to election law in Brazil. The winner has to have 50% of the votes plus one to become president.

Nonetheless, we knew who had won the local seat at 11.00 that night as the supporters were out celebrating – noisily, so it was a good day all around!

Weekend at Poços de Caldas

Recently we spent the weekend at a spa town called Poços de Caldas (literal translation, Wells of Hot Water), about 2000 feet higher than here and therefore much cooler. About two and a half hours' drive away, it is a volcanic region with quite a number of thermal springs in the area. I guess the town grew up around the thermal spring during the era when 'taking the waters' for one's health was in its heyday. There is a large, old (by Brazilian standards) building labelled Thermal Baths in the town, and next to it a large (and once upon a time very smart) hotel called the Palace Hotel, which we stayed in. (The nightly rate was quite reasonable – £50ish for the three of us for the night including three meals.) The baths were closed for renovations, but the hotel had its own 'sulphur' pool, which we went and wallowed in. The hotel had a certain decaying elegance about it with spacious rooms with balconies overlooking the pleasure gardens surrounding the area.

The foyer has dark wood panelling, high panelled ceilings, and a revolving door with brass fittings. There are lifts with sliding grills, which one pulls across by hand, and the lifts themselves are manually operated. There is a marble staircase of course, but very plain. Marble floors and sink surrounds in the bathrooms, with basin, toilet and bidet decorated with blue floral swags. And the shower ... oh, what luxury; I want one just like it! There is the conventional showerhead up above, but there is also what I can only describe as a walk-in cage made from four or five tiers of pipes from about knee level to just below my shoulders, and these spray water at you from all sides! Just the sort of shower I like where you are sprayed all over with hot water instead of having to heat one side of your body while the other freezes, only to then have to turn round and repeat this on the other side.

The town has various tourist attractions, not least of which are the Japanese gardens, and these are modelled on the imperial gardens in Japan. All very Japanese with large bonsai, a pool with Koi carp in it, three spouts of water falling into another pool, a meditation retreat made of wood (metal won't do) with a pyramid roof to enhance the right sort of energies, and wonder of wonders – trees from cooler climes which shed their leaves all at once! This shedding the leaves business is obviously a source of fascination to a culture used to more tropical foliage, because our guide told us about it several times.

They have a Cristo Redentor (Christ the Redeemer) perched on the highest hillside here, styled after the figure of Christ in Rio de Janeiro (as are most of the figures of Christ on hilltops here in Brazil).

The town is also known for its 'crystal', by which I mean glass, not stones. One can find plates and vases in various peculiar shapes made of coloured and clear glass, fashioned in a style similar to Murano glass in Italy, and here there is also cut glass, where a layer of coloured glass has been cut through to expose clear glass underneath.

I don't know who buys them, because they were expensive even by our standards. They also produce glass animals, which were quite attractive – toucans and hummingbirds amongst others, and you can watch them being made by an expert glassblower. One of these chaps was operating literally out of his garage!

Spring is very definitely here, with all the trees in flower. Driving up the road to Poços de Caldas, we passed through an orange growing region, with lots of trees in flower. The smell of those orange blossoms wafting in through the windows as we drove by was heavenly.

The pleasure gardens behind the hotel were full of flowering trees surrounding an amazing fountain. Various jets set into the pool would squirt water to different heights in a random sequence – a dancing fountain you could call it – and to add to the effect, there were coloured lights at nighttime, which changed in a varying sequence. I could have sat and watched it all night.

Parrots were flying from tree to tree in the gardens outside our hotel window. They also sit in trees and chatter. I think you could perhaps describe parrots as the chatterboxes of the avian world. These were the smaller green variety, not macaws. Such noisy creatures – they seem incapable of flying without shrieking at the world! Last year at Christmas in Barra Bonita, we heard a tree full of squawking, but we couldn't see a single bird in it. It was a tree covered in green leaves full of green parrots – and very noisy parrots they were at that!

Speaking of noisy trees, we frequently hear a high-pitched whining sound in the trees here in Piracicaba. We heard it this time last year when we arrived and were totally baffled. It occurs down by the river, and we thought it might be something electrical, or maybe something to do with the water museum. After my walk in the park by the river this morning, I've decided that it must be a certain kind of insect that comes around this time of year. It is not a continuous sound at a steady volume, but rather it ebbs and fills. As I walked round the lake today, the sound got louder and louder until I approached a certain tree, and then it started getting softer. As I passed under the tree, I also heard a noise that I can only describe as clucking or quacking – almost as if whatever was making the noise was taking another breath to continue the symphony. All very mysterious, but you can hear the noise from various directions, presumably from different trees. To add to the mystery, when I passed under that same tree on my second lap, it was completely quiet!

Spring is putting on an exuberant display of new life in flowers and young animals everywhere. Last Saturday when I was walking in the park by the river, I saw the burrowing owl standing above her burrow, and there, peeking out over the edge of the burrow, were three fluffy youngsters looking all around with wide-eyed eagerness at the world about them.

Burrowing owls on the edge of their hole. These are not the ones described above, but they are young owls.

I have discovered the source of the whining noise I've been hearing in the trees round the park. They are very big cicadas – about two inches in length – and boy, are they noisy. They sing in the trees mostly at dawn and dusk, but at any time of day there is usually a tree somewhere full of singing cicadas. Whole groups of them seem to congregate on one tree and sing at full volume. As someone pointed out, you rarely see them flying, but they must move from tree to tree at some point. God help you if they decide to move en masse and you are in the way! The ones I saw were clinging to the tree beside empty, beetle-shaped husks, or shell-like cases, which I assume they had just emerged from.

Our hot weather has cooled a bit. The forecast said that the hot spell would continue until the 20th. It did that alright, with Monday being the hottest day we have recorded on our balcony (in the shade) at 36°C! Monday night was wet and windy, and last night we recorded a temperature of 16°C. That's a 20°C difference between day and night. Even with the temperature at midday being about 26°C, that is quite a fluctuation.

Weekend at Caraça

One of the best things about living in Piracicaba is its location. So many fascinating destinations lie within a few hours' drive, making it easy to plan weekend jaunts and adventures. This time our destination was Caraça in Minas Gerais, the state adjacent to the one where we live in Piracicaba.

The state of Minas Gerais is mostly mountainous, though nothing very high. Belo Horizonte, the state capital, is about 120 kilometres from Caraça, and it is a large city – in excess of 2,000,000 people now. It was probably well established when the Santuário at Caraça was founded in 1779 as a seminary for training priests. There are a couple of small settlements fifteen to twenty kilometres away, but otherwise, apart from the one road to the Santuário, there is nothing but scrubby forest, mountains and rivers. Caraça is very remote, sitting up in the mountains, so that if any would-be priests decided the monastic life wasn't for them, they would have had a difficult time running away.

Getting to Caraça involved a much longer drive than most of our weekend trips – 800 kilometres and eleven hours driving to get there, one hour of which was spent travelling 40 kilometres because of a tail back caused by road works – but the journey was completely worth it for the beauty of the destination.

Our main reason for going to Caraça was to see a maned wolf. Some years ago, a padre there started putting out meat each evening to feed the wolves, which then became a tradition and is now a tourist attraction.

The place consists of a church with a tall steeple, flanked on either side by sleeping accommodation, with the kitchen and refectory at the back of the structure, all built from thick stone walls, which is unusual for Brazil. It is set in a corrie/cwm/coomb in the mountains, and is completely surrounded by forest. The Santuário sits at an elevation of 1300 metres, and the highest peak nearby is a little over 2,000 metres. The mountains here are more rugged than any we've encountered elsewhere in Brazil, with lots of rocky outcrops and bare rock faces (not unlike Connemara in Ireland).

Accommodation was basic, but all the perceived necessities of this day and age were there – beds, showers and toilets. There was even a TV room! The office was computerised, but this was no surprise as everything in Brazil is for the most part.

Santuário do Caraça

Back courtyard at the Santuário

Food was provided (all meals are included in the price), and meals are served with refectory style seating (complete with the pulpit for the monk to read meaningful Bible passages). Guests are free to help themselves from pots set on a large wood-fired stove. The menu consisted of rice and beans (a staple of any Brazilian meal), stewed meat, assorted vegetables, and of course there was the usual lettuce, tomato and a dish called mayonnaise (which is more in the nature of a potato salad with carrots, peas, onions, etc., mixed together with mayonnaise). They provided chips with every meal, which I'm sure were cut by hand! (And they were feeding in excess of a hundred people that weekend.)

Breakfasts were fun, and once again, it was all done farmhouse style: you choose from an array of fresh fruits, which we ate first, and then you select a bread roll, cheese, ham and an egg to cook directly on the wood-fired hot plate.

There are lots of walks in the mountains with trails of various distances, and we were delighted to find this natural pool set in a clearing surrounded by grass.

We were there on a holiday weekend, and the place was full, with more people coming just to spend the day there. On Saturday we explored the swimming pool and took in the view from above it, then came back to the Santuário for lunch.

Sarah wanted to sit outside and read for awhile, so we found a vine covered trellis and sat comfortably in the shade. There was a pleasant semi formal garden surrounding the Santuário, with a small museum at the back, and a small playground for children.

Later we decided to go and find a grotto marked on the map, which seemed to be about two kilometres distant. We went up, up, up, and then much to our consternation, down, down, down through thick trees; just when it seemed that surely we must be getting close, we realised we still had to cross some rocky outcrops. We found the grotto eventually, but the trail seemed little used and was not well marked.

Jungle along the trail to the grotto... and finally, the grotto

The map is more a guide to what is available, rather than a means of finding your way around. This rigorous trail is more suited for an experienced hiker and not an average day-tripper who is expecting a comfortable hike on flat terrain.

We were a bit concerned about getting back before the light began to fade, as we would be returning through trees, but as it turned out, we made it back in time.

Supper is served from 6.30 to 8.00 p.m., which is early for Brazil. After supper (and after mass), the priest puts out a tray of meat in the courtyard in front of the church. Lots of people were sitting round expectantly waiting for a wolf to appear and take the meat. This is part of the tourist attraction of this place now, though as I said before, it started with one of the priests just deciding to put out meat for the wolves every evening. It would seem that the average tripper here has no idea how to wait for wild animals. Too much noise and moving around. Needless to say, the wolf did not show up. Later we heard that someone actually waited until 4.00 a.m. The meat was gone by 6.00 a.m., however, so something made a meal of it. Friday night was apparently the same story.

Sunday, we followed a fairly well used path to a small (derelict) chapel perched way above on the hillside. This was another interesting path to climb. About a third of it used a natural rock ledge travelling diagonally across the hillside. The clearing where the chapel was built had been augmented by the addition of large stones. In fact, they had built a large wall of massive stones and filled in behind it to make the clearing big enough. How they manhandled boulders that size without the aid of modern lifting gear is anyone's guess, but then I suppose we are spoiled with all the various lifting devices available to us now, and have forgotten about blocks and tackle and shear legs and all that.

Trail to the old chapel ... and, the old chapel

Coming back from the chapel we came across a series of what looked like ants' nests, though it was more probably spoil heaps.

Every now and then, an ant would appear from inside, carrying something, which it would leave at the top of the ridge. It was fascinating to watch.

After lunch, we went to the nearest waterfall marked on the map, and found a tiered cascade with a large pool at the bottom of each tier. One look and we just had to go for a swim.

The water was cool but not icy. Sarah and I swam with the tadpoles, which were about two inches long, so it makes you wonder: what size are the frogs?

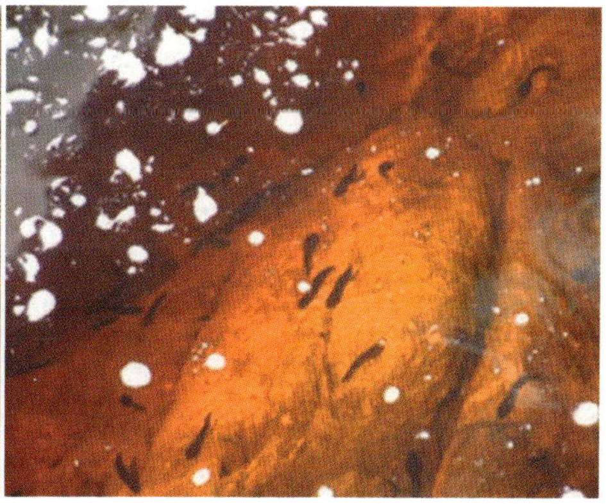

Then it was back to our room and time to put our feet up for awhile before supper. The heavens opened – talk about torrential! Thunder had been rumbling around all day, giving us small warnings of what was to come, but when we opened the door and looked out, we were stunned to see hailstones mixed in with the rain – big hailstones, about one cm across! The rain was still streaming down when we decided to go for supper. Our direct route across the yard was flooded, so we went the roundabout route. Three under an umbrella isn't really the best way to keep dry, but we managed to circumnavigate another flood and eventually reached our supper.

There were about twelve people dining with us this time, as most others had gone home to return to work the next day. The rain had eased by the time we finished, but we still found a frog in the passage, which we duly escorted outside.

I think the padre had decided that no one would be wolf watching on an evening like that, so he didn't wait to do his usual little talk, but just put the meat out. He calls the wolves by calling out *guará* several times. The Portuguese name for a maned wolf is *lobo-guará*, the guará bit being an Indian word meaning red. This time there wasn't a noisy throng gathered waiting for the wolf to appear, so the chances of one showing up seemed likely. We opened a door to the courtyard, pulled a sofa directly in front of it, and waited to see if the wolf would appear. A couple of other people did the same at the door on the other side of the courtyard. After about twenty minutes, a wolf came up the steps, making his way gingerly toward the meat, but paused and nearly fled when he became aware of people watching him, but the lure of the meat was too strong. He grabbed a piece, ran off to eat it unseen, then came back for another.

Then someone at the door across the courtyard dropped something, and this was enough to scare off the wolf. We waited another hour, hoping he would reappear, but he didn't come back. Sarah had fallen asleep by this time.

They are not like northern wolves - greyish and woolly - but as the padre pointed out, they are more akin to a dog than a wolf. They are lightly built, of a reddish-brown colour, and have extremely long legs. The legs are black. They seem almost dainty when walking. I guess they must stand about one metre at the shoulder, if not more. Seeing that wolf was one of the highlights of the weekend.

The ceiling in our room leaked during the downpour, and as Alan put it, his shower continued after he had turned the tap off! We were offered another room, but they didn't seem appalled by the fact that the roof was leaking. I suppose it's a common occurrence when it rains this heavily, but damp generally isn't a problem in this climate. As the leak was not over the bed, we stayed put.

Monday was blissfully quiet. It seemed as though we had the Santuário to ourselves - just the three of us and the people who work there. A bus brings most of the workers up the valley, arriving about 6.45 a.m. A number of them live at the Santuário. The bus driver also works there, which is convenient, as he can then drive everyone back down again in the evening. We went for a couple of shortish walks, but one had to be curtailed as the stone bridge we had intended to cross was under water because of the rain the previous night. I think it was more in the nature of stepping stones, but we couldn't even see them under the water, and it was quite a fast flow of water too.

The Santuário was built on a raised area of ground with a surrounding parapet that looks out over a profusion of natural growth. These aren't small scrubby plants; instead, they're more like trees, actually, and we saw some extraordinary birds which I think are a species of curassow.

The padre has a parrot and keeps several songbirds, in cages. The parrot was allowed out of his cage for visitors to interact with him, and he would walk up your arm if encouraged. He seemed to spend most of his day in a tree in the centre of this internal courtyard. Caged songbirds are very popular in Brazil. The Honda garage where Alan bought his motorbike has at least four suspended in cages round the walls.

There are wild parrots about, too. It doesn't seem quite right for green parrots to sit perched on the roof of a European looking church, particularly because they are such a noisy lot.

We tried wolf watching again Monday evening, but one man kept going to the edge to see if the wolf was coming (which was certain to keep the wolf away), so we gave up and went for a short walk instead. By this time the sun had gone and evening had set in, but it was almost a full moon and a lovely clear still night, and not cold. We thought we could hear the ducks on the pond, but as we drew nearer, we realised the sound was frogs. So we sat and listened, and soon, more frogs joined in. What a lovely, rhythmic sound they make; now I understand what is meant by a symphony of frogs, for that is indeed what it was. It was amazing. Some of them like a drum, others a bit like ducks, and some make a scraping sort of noise, while still others produce an almost bell-like sound. It was wonderful to be treated to such a magical performance.

Whilst on the subject of wildlife, we have seen some interesting insects and spiders here at the Santuário – large ones, some with great long feelers – but the best one was a large hairy spider that caught me by surprise in the ladies' toilet! When I turned to flush the toilet, there was this black blob on the wall about two inches or more across, solid and hairy.

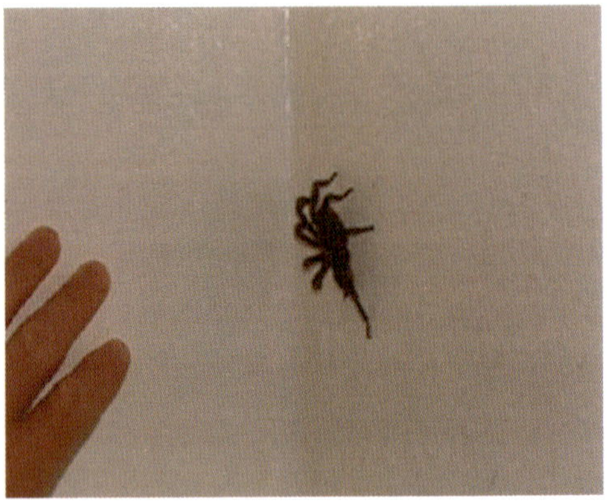

I had to call Alan to have a look. Luckily, there were no other ladies about to object! After photographing it, he tried tickling one of its legs to make it move, and when it did, he was the one that jumped! They can move extremely rapidly when they want to. It just launched itself off the wall and on to the floor, barely missing Alan's shoulder as he jumped out of its way. There was another interesting insect waiting on the toilet door, too – something like a grasshopper but with long antennae and blue in colour rather than green. Maybe it has camouflage abilities and was blending in with the blue door to protect itself from us frightening humans!

Then there was the frog that I nearly trod on in the dark one evening. I must have really frightened it, because when Alan photographed it, he noticed a small puddle behind it where there had been no puddle previously. Yes, frogs do pee. This was a six-inch long greenish frog, in marked contrast to the tiny black ones we saw on rocks on the hillside. Those were an inch long if even that, and apparently are able to live in dry conditions, very unusual for frogs.

We went exploring up behind the complex and came across a vegetable patch, but on the way to it, we found a huge flower, Latin name *Aristolochia Gigantea*, also called Brazilian Dutchman's Pipe – quite amazing.

On Tuesday morning, we departed this lovely sanctuary that had been our temporary home amidst mountains and nature for three days and four nights, and headed back to Piracicaba and everyday life. We made the trip home in nine and a half hours this time, stopping along the way to buy a cotton bedspread I spotted along the roadside. They were displayed draped over a rack at the back of a van, nowhere near any town. Most of the journey is along one road. If you can imagine a dual carriageway from one end of Ireland to the other, it's about that long – actually a bit longer!

The Amazon!

As with last year, I couldn't get into the Christmas swing of things because it falls in the middle of the summer season here in Brazil. Christmas should not be hot!

My sister, Lu and her partner, Matt arrived on schedule on December 18, and we headed north east on the 22nd to Natal (which translated means Christmas), which is situated in the area where the top of Brazil turns a corner and goes south. We were assured that it would be very hot (I say assured because we were headed to a beach resort) - but in fact it was cooler than Piracicaba. It stayed more or less around 28°C the whole five days we were there. It is the cooler season there at the top of Brazil, after all, because it is just south of the Equator, and at this time of year, the sun is over the Tropic of Capricorn, nearly as far away as it can get.

Our hotel, the Rifoles Praia Hotel, was very smart, and built overlooking the beach, and what a lovely beach it is with the blue-green sea lapping at miles of pale sand fringed with palm trees. The hotel provides loungers, and a member of the hotel staff is always at your beck and call, ready to serve cool drinks (at a price, of course) whenever the fancy takes you. And if the pristine beach isn't enough, the hotel has three swimming pools, one with a bar alongside so you can sit in the pool on submerged stools and drink at the bar.

The climate in this region is so temperate that the restaurant is practically open air: whilst it has a roof supported by tree trunk-shaped timbers at intervals, there are no windows or walls on the seaward side. It was very pleasant having breakfast there, overlooking the sea, although I could have done without the Hallelujah Chorus every morning, which was part of the background music. The tape must have been very short. Maybe that was to encourage the guests not to linger over breakfast.

One day we walked to the end of the beach, paddling, swimming and body boarding along the way. Sarah adores body boarding, as does Matt. It's just as well they were rented boards; otherwise, the two of them would still be there.

From the hotel, we could see a huge pale green outline of a Christmas tree, which was lit up at night, on the side of a dune at the end of the beach. On closer inspection, we could see that it was made of used plastic drinks bottles. They do the most amazing things with these bottles here. Sarah's school made a Christmas tree by cutting bottles into strips, up to the stopper, and stacking them on top of one another.

Another day we went on a town tour. They have a 400-year-old, star-shaped fort complete with grisly stories about what happened to the prisoners kept there. Some of the buildings in the town are quite old. This corner of Brazil was one of the earliest to be colonised. They have turned the gaol into a craft market with each cell being a separate craft vendor's stall. I saw lots of very attractive embroidery and lace, but could only think, W*hat would I do with it?* – so I didn't buy any. We did buy a couple of hammocks, though, as they are much cheaper in this area than in our corner of Brazil.

We spent Christmas Day snorkelling over a reef about seven kilometres off the coast. Before we got to the reef, however, we were taken to another beach with a small hotel, pony rides for children, canoeing and trips in a microlite, all designed to keep us entertained while waiting for the tide over the reef to be just right for snorkelling. I guess the tour company has some deal with the hotel, bringing in 'captive' guests as part of their daytrip. We built a sand castle much to the amusement of many. Building sand castles is not a typical beach activity here in Brazil.

Then, it was off to the reef at last. About thirty of us were taken in two open boats to a platform moored out on the reef. There, we were given snorkels, mask and flippers for those who wanted them, and after a few brief safety instructions, more about protecting the coral than us, we were let loose. The water is about two or three metres deep there, with not a huge variety of coral but lots of fish, and I saw a small octopus and a large sea slug. Flotation devices were available for those who desired. Sarah had a small life jacket wound round her middle and we all paddled about happily. We must have spent over an hour in the water before some of us started to get cold, which says something about the temperature of the water. We all loved it, and Alan and I are already looking for more places to snorkel.

A couple of mornings I went for a walk along the beach around 6.00 a.m. The second time, I noticed small piles of freshly dug sand and went to investigate. As I approached, two little black dots on top of the pile disappeared rapidly. Crabs! – ranging from about one to five centimetres across (which is about two inches) – including their legs. They were a pale creamy colour – almost translucent – and they live in the sand. They dig their way out (at one point I saw bits of sand flying out of a hole) and sit on top of the pile next to the hole presumably waiting for something tasty to come within their reach. Most visible were their eyes, nothing more than two little black dots on the ends of stalks. I could get within about two feet of them and they would scuttle rapidly sideways down their holes. I did this for several minutes – playing hide and seek with crabs. Every time I went to seek, they hid!

The following day we took a taxi to a beach further south, just for a bit of variety. On the way, we passed the biggest cashew tree in the world. It was huge, but not in height so much as in spread! It must have covered at least the equivalent of one block (as in a block of houses), and a block here measures about 200 metres square. We didn't stop to look, but got a good look as we drove by. There was a small but permanent craft fair there, no doubt some of them selling T-shirts to prove that you had seen the biggest cashew tree in the world.

Cashews look very different in their natural habitat compared to how they look when packaged. The nuts are not found in the middle of the cashew fruit, which is most common with such seeds, but appear as a hard grey/green kidney shaped protuberance on the end of the fruit. The nut is inside a hard casing with a toxic resin in it. Generally, these casings have to be heated to extract the nut without contaminating it with the toxic resin.

The fruit is shaped much like a small pepper (the red, green and yellow sorts) and ranges from yellow to red in colour. It is a most peculiar fruit. Sarah was given a couple by the resident artist in the hotel. He had done several still life paintings of cashew fruits, as they are very much a part of the region. The inside is like a fibrous sponge. I tried biting into one, but it just squished, and a load of juice poured out (not very sweet juice either, but still quite tasty, nonetheless). Cashew juice is commercially packaged and frozen, and is easily available in supermarkets and restaurants. This corner of Brazil seems to be a large producer of cashew nuts, which are cheaper to buy than walnuts!

The beach we went to was not much different from the one we had just left, but I preferred it because it was quieter, had fewer people, and was not as built up, but the sea was more dangerous. Thankfully, Sarah has a healthy respect for waves, and won't venture out very far.

We returned to our hotel to pack and have an early night in preparation for a 5.00 a.m. flight to Manaus (via Brasilia). The next day, as we made the approach to the airport in Manaus, we kept seeing rivers ever increasing in size and wondered which one was the Amazon. (None of them, as it turned out!). There is a lot of water in the Amazon area.

We were met at the airport by another tour company and taken to a hotel on the shore of the Rio Negro, one of the two main tributaries of the Amazon (the other is the Rio Solimoes). There we spent two nights. The amenities were luxurious - several swimming pools, a bar, a restaurant/snack bar and a supply of waiters to do your every bidding, but this hotel also has its own mini zoo. The river at this point is five miles wide, and the sea is a thousand miles away! It is big.

We did a tour of Manaus that afternoon that included the municipal market and the opera house. The municipal market was modelled after Les Halles, in Paris, France. It was interesting to see so much local Amazonian produce stacked around the fancy, European designed wrought ironwork of the market. It certainly makes an interesting visual contrast.

Our next stop was at the opera house.

Opera House, Manaus

The opera house is an amazing bit of European nostalgia, with practically everything for its construction brought to Brazil from Europe during the years from 1880 to 1890. It is hard to imagine transporting building materials a thousand miles up the Amazon, an area with no roads whatsoever. This was during rubber boom time, which lasted about forty years, until someone took some rubber tree seeds to Malaysia, and that cut Brazil's monopoly of the rubber trade.

Manaus Zoo (which we didn't go to) is run by the army. Seemingly, it is an offshoot of their jungle warfare training. I guess it is advisable to let the raw recruits know what sort of animals they should be looking for (or avoiding) before they are let loose.

In the hotel, working in one of the posh jewellery stores there, we met a lady named Dora from Belfast, and we immediately felt like kin! Her husband had come out to Manaus thirty-five years ago to install textile machinery from Mackies, and he kept being asked to stay on. She has no desire to return to Belfast. What is more, a gentleman who came out at the same time to help install the machinery now works in F.G. Wilson's in Larne! Alan of course is currently working for F.G. Wilson-Brazil! This gentleman remembers going to Dora's house in Manaus to play cards with her and her husband! I don't know who was more gob smacked that they had a mutual acquaintance - Alan or Dora.

Dora told us that up until about ten years ago, Manaus was a relatively small place, but now is expanding because of government tax incentives to bring employment to the area. They are pushing eco-tourism as well, with quite a number of 'jungle hotels' springing up. The airport where we landed was built in 1976, as was the hotel where we were staying. (The hotel seems to be an airline off shoot.) Up until then, there was only a military airport.

We had another full day before going upstream to our jungle hotel, so we opted to do a river trip, the main thrust of which was to see the 'Meeting of the Waters'. It was quite impressive. Manaus is not actually on the Amazon proper, but on the Rio Negro, which as the name suggests, is dark in colour. About an hour downstream, the Rio Solimoes joins the Rio Negro. (The Solimoes is sometimes referred to as the Amazon.) The Rio Solimoes has a lot of pale sediment suspended in it, and so is creamier in colour. At the confluence of the two rivers, the waters do not mix because of differences in temperature and density, but they continue running separately alongside each other for up to twenty miles, though they usually combine sooner, at which point a lot of the sediment settles and the water is a light brown colour. The Negro is warmer than the Solimoes, which comes from the Andes bringing the snowmelt from Peru. 'Coffee and cream' was one description of the difference in colour, and that is pretty accurate.

The Meeting of the Waters

We were also taken to see an area where the Victoria lily grows. That's the one with the huge leaves. It wasn't desperately impressive, as all the leaves were looking a bit tatty. Spring, we were assured, is the best time to see the plant, as that is when it's in bloom. We were more interested in the alligators lurking in the pool. In the same area they had a craft shop with lots of locally produced stuff: seed jewellery, grass skirts, blowpipes, fish scales to be used as nail files, and of course, the ubiquitous T-shirts. We were also taken for a brief excursion in what were described as canoes, but they were actually small motorised wooden launches. The purpose of this activity is to get you to give money to the local kids! They would come up to the launches, paddling in their own (proper) dugout canoes, each child clutching a small animal of some sort which you could hold and take photographs of, and you were expected to hand over some money in return. We got a small alligator, and another boat had a sloth to play with.

We also were taken on a short walk through the jungle! We managed to be in the front of the line and so heard first hand from the guide (who did not speak any English) what was going on. He cut a piece of bark off a tree, inserted it into a fork he had made in a stick with his machete (you can't go into the jungle without your machete), and set fire to it – the bark, not the machete. The resulting smoke was a natural insect repellant.

He showed us the local jungle telephone: a tree with large buttresses at the bottom that you hit with a large stick. The resulting sound carries for miles. The locals use a code to communicate with one another. At one point our guide stopped and wriggled a stick in a hole at the base of a tree, and out came a large (and probably irate) hairy spider – a Tarantula, I think!

At some stage in the trip, we stopped off for lunch in a small hotel set completely by itself across the river from Manaus, and I think it existed solely to feed the day-trippers on this boat trip, and maybe the occasional private tripper. I also think it is affiliated with the hotel we were staying in, as they had the same pattern on the door handles. The pattern also appeared on the hotel stationary. They did emphasise that there were rooms available if anyone wanted to stay the night. There was of course the obligatory craft/gift shop.

We cruised past Manaus (and back again during the trip). The shipyards there are quite impressive, busy and thriving, and not just from making small pleasure crafts. They manufacture large ships as well. Ocean-going vessels come up river to Manaus, which makes it plausible to build them here too. That gives an idea of the sheer vastness of the river. There was activity around at least half a dozen partially built ships. There is an annual rise and fall of the water level in the river of about forty-five feet, so the shipbuilders have to work with the river and have a vessel ready to float by the time the river rises. Needless to say, there are docks for loading and unloading cargo ships, the same size as the ships you would see in Belfast docks.

The river rules every aspect of life here, and to get from your village further along the river to Manaus, you take a bus. The buses just happen to be boats, and the roads just happen to be rivers. The villagers wouldn't have cars. They would rather have boats instead.

Next day we spent a leisurely morning exploring the hotel grounds, the zoo, the orchidarium (in which very few plants were in bloom), and we also had a go at archery. (I didn't, but everybody else did.)

After lunch, it was time to move on up the river to the Ariau Jungle Towers Hotel. This journey takes two hours by boat travelling about 70 km upstream from Manaus.

The hotel is a series of circular towers on approximately thirty-foot stilts, all connected by walkways on stilts.

At this time of year, there is a lot of space under the walkways, but come May that space is filled with a lot of water, and you might even find yourself paddling along the walkways. The river has been known to rise sixty feet. The hotel boasts eight kilometres of walkways. Accommodation is in the various towers, and the administrative office, restaurant and museum are all located in another tower. There is also a central area with bar and television, gift shop, and would you believe it, a beauty salon. There are lots of hammocks hanging around the place, too, if you just want to lie about and vegetate for awhile.

We tried to explore all the walkways, but we missed a few. We'll just have to go back again! Exploring after dark was interesting. There are fluorescent lights set at intervals along the walkways, and of course, this attracted flies – and some large beetles. In the area below the lights, we saw inch-long black beetles lying on their backs waving their legs in the air. As for the bats, the flies and all the helpless beetles were an absolute gift. Talk about fast food! We encountered several bats flying along the walkways, having their dinner. We are not talking about pipistrelle-sized bats either. These bats have a twelve-inch wingspan, if not more. Dodging the bats made for interesting walking, though they of course were better at dodging than we were. Bats could also be found in the central television/bar area doing fly-throughs in search of dinner.

Another excitement on our evening ramble was spiders. We met two large (four inches across) hairy ones at different places on or under the handrail. We waited to point out one of the spiders to an American family who were approaching because we thought they would be interested. They were terrified and couldn't get away quickly enough!

As I mentioned previously, the towers are circular. Each floor has a central circular hall and the rooms open off this. They are of necessity wedge shaped; each room has its own shower and loo and a small balcony, all with wire mesh screening to keep the squirrel monkeys out! There is no hot water, but that is not a hardship because in this tropical climate, one is quite happy to take cool showers. All the doors are beautifully carved with animals native to the region. They also have various suites for those prepared to spend the extra for plushier rooms, not to mention the Tarzan houses. Dare I say it, but there is even a football pitch on stilts - and a helipad.

There were several macaws hanging around the place, which you could talk to and every now and then, a troupe of squirrel monkeys would come by, amusing everyone with their antics. The best we saw was when several of them were playing in a hammock, leaping onto it and hiding in the middle, and then chasing their friends all around it. They were having such fun.

The Ariau Hotel offered various day trips for exploring the area, all by boat. There are no roads whatsoever this deep in the jungle. The boats are long, narrow and motorised. (Before seeing what kind of boats were used for these trips, we had wondered if we would have to paddle!) On arrival at the hotel, we had been assigned to a guide, and we went with him on whatever trips we were booked in for. Each guide seems to work in partnership with a boatman, so they know each other's quirks. Our boatman, Francisco, was fairly new to the job, I think. He was young and a bit shy, and our guide, Rui, patiently spent time explaining things to him.

We went on several day trips during our stay at the Ariau Jungle Towers Hotel: we journeyed to a native village, went piranha fishing and jacaré hunting (a jacaré is a type of alligator); took a boat trip at dawn, a trip to a native house and a walk in the jungle. I would pass on the piranha fishing if I went again. They are easy to catch – you stop the boat and just drop a hook baited with raw meat over the side. If they are in the mood, they bite – almost immediately.

I'm not keen on fishing, but the craic in the boat was good, in spite of the torrential downpour. We had Belgians and Americans in our group as well as Brazilians, and almost everyone spoke English. We were doing so well with our catch that most of the group was reluctant to leave when our guide, Rui, said that our time was up.

We had quite a good haul, and the hotel kitchen staff made the fish into soup for us to eat at teatime. The fish were simply gutted and cooked whole with some vegetables and flavouring. Eating piranha is reputed to be an aphrodisiac.

I should perhaps point out that the people described as natives are not the Indians of the region. The natives are of very mixed ancestry, starting with the Indians, and mixing with Portuguese, Bolivians, Peruvians, Columbians and various others, and of course the Africans who were originally brought over as slaves. These were all pioneering peoples who found their way into the region before the rubber boom at the end of the nineteenth century. The result is a brown-skinned group of people who are as knowledgeable about indigenous plants and animals as the Indians are, but they also have retained the knowledge and traditions that have been passed down through generations of people descended from the various cultures that settled here. Both Francisco and Rui would describe themselves as native, in spite of the fact that Rui appears to be Negro and Francisco is more Indian looking.

Rui and Sarah

The native village we visited was a collection of small houses, wooden and brick, set well up from the river and raised on short stilts about three feet high, not so much as flood defence but more to allow air to circulate underneath the houses to keep them cool. There was a school and a church in the village as well. When I asked Rui how the people adapt their dwellings when the river floods, he said that if the water rises high enough to cover the first floor, they simply add another storey to the house. Apparently, a lot of native peoples migrate to Manaus for a couple of months when the river is at its highest, and thus is probably flooding their houses.

There is no mains electricity, needless to say. Alan of course asked to see the generator. (I could just hear him thinking, *Is there an untapped market in the area?*) Lo and behold, it was an F.G. Wilson generator made in ...Larne! The mind boggles at the logistics of getting it here. By boat from Ireland to Manaus – okay, that's not too difficult – but from there, the generator had to travel three hours up stream on a small boat, and then from the small boat to the shed where it now resides. How did they accomplish this feat with minimal lifting equipment? These generators are not small. One can only admire the hard work and determined effort involved in such a process. Guess what the next F.G. Wilson newsletter will have an article about!

Tourists do provide a substantial amount of revenue for these people, so there were a couple of gift shops selling authentic items made in the village, such as seed jewellery and feather head dresses, but thankfully, no T-shirts! The proceeds from their sales were going towards the upkeep of a health centre. Apart from the gift shops, no attempt had been made to smarten the place up for the tourists, but this made the visit to the village all the more pleasing, as it gives tourists a chance to see the unspoiled natural environment that the natives live in. Everyone went about their daily business, but there were not too many people about. I would guess that living this close to Manaus, many people work there during the week and come back to the village at weekends.

An added attraction was the weaverbirds and their amazing nests, hanging from a nearby tree. These birds were black and yellow and were about the size of a thrush.

Our jacaré (alligator) hunt was not with the aim of killing said beast, but to let us all see one. It was an evening trip, and their eyes glow red in torch light, so Rui and one other were at the front of the boat searching for jacaré with a torch, and Francisco was at the back awaiting commands as to where to take the boat. It only took about fifteen to twenty minutes to locate and catch one, so there must be quite a few around. It was a small one, and the poor creature was then passed from person to person along the length of the boat so those who wanted could have a good look at it before it was put back into the water.

We saw a big one (well, the eyes of it) crossing the river in front of the boat, but our catch was a small one. The other excitement of this night trip was the suicidal sardines, which, as we were entering a lake, leapt into the boat. This behaviour apparently is actually a survival mechanism, trying to escape predators. The boat would seem like a predator. Rui had warned us that this might happen, so that people wouldn't panic. They were up to six inches long!

The native house we visited was set by itself, up from the river, wooden and again on short stilts for air circulation rather than flood avoidance. There was no glass in the windows, but that is fairly common in rural Brazil generally.

The family who lives in this house had burnt their bit of land to clear it and were growing mandioc as a staple crop. Apparently, once the root of the mandioc matures and turns yellow, it is full of cyanide. We were taken to where the plant is processed to make it edible. This involves lots of boiling and squeezing in a special tube woven from palm leaves. After boiling and squeezing, it is then roasted and ground into flour, which is quite tasty actually. The family lived in what seemed to be two rooms, but we didn't go into the house.

We also saw a Brazil nut tree. It is potentially dangerous to stand underneath one of these trees after a rainfall, as the seedpods, which contain about twenty nuts on average, are liable to fall. Imagine a container of twenty Brazil nuts being dropped on your head from a height of about twenty feet! Francisco peeled individual nuts with his machete for us all to try. They are much juicier, fresh from the tree than shop bought Brazil nuts. The family had built a separate hut (from wood and palm leaves) from which they sold seed jewellery, made by the family. They never take money for the tourist visits to their villages and homes, so buying something from them is a way of saying thank you for their hospitality. I did buy, as the jewellery there was a lot more imaginative than any other I had seen.

The trip up to this house was very interesting too. The whole area is a maze of waterways that change with the rise and fall of the river. We did not go directly up the main river (though we returned that way), but through a lake that is connected by small waterways to the main river. I would guess that two weeks earlier we would not have been able to go that route because there would not have been enough water.

Access to the lake was clear enough, but the next section, from the lake to the next open expanse of water, was overgrown with a waterweed that is a relative of sugar cane. Apparently, this is what the *peixe boi* (as the

Amazonian sea cows are called) feed on. They are very shy and difficult to catch a glimpse of (and endangered as well). There was a narrow deeper channel through this weed, which twisted and turned frequently. Our boat was about twenty feet long with an outboard motor at the back, and trying to negotiate the channel without getting weed wound round the propeller was not easy. Francisco did have to clear the propeller several times, but generally, he was very good at keeping the motor in the deeper water so the boat could glide through the weed in order to get round corners. The biggest hazard was various other boats trying to negotiate the same channel - in both directions.

We visited (or passed through) that lake several times. On one occasion, pink dolphins surfaced close by. They really are pinkish in colour, but have much longer noses than their sea-going cousins. There are various legends about them, much the same as those about the Silkies in Scotland. Supposedly, they can turn into handsome young men who come ashore to seduce the maidens. Our guide explained that the local population has a healthy respect for them, evidenced by superstitions, such as if one crosses in front of an unmarried girl, she will be married within the year, and there are various fertility superstitions as well.

We also saw some Hoatzins, which are a species of birds said to be akin to archaeopteryx. They have two stomachs, hooks on their wings, and are very clumsy in flight, flying only very short distances from tree to tree. I must confess they are fairly bizarre looking.

Our walk in the jungle was very interesting (no tarantulas this time!). It was secondary rather than primary forest, and had been cut down at some time and allowed to re-grow. We discovered another natural insect repellant: ants, very small ones. You let them crawl over you and then crush and rub them into your skin. Squishing them releases the formic acid in their bodies, a smell that says 'keep away' to other bugs.

We came across another telephone tree. The prominent buttresses are very useful as a safe place to spend the night; they form a sort of triangle, and if you made a campsite within the safety of the buttresses, you would have protection on two sides of the triangle, and would only have to worry about the third. We were also shown rubber trees - the real ones, not those sold as pot plants in Britain - though that variety does grow in enormous quantities here.

There are plants used for medicinal purposes, such as to counteract malaria and to calm stomach upsets. Another tree contains sap, which the natives drink to stop hunger pangs, though I think it is of little nutritional value.

Speaking of malaria, the general advice here is that the side effects from the anti -malaria drugs are worse than the disease itself, so don't bother dosing yourself. The medical centre at Caterpillar provided us with lots of insect repellant and vitamin B tablets before we took off for the Amazon. Vitamin B is supposed to make humans less tasty to insects. In that particular area of Amazonas, however, on the banks of the Rio Negro, insects are not a horrific problem. The water is so acidic (pH 4.3 was quoted) that the larvae cannot survive. It certainly felt soft, which is an indicator of water that is acidic.

Our dawn trip on our final morning was very peaceful, just our family and the guide. We went up through the lake again, though we didn't see anything spectacular, but it was very pleasant in that pre-dawn stillness. Our guide had hoped to find the pink dolphins again, but they weren't playing. Everything was still and the water was like a mirror. We nearly missed the boat back to Manaus though, as the motor started playing up.

We had booked an extra day at Ariau (in addition to the standard tour), so we asked for a day in the jungle, hoping to get more information about medicinal plants. What we got was a survival expedition, which was like playing boy scouts in a tropical forest. It was quite fun.

Our guide that day was an Indian who spoke no English. We made a shelter using palm leaves and vines, and then he showed us how to make the local equivalent of origami using palm leaves.

We had also opted for lunch in the jungle, rather than back at base, so while we were playing, our boatman cooked a large fish (brought from base) over an open fire. We had gathered the firewood first and our guide had lit the fire using the flint and tinder method, before we went off to play. He also showed us how to light a fire using steel wool and a battery. You take a piece of steel wool and extend it so that the two terminals are covered, and the bit in the middle catches fire!

The fish was excellent, eaten with fingers off a piece of plastic (a bin liner) with some mandioca flour and tomatoes for added interest. It really should have been a palm leaf plate to make the experience truly natural and organic, but it was an amazing way to have lunch nonetheless.

The trip to and from our jungle playground was interesting. We passed through the lake and negotiated the narrow weed-choked waterway again, and then proceeded on through some trees – meaning, the area had started to flood, and there were trees literally rising up out of the water!

The water rises three to five centimetres a day, on average, starting in November, with May having the highest water level. We could notice a difference in the four days we were there. It seemed a bit strange to be floating through the forest. You can see the previous year's high water mark on the tree trunks. Above the water level, the bark is whitish, and below, it is dark – bark coloured! – and we were floating well below that level.

To cap off our Amazonian holiday, we had the most memorable New Year's Eve imaginable! The hotel provided a show at no extra charge. This took place in yet another tower, and was performed by a dance troupe whose repertoire is an interpretation of various Indian legends. Their costumes for the most part were minimal but very colourful, comprised of feathers placed in strategic spots for both male and female, and little else. It was quite spectacular, very energetic and exuberant, with lots of lighting effects, including fireworks and fire-eaters who would appear on stage dancing with their mouths full of flammable liquid, spouting flames at the appropriate times. How they manage not to swallow the liquid, I don't know. This was all taking place inside a wooden structure; talk about a major fire risk! They also had mini candles in plastic cups all round the edge of the dance floor, to add to the effect (and the fire hazard).

I was never quite sure what the stories portrayed, as I couldn't understand what was being said over the microphone. Certainly there were some magnificent costumes, which could have been god/goddess type figures, and I think there were some demons too. I was waiting for them to catch fire! At one point, some of the troupe appeared in long dresses carrying parasols. Presumably this performance was a legend involving the colonials. There were also two cow costumes – but I never did get the significance of the two large cows. I know it is some sort of tradition in the area, perhaps involved with a story of the fazenda owner's daughter who fell in love with the wrong boy. Maybe that is what the colonial costumes were all about.

Added interest in the show was the poor bemused bat, which had managed to find its way in. It would flutter round for a bit and then roost somewhere, until disturbed again by a loud noise, more smoke, a jet of flame or whatever, which would send it fluttering off again. It certainly would not have found any flies in the vicinity, what with all the fire!

We were then invited to go down to the beach below, so we all made our way down the stairs at the side of the stilts and followed a path lined with more mini candles in plastic cups. On the beach they had set up a stage, and the show continued in the sand and on the stage, with the fire eaters spouting fire from above, round the edge of the tower building that we had just left. The story here was the arrival of the Portuguese and their mal-treatment of the Indians. This all culminated in a fireworks display over the river at midnight. The hotel provided champagne and wine. You stated your preference; the chosen bottle was removed from the ice in the polystyrene box; and then you collected as many glasses as you needed and went off to join your group. The band continued to play, and soon everybody got up on the stage and danced, and a good time was had by all.

The trip back to Manaus on the ferry at the end of our stay at Ariau was a marked contrast to the outward-bound ferry. On the way out, everyone had been excited and full of chat, and there was a guide from the hotel on the boat telling us things such as where we had to be when, smoking regulations (given that everything is made of wood), and so on. The return trip was very subdued by comparison. It left at 7.00 a.m., and most of us had been on the go nonstop since our arrival there. It was quite pleasant just to sit and watch the river glide by knowing that we didn't have to do anything for a couple of hours. The ferry took us back to the hotel in Manaus where we had stayed earlier.

Our flight back home was yet another adventure in this journey to and from the Amazon. We crossed two time zones, so what looked like a seven-hour flight on paper was actually only five hours, and that included a stopover in Brasilia. The food was terrible. We arrived behind schedule in São Paulo and thought we would miss our connection to Campinas. Not one bit of it. The airline was clued up and there was a man waiting at the bottom of the steps for passengers trying to get that flight. He knew how many he was waiting for. We were directed to a mini bus and taken straight across the tarmac to the waiting Campinas flight, which left immediately, only a few minutes behind schedule. What impressed us even more was the fact that our baggage also made it onto the flight - and our taxi was waiting for us at Campinas. We arrived home about 11.00 p.m. after a 7.00 a.m. start that had included about four hours hanging around the hotel in Manaus waiting to be taken to the airport.

Throughout all the waiting times of our journey home that day, my mind kept drifting back to the adventures we had experienced. I can understand why people get so excited by the Amazon. It has a timeless quality. Life is dominated by the river and you ignore it at your peril. It is big, and has a substantial rise and fall every year. Many of the animals and plants depend on this for survival. Man hasn't managed to change this. It is an awful lot of water to try to divert or dam up. We saw it at low water - more or less. I would like to go back in May when the level is up. I imagine it would be a very different landscape.

And what a fantastic way to bring in the New Year - no rain, no cold, just a warm balmy evening on an Amazonian beach, with a party going on, and the whole evening was so totally Brazilian: the noise, the exuberance, the slightly ad hoc manner of doing things, the relaxed attitude toward potential disaster. It could only happen in Brazil!

Passeio Ecologico

We had a good holiday up north, and when we got back here, Lu and Matt hired a car and went looking (unsuccessfully) for places where Matt could paraglide. Out of twelve days, he got four days flying. The weather was diabolical, with nothing but rain, rain and more rain. Even the locals have been commenting about how much rain we have had. I know the wet season is supposed to last through December and January, but I don't think that usually means two months of nothing but clouds and rain like we've had this year! Then, as soon as February arrived, the sun came out for the first time since the beginning of January. We have had almost a month of sub 30°C temperatures, and suddenly now we have high thirties.

Sarah had her birthday party, to which we invited everyone in her class, all fifteen of them, and her teacher. Only about half turned up. It is peak holiday time, and it seems as though the compunction to reply to invitations is not felt as strongly here as we're used to, which makes catering a bit difficult. We had rented a Cama elastica, which is a small circular trampoline ten feet in diameter. It wasn't used as much as expected because of lack of numbers, but certain big people had a go when the smaller ones were elsewhere (like in the swimming pool). I bounced, Matt bounced, and a couple of others bounced.

Lu and I made a crocodile shaped birthday cake, using Brazilian recipes. Novelty cakes are rare here, and icing the cake with a mixture made of condensed milk and chocolate was interesting. In the end, we used fingers for smoothing. I had made a cake last year and iced it with butter icing, but that hadn't been received very well, so we decided to use local recipes.

Weekend before last, we watched the start of an annual event called a *passeio ecologico* – an ecological trip. It consisted of floating 15 kilometres down the river in whatever one cared to float in. Most people had large inner tubes. Some were individual. Some had a second inner tube for their cool box of beer to accompany them, and some groups had tied their inner tubes together to keep each other company. There were also some interesting looking rafts, put together by various groups. Some had portable barbecues, all busily cooking, with their savoury smells wafting through the air as they floated downriver. Everybody was out for the fun of it and the atmosphere was good. They had a good send off, with lots of noise, music and firecrackers, naturally. We are not talking about 50 to 100 people here. We are talking about 5000! It is a big river!

A great way to relax on a Saturday afternoon!

It takes teamwork … and don't forget the BBQ and beer!

São Paulo, a Beach Trip and the Museums of Rio

A chap from Larne came to stay with us for a bit, but he didn't need much entertaining as he was here to work. We went to São Paulo for a weekend in February to coincide with picking him up at the airport. I was particularly interested in exploring a gem stone shop I had heard about, and there was also a theme park we had seen from the ring road. It didn't have a particular theme; just fun rides and things.

The gem stone shop was amazing: masses of amethyst geodes bigger than you have ever seen, and all sorts of semi-precious stones on display.

Amongst other things, the theme park had a spectacular water splash. Brazil has the climate for that sort of thing. You get soaked but dry off fairly quickly from the intense heat of the sun.

We also visited an antique market that is held every Sunday morning, with lots of stalls selling all sorts of interesting things. Some items are of quite good quality; others are definitely bric-a-brac.

We had hoped to see Carnaval in Rio, but the tickets fell through. In truth, it is spectacular touristy event with the most incredible floats and costumes - and all for a short parade on one night of the year. There are actually three nights of parades because there are so many floats, and the parade goes on all night. It starts as late as 10 p.m. or even midnight, and by the time it is over, the revelers are going home with the dawn.

We went to the beach instead and spent three days being beach bums. We went to the north of São Paulo this time, a good choice, too, as the beaches are fabulous there. I think what makes it so stunningly beautiful is the backdrop of the mountains along with the palm trees fringing the beaches. As with our trip to the beach last March, the drive to the coastal strip was spectacular, as you descend approximately 2000 feet in a comparatively short distance. The road down was wonderful: lots of hairpin turns, all through tree clad slopes, which at this time of year have one particular tree in bloom with a wonderful display of purple! At the bottom of this steep descent, the first thing you notice are lots of mini businesses set up ready to sort out your brakes, especially after you have been rescued half way up with no brakes.

One day we took a trip to an island called Anchieta and went snorkelling. To get to the boat to take us there, we waded out from the beach to an inflatable launch that took us to the boat. The outboard motor broke down on the way back to the beach to collect the next lot of passengers, so it had to be paddled out again. Things got a bit delayed because of this, but we finally got going. It was about a forty-minute trip out to the island, and it was very pleasant watching the waves go by with a warm breeze blowing over us. We didn't have much time on the island, but we did manage to get in some snorkelling, then had lunch and looked at their 'ecological exhibition'. Soon it was time to go back to the mainland.

On the way back, I saw a flying fish! It seemed to fly for an incredible distance before disappearing into the sea again. As before, the boat was anchored, and one gingerly transferred from it to the inflatable, which took you back to the beach. The 'captain' suggested that if anyone wanted to 'help' they could swim back to the beach so there would be fewer trips paddling the inflatable. Alan and I looked toward the shore and guessed it to be about 150 to 200 yards. With that, we made a quick decision: we put Sarah's flippers on her, and she and I swam back to the beach. Alan waited for the inflatable with all our snorkelling gear.

Later as we were leaving our room at the pousada (a B & B) to go out for dinner, Alan noticed a frog sitting on the railings outside - a small frog about one and a half inches long, and green. He was still there when we came back. Ours was an upstairs room, though the stairs were outside. Alan tried to photograph him, but he jumped and landed on a vertical railing about three feet away - in the dark! He must have had suckers on his feet! This time he stayed still long enough to be photographed.

The next day we did a little bit of snorkelling close to some rocks at the end of the beach, but the water was not very clear. Alan did manage to see a marine turtle about a metre long.

After that, Sarah had a tattoo done on her leg - a henna tattoo, so it has just about disappeared now. You can get all sorts of things on the beach, from bikinis and beachwear to barbecued cheese!

We went into the town that afternoon and visited the aquarium and another place where they have marine turtles. There is an ongoing project in Brazil to preserve marine turtles, and one way of raising awareness and gaining money to fund this conservation effort is to have them on display in an aquarium in a busy tourist centre. They are lovely creatures. The big ones, the Leatherbacks can grow up to two metres long! I didn't realise that they were so big.

When we weren't boating, snorkelling, or looking at turtles, we were sitting on the beach under the cooling shade of an umbrella at one of the numerous cafes that line the beach, drinking fruit juice and taking it in turns to keep Sarah company in the water. We bought her a cheap body board, which will probably last the duration of our stay here.

One of Alan's team at work has a *sitio*, which is like a small holding. He grows all sorts of things: soya beans, pineapples, oranges, coffee and peanuts, to mention a few, and he also has about a dozen banana trees. It was banana harvest time a couple of weeks ago, and Alan arrived home with about eighty green bananas! We put them in a box to ripen and I ate two or three bananas every day. I made banana ice cream, I dried bananas, I made banana bread, I gave some to my maid. The effort to put the bananas to good use was entirely up to me, as neither Alan nor Sarah eat bananas! Apparently the Brazilians do savoury things with green bananas, but I don't know how to. They also serve deep fried bananas coated with breadcrumbs at some of the restaurants, which are very good.

Luckily, through it all, I haven't gone bananas yet!

We did another of our long walks recently, twenty kilometres this time, through lots of sugar cane as usual, but there were various mini wooded areas too to add to the interest. Alan made a very good friend. A butterfly thought he was the best thing since sliced bread and wouldn't leave him alone. It landed on his face first, and then on his hand. He must have been extremely tasty. We could actually see the butterfly's tongue licking him!

Our destination that day was the Festa de Milho Verde, which means the Sweet Corn Festival. I suppose it was originally like a harvest supper, when all the crops were gathered in and it was time for a party. Now it is more a food festival, and they put on live bands in the evening. It goes on for two consecutive weekends. I tried Suco de Milho – a drink made from sweet corn, which was quite nice. They also have a sweet corn ice cream, which I am quite partial to. And then there is sweet corn cake and sweet corn puree, which can be sweet or savoury. As with all such festas, it is an excuse to indulge in that Brazilian pastime of going out with your friends and *talking*! Drink comes into it too, but that is not the reason for going. You go out to socialise with your friends. On the whole, Brazilians don't drink much.

Our friend Jo arrived the next day, so it was an early start for us, 4.30 a.m. to get to the airport for her flight coming in around 6.30. Then we dragged the poor girl round an exhibition that I wanted to see in São Paulo. Some of the warriors from the Terracotta army had been allowed out of China for the first time. Some went to New York, some to Rome and some came to São Paulo. It was very interesting! There were eleven warriors, two horses and lots of smaller artifacts. I didn't realise they were so big – life size, actually – and that means all different shapes, sizes and heights, just like the real warriors they were modelled after.

Last weekend we went to Rio again, because it was one of the things Jo wanted to do. We flew out at 8.30 on Saturday morning and back again at about 7.30 on Sunday evening. It is a 45-minute flight from our local airport, which is about 45 minutes' drive away. We organised a taxi for the Saturday and did the tourist traps. We managed to go up Pão de Açucar (Sugar Loaf) this time, the tall pinnacle of rock synonymous with Rio that one reaches by two cable cars.

We saw some marmosets on the tables at the halfway point where you change from one cable car to the other. They were being encouraged by one of the workers there who was feeding them with bananas. One had two babies on her back.

Both the top of Sugar Loaf and the halfway point have cafes and souvenir shops. We also noticed a separate cable car system for bringing the supplies up to the outlets.

Then we went to see Cristo (Christ the Redeemer) on his lofty perch high above the city. He is not perched on Sugar Loaf, as everyone thinks simply because those are the two famous landmarks that most people think about when they hear mention of Rio. Cristo actually looks down onto Sugar Loaf instead. We took the tram up this time. That was fun. It was very steep, and I reckon that if I had been wearing trousers not shorts, I could well have slid off my seat. The last time we made this journey, we were taken up by car and it was a very twisty road. You can imagine the traffic chaos with lots of tourists trying to drive up and down this road. There were not too many tourists today because the weather was quite changeable, and low cloud was threatening to engulf the Cristo at any minute. It was very windy and cold, and we didn't stay long.

By the time we got to the bottom it was spitting with rain and that set the trend for the rest of the afternoon: Time to go to a museum. We visited three museums over the two days we were in Rio, and I was impressed by the standard of all of them. One was devoted to folk art and was full of native paintings, sculptures, and costumes used for various festivals. Another was the Museum of the Republic, which hadn't been on our itinerary, but was next to the folk art museum and so it was convenient; besides, it was still raining. It is a beautiful structure built in the neo-classical style, and its theme is, as the name suggests, that of political history.

The museum is housed in what had been the home of the presidents (when Rio was the capital), until President Getúlio Vargas committed suicide there in the 1950s. A lot of the displays were devoted to him, as apparently he was one of the more notable figures in Brazilian history. One of the rooms that draws the greatest attention is the one in which he committed suicide. A lot of the history went over our heads simply due to lack of familiarity, but many of the rooms were extremely ornate, almost what I would call baroque style, and that in itself was worth looking at.

That was Saturday's entertainment. The only thing left was to find something to eat and go to bed or go out on the town with Omar, our friend in Rio. Alan opted for the latter option, and was taken to an Irish pub!

Sunday was a visit to the botanic gardens, the Jardim Botânico do Rio de Janeiro, and The Museum of the Indian. The garden was founded in 1808 by the Emperor Dom Joao VI, and is one of the great tropical botanic gardens of the world. The walkways are lined by 100-foot-tall palm trees, serene and impressive in their stately beauty. These royal palm trees date from when the gardens were first laid out, and they were all propagated from one tree known as the Palma Mater.

There is so much natural beauty to take in while visiting the gardens: There is an orchid house, a bromeliad house, a Japanese garden, a lake with Victoria lilies, a rose garden, and so much more. It was pleasant ambling among the plants and trees and spotting a toucan, some squirrels and some wonderful iridescent blue/green birds – finch sized.

It is well worth the visit, but as with all such places, you can see much more in the way of colourful blooms if you go in spring and early summer. For those of us from the northern hemisphere, the trick is remembering that the seasons are reversed here! April – the month we envision when we think of springtime beauty – is autumn here, so if you want to visit the botanic gardens in spring or summer, you must come sometime during the months from November to February.

The Museum of the Indian, or the Museo do Indio, which we visited after lunch, is very interesting. It contains over 12,000 exhibits, including baskets, objects crafted from birds' feathers, pottery, musical instruments and weapons. There is also a library and collections of photographs and microfilms. The Museum sells Indian craft products. The museum had an Indian hut built in the garden, consisting of supporting poles and a palm leaf roof. The tribe that this hut is representative of lives in the north of the country near the equator, and there are only about 500 members of this tribe left.

We went back to our hotel and put our feet up after so much walking, and then what did we do next? Yes, we *walked* to the airport by way of traipsing along the beach! (Actually, we went through the park that runs alongside the beach.) You can't do that easily with many airports, but this was a smaller domestic airport, not an international one. It sticks out into the bay, and it is one of those airports where, as the plane flies in on approach, you wonder if you are going to land in the sea because you can't see anything solid to land on!

It is now the end of March. Weather turned cooler last week, barely reaching 30°C at mid-day and falling to below 20 at night, which means I am looking for long sleeved tops to wear. How are we ever going to survive an Irish winter again?

Our next visitor arrives later in the week: another Alan. He and my Alan are going to the Grand Prix at the weekend. Time to wash the sheets and make the bed up again!

Sueli's Sitio

Alan Soutar arrived as scheduled last Thursday. He and my Alan went to the Grand Prix this weekend and got absolutely drenched, and Sarah and I ended up spending Saturday night at the family home of a friend of ours named Sueli. She came to call and ended up inviting us to go out to her *sitio* for the night.

The sítio turned out to be the original family home, set in the midst of a massive sugar plantation. It is not an ornate 19th century historic house, but rather an unimposing one-storey dwelling that Sueli's grandparents had bought and which her parents had modernised. There is a wide shady veranda along the front of the house, and the front door (which we didn't use) opens directly into a sitting room, which seems to be the equivalent of a front parlour and is little used. The back door (which we did use) is round the side of the house and opens into the kitchen. From the kitchen you can go to a patio outside with barbecue facilities or to another sitting room (with television), and from there, to the four bedrooms and two bathrooms. There are tile floors throughout and no glass in the windows, just fly mesh and shutters. The walls are painted an off-white colour. It all seemed a bit empty and spartan, but then no one actually lives there during the week.

Sueli's parents had died in the late 1990s, and now she, her three sisters, and one brother, along with their spouses, jointly own the property and use it as a weekend retreat. It is about fifteen minutes from our flat, but you would think you were way out in the country. There is, conveniently, a sugar processing plant just down the road. This factory rents all their land and grows – what else? – sugar cane.

One sister and her family arrived just after we did, and a bit later, as we were tucking into carryout pizzas, another sister and her husband arrived. They were all very hospitable and welcoming. I got Sarah into bed by about 11.30 and followed suit shortly afterwards.

Sunday started with a lovely leisurely breakfast of fruit, cheese, ham, bread, cake (and much more) on the patio outside the kitchen, followed by a tour of the property immediately surrounding the house, including an orchidarium, a mini vegetable patch full of mint, spring onion and parsley, and one or two fruit trees. There is also a massive birdcage about two yards diameter and eight feet high, with various specimens of the local birds perching and flying about: budgies, zebra finches, and a lovely bird with a red and black head and golden tummy and lilac bits, to describe but a few. (Brazilians are very much into their songbirds. They are a very common sight, and many homes as well as businesses with larger premises will have a cage or two with singing birds.)

Let's not forget the football pitch, which is part of the garden. I think small boys here are born knowing how to play football. Sueli has a three-year-old nephew, and he packs a powerful - and accurate - kick, and is fairly proficient at dribbling the ball and saving the goals, too. The fact that his thirteen-year-old brother is football mad might have something to do with it. Sueli has a two-year-old daughter, but she hasn't been smitten by football yet.

The house is not in splendid isolation, as there are various relatives living close by. The extended tour started with the neighbour's chickens. Their four-year-old son quickly joined our party and tagged along with us. In the corner of the chickens' enclosure was a tree that seemed fairly unassuming when you were underneath it, but which was most attractive when you could see the canopy. It is seedtime now, and this tree must be of the legume family. The pods, about four inches long and half an inch (or less) wide, are dark brown, but then they open and curl back to reveal a creamy green interior dotted with bright red seeds about a third of an inch across. It almost looked like the tree was in flower with the pods and seeds striking a colourful contrast against the leaves.

After admiring chickens and trees, we went down past two ponds. There were no ducks on the ponds, which seems to be the norm in Brazil, but there were fish. There are always fish in ponds in Brazil. Fishing is second only to football as a national passion here. We crossed a bridge over a small stream in which a white egret was highstepping along in slow motion, picking its way as it went, and a large brown cow with floppy ears and droopy horns was wading up to its knees. Then we walked up a short hill to an empty house where Sueli and Sarah left me holding the babies - her two-year-old daughter and four-year-old nephew - while they disappeared into the unkempt wilderness of the deserted garden from which they soon reappeared laden with passion fruit and unripe tangerines. The return journey was interesting with a t-shirt full of tangerines and passion fruit and small children all wanting to be carried! Round the other side of the pond was a disused pinga distillery. Apparently, every sugar plantation used to have its own distillery. There were not a lot of the workings left, but there were three large tractors inside, the sight of which brought life to weary children. Having made a few imaginary races round the shed on the tractors, we returned to the house to find lunch preparations on the patio.

Our choices were meat, meat, or meat, some egg pâté as a starter, and some rice cooked along with very fine pasta strands, which made an interesting combination. It was all very leisurely; the temperature was not too hot. We women sat and chatted in the sunshine, a very pleasant repose with the birds singing in the cage nearby, and the husbands drifted between the meat and the television where the Grand Prix was on.

After a communal washing up, Sueli said it was time to go home, to Sarah's immediate dismay; she protested that she hadn't got her sugar cane. Right enough, Sueli had promised Sarah some sugar cane and we had forgotten about it. The rain was starting, and just as we had persuaded Sarah that Sueli could get some during the week and bring it into school for her (Sueli works in the office at the school), Sueli's sister suggested that we could all get into her car and drive up to the section of the plantation where we could find the correct variety of cane. So, all the children were bundled into the car and I was installed in the front seat with a knife, which looked more like a machete, and off we went. It wasn't far, but the last 100 yards was up a very rough track between two stands of cane. Sueli was dispatched to cut the cane, just outside the car, with the rain getting heavier by the minute. She returned, drenched, and then loaded the boot with the cut cane and off we set again.

Thank goodness, the track was down hill. Within those few minutes of rain, it had turned into a stream and we slithered down to the road at the bottom. We would not have managed to drive up it if we had arrived a few minutes later.

Sugar cane is about one to two inches in diameter and looks like bamboo with growth marks at regular intervals. Unlike bamboo, though, you can cut sugar cane with a sharp knife. The inside is fibrous and juicy. Sarah likes chewing the raw stems, and this variety is particularly suited for this. It is not too hard to chew and rewards your efforts with lots of sweet juice. You take the outer skin off, cut across above and below the harder intersections, split the resulting piece into four (or more) along its length, and gnaw at it to release the juice. It is lovely. You are then left with a dry, flattened fibrous stick, which goes into the bin.

This variety is softer and juicier than most and is good for chewing on. Other varieties are harder and less rewarding to chew, but each variety is used for a specific purpose, whether to make sugar, or pinga, or to make alcohol for car fuel, or for squeezing for the sugar cane juice drink you can buy at roadside stands flavoured with lime or pineapple. I'm not a cane expert ... yet!

Sueli left us home laden with goodies: passion fruit, tangerines, avocados, and of course the cane. The flooding on the road back to Piracicaba was a good indication of how heavy the rain was, but this type of torrential downpour is always short lived, and the roads were dry again within the hour. Meanwhile, the two Alans had been out in it at the Grand Prix, but they duly arrived home a bit damp, but nothing daunted, they got changed and went in search of food.

It was a great weekend, but alas, no photos ... Alan had the camera at the Grand Prix! We had planned a weekend at home, maybe with friends coming to play, and we ended up elsewhere in very pleasant surroundings. It was fantastic. I have been ordered to bring Alan for a cervejinha some weekend. Cerveja is beer, and cervejinha is their way of saying 'a wee beer'!

Tropical Bounty

Our friend Kaye has been and gone, and Alan's new boss has been and gone, so I now have the place to myself again. I think we ran Kaye off her feet and she was probably glad to get back home for a rest. We packed in quite a lot, in spite of the fact that we were bound by school hours. She arrived on Sunday, April 13 and Alan Soutar (Sooty) left on April 12. Alan drove Sooty to the airport, stayed overnight in São Paulo and came back with Kaye the next morning.

The day after she arrived, we took her to see the Passion Play that we went to last year, and she enjoyed that. Wednesday that week I took her to Pedreira, the town where we got the agate wind chimes. Its main claim to fame is cheap 'porcelain', and it certainly is full of shops selling all sorts of ceramic ware. I found some nice things, very tempting, but I don't think they would survive shipment home.

The coming weekend was Easter, and since both Sarah and Alan had Friday and Monday off, we took advantage of this and headed for Penedo, a small town settled by Finnish immigrants in 1929. The town founders' vision was to provide a better life for its inhabitants: a place where everyone pulled his or her weight, and they lived more or less self sufficiently, free from commercialism. If the original inhabitants could see the town now, a thriving tourist trap with commercial outlets everywhere, they would probably be quite dismayed at how much their vision has been corrupted.

Peneda does have a Nordic flavour to it, though, which is an interesting diversion. There is a mini tourist village in the centre, which is all shops and restaurants in sized down Finnish style buildings. There are also at least three chocolate factories, which are really more like small kitchens.

We did have a giggle to ourselves one evening. What an interesting picture we made - four people from Northern Ireland sitting in a restaurant in a Finnish-style village in Brazil eating Japanese food!

Penedo is just across the state boundary from us, in Rio de Janeiro state (we are São Paulo state), but it was a five-hour drive to get there. It is nestled in the foothills of the mountains, which comprise most of Minas Gerais, the state to the north of Rio de Janeiro and east of São Paulo state.

Approaching Rio State

One of our trips out from Penedo took us up to the mountains and to another series of small towns, settled (this century) by Swiss and German immigrants and developed deliberately as tourist traps. It was some road up: a dirt road, twisting ever upwards, occasionally a bit narrow in places, and this is the main access! Everything has to be brought up that road in lorries. Tourists come in buses, and lots of cars come too. Apparently in the past, hoteliers from these villages used to come down to the town on the main road to collect their guests - on horseback. It would have been some trek. You can imagine the traffic problems in these small towns, where, because of the nature of the terrain, there is nowhere to put a by-pass, or build car parks. It was interesting.

We were hoping for some sort of park, with trails for walking, but I think you have to be a very serious walker, prepared for a 6-hour minimum walk, with a guide. However, we explored the town, paddled in the natural swimming pool (in the river), and came across yet another chocolate factory. This time it really was somebody's kitchen. We went in for a bit and watched them busy at work coating truffles, bought a small bar of chocolate each and continued on our way.

We tried to visit a waterfall, but the road we were following got narrower and narrower and rougher and rougher, and it had started to rain. We decided that discretion was the better option rather than being stuck in the middle of nowhere with sub-zero temperatures at night, so we hair-pinned back down the dirt road to Penedo instead.

We had fondue for tea, going for the option of trying the three types of fondue offered: cheese, meat, and chocolate. There was bread to dip in the cheese sauce, meat to fry in oil, and fruit to dip in the chocolate sauce. We were stuffed by the end of it.

We returned to Piracicaba on the Monday. Alongside the main road we were travelling on (the São Paulo – Rio de Janeiro road) is a town called Aparecida. It has a massive church, described in the guidebook as a Basilica, and has the capacity to seat 45,000 people. It is a centre for pilgrimage, and come October 12 is absolutely bunged with people. Nossa Senhora de Aparecida is the patron saint of Brazil, and October 12 is her day. We nearly stopped, but decided that we would like to get a few more miles (or kilometres) behind us before stopping.

Wednesday that week, I took Kaye to the top of a scarp slope about an hour away to see the countryside. The view is quite spectacular, and on a clear day, you can see Piracicaba. We can see the slope from our flat. There is a hang gliding/parascending take off point there, which Matt got quite excited about, but never managed to fly from. Weather permitting, he would have flown from there to Piracicaba's miniscule airfield.

We visited a couple of waterfalls while we were there. It is an amazing tract of country. These were not over the edge of the scarp as you would imagine, but further back from the face, where, for no apparent reason, it seems as if a huge chunk has been cut out of the ground. These waterfalls fall over the edge into this chasm and disappear to I'm not quite sure where.

Kaye came to my choir practice that week and enjoyed herself. I asked Sueli, who also sings in the choir, if we could visit her sitio again, as Kaye was eager to see it. Of course, Sueli said we were welcome to come and visit, so on Saturday, off we went. Once we were there, we did a five or six kilometre walk at a very leisurely pace through sugar cane fields and through the nearest small village, and then we visited the church where Sueli used to go as a child. We looked at some photos there of various functions which involved her parents, got invited to a party at the church by a group who were doing some maintenance to the building, and saw the local school (now closed down) where she went as a child.

Sueli's sister is an orchid fanatic, and there were all sorts of wonderful plants round the place. I took masses of photos. I can see how so many people get hooked on growing orchids. They are quite extraordinary, and there are so many different shapes, sizes and colours.

I had asked Kaye to bring a bottle of Black Bush as a thank you for the generosity Sueli's family had shown when Sarah and I ended up staying there at short notice. Sueli responded in kind with a flagon of pinga – the local hooch brewed from sugar cane. It was brewed about five years ago on the farm, which had a small-scale commercial distillery. Production stopped when her father died four years ago. Now most of the equipment from the distillery has been sold off, as none of the family is interested in keeping it going. The building is still there and she showed us where the cane used to be crushed; where the fermenting tanks used to be; where the 'worm' had been housed, with the boiling vat beneath; where the storage tanks were; where the runoff from the boiling vat went, and that the 'waste' was used to fertilise the next year's crop.

Speaking of sugar cane, having been here over a year now we are more in tune with the goings on of how the cane crop is managed. The sugar cane harvest has started in earnest now, and we can see plumes of smoke from our flat (the joys of being high up), at various points around the countryside. As you drive around the countryside, you can see piles of cut cane waiting to be loaded, which is done by trailers using a grab on the front of a tractor. On the roads, you encounter the vast lorries, with two trailers behind the main truck, transporting the cane to the various factories to be processed. These lorries are 30 metres long, and must be carrying a colossal weight. Interestingly, the majority of the sugar cane is processed into alcohol for car fuel.

The day after our leisurely six kilometre walk at Sueli's sitio, we had arranged with Carlos to do a mini calango (long walk) based on the route of our last calango in March. We set off at 8.00 a.m. (rather than the usual 6.00 a.m.), and right enough it is a lovely route along a dirt road all the way through the countryside. In one area there was a signpost to a condominium called Little Switzerland, which gives an idea of what the area was like, but I think that whoever named the condominium had never actually been to Switzerland. There are a few nice hills in this area, but no towering mountains!

What I noticed was the abundance of butterflies along the route. It was lovely. We took turns driving the various cars. There were eleven of us altogether, and we finished by visiting a waterfall, which we reached by walking along the streambed for about 200 yards. Carlos, Sarah and I took advantage of the waterfall and got totally soaked. In this climate, you soon dry off, no matter what you are wearing. The finale was a barbecue at a sítio belonging to a friend of Carlos. All in all, it was a very pleasant day.

Kaye now had less than a week left. On Wednesday, we took a spur of the moment decision to go to São Paulo to see the terracotta warriors on display. Kaye had missed out on seeing them during her trip to China, and so was quite keen to go. We took the bus, as there was no way I could be compelled to make that drive, but the bus ride was another new experience for me. I've tried the local bus service a couple of times, returning from a calango, but this was my first time on a long distance coach. Very comfortable, and very efficient – once we had worked out where to buy the tickets.

Each bus company that operates out of the bus station in Piracicaba has its own ticket office. We couldn't buy a return ticket because we didn't know what time we were coming back, and this is necessary, as you are allocated your seat on that particular bus. Our tickets to São Paulo were duly printed out, and on them, in addition to the time and date, were our seat numbers and also the departure gate at the bus station – none of this standing around watching a board for departures.

I almost felt like a naughty child that had escaped for the day. There were Kaye and I in our shorts and T-shirts, carrying a small bottle of water, and everyone else was more respectably dressed in long trousers and carrying luggage of some sort.

It took us nearly three hours to get to the bus station in São Paulo, by the time we had sat in the slow traffic on the inner ring road. Once we got there, we then took a taxi, which was easy to do as there were lots of them lined up, waiting. We took taxi *commun*, as opposed to a taxi *especial*, the difference I think is that the special ones are more comfortable and have air conditioning, but of course you pay more for them. Twenty minutes took us to the exhibition. The traffic is a nightmare! That twenty-minute taxi ride cost us marginally more than the three-hour trip in the bus: bus fare, 21 reais; taxi including tip, 25 reais. That is little more than £5 for the taxi.

We took the precaution of buying our return tickets before we left the bus station. Again, the difficult part was finding where to buy the ticket. Piracicaba, a moderate sized town, has about six companies operating out of it. You can imagine what it is like in São Paulo, a huge city by comparison. There are seemingly hundreds of ticket offices, but we found the right one and bought our tickets. It is no cheaper buying a return ticket. We did briefly consider getting on a bus to Santiago – in Chile, or maybe taking off to Uruguay, because there were ticket offices labelled with those destinations, but we thought better of it.

Kaye enjoyed the exhibition and the return journey was just as easy. It was just as well we did buy the tickets earlier, because I don't think there were any seats left. Again, there is no rush to get the best seats, because they are allocated at time of purchase.

The next learning curve will be using the metro in São Paulo, I think, but I'll leave that for another time!

The next day, Thursday, was May 1 and a holiday. We went to visit a coffee *fazenda* about an hour away. The coffee plant is a large bush that grows up to ten feet high with dark green shiny leaves. It has a white flower, which turns into a green then red berry in autumn before it shrivels to dark brown. The berry is quite sweet. The coffee 'bean' is actually the seed inside the berry. Legend has it that some goatherd had observed that when his goats ate this particular berry, they started behaving in a more hyperactive manner, so he tried it. Why he decided to chew the seed is anybody's guess; maybe he wanted to replicate the same experience his goats had.

Coffee bushes typically have a twelve-year economically productive life. They start producing when they are three years old, produce for twelve years, and then the bush is cut down about a foot from the ground and the roots send up new shoots. This will be the bush for the next fifteen years. After that, they are pulled up, roots and all, and the ground is left fallow for a year. Young plants from the nursery are put in and the whole process starts again.

As with any crop, there are pests, but they have natural pest control in the form of a climbing plant that attracts the insect which would otherwise eat its way through the flesh of the berry to the seed.

Harvesting starts in mid May and they bus workers in from Bahia, a state about 1000 miles further north. Apparently it is more or less the same families who come each year and stay for about three months. Machines are used to beat the berries off the bushes, but they leave behind about thirty percent of the crop, which then has to be stripped by hand. If the bushes are too tall, the machine can't cope. The machines are basically two sets of what looks like large revolving brushes, except that the 'bristles' are plastic coated spikes fairly closely spaced. These pass either side of the bush. I hate to think how many leaves are stripped at the same time.

Hand stripping is obviously much gentler on the poor bush. Green and red and brown are stripped, with the different colours producing different qualities of coffee. Different varieties of bushes produce different flavours of coffee.

When the berries are stripped off the bushes, they tumble down to a large cloth/tarpaulin and then are winnowed to get rid of the unwanted stuff such as leaves and small twigs. Each worker has a large sack with a number on it. When the sack is full, the worker takes it to a waiting truck and empties it. The worker's number is noted, and they are paid by the sackful. At this stage, it is done by volume rather than weight, as the dried berries weigh a lot less than the red or green ones. A fit worker can average about fifteen 70-litre sacks per day and they are paid four to six reais per sack depending on whether it is a generous 70 litres or a scant 70 litres.

The truck then empties the berries into a concrete collecting tank, which has a hole at the bottom over a conveyer belt which takes the berries to a waiting water tank. The different colours of berries behave differently in water. Red and green berries sink, but the brown dried ones float away along pipes to the drying ground. The red and green ones are put in a revolving drum that removes the pulp from the red ones.

As an interesting side note, the best quality coffee is made from the brown berries because they have already started to dry on the bushes. Red is next best and green berries are used to make instant coffee! The best quality coffee of all comes from Columbia because that country is higher in elevation and thus the climate is cooler. Also, the berries there are picked by hand individually, instead of being stripped from the bush by machine, so there is less chance of immature berries getting in. Why are there dried berries and ripening berries on the same bush? - because coffee bushes flower twice a year, and the dried berries are from the first flowering.

After the berries have been through the water tank, they are dried. The old way has stood the test of time - it is still best to leave the berries out on the ground in the sun for three days before putting them into the drying machines. To this end, in front of the house, is a huge flat area of tarmac, and the berries are laid out on it in the sun.

The drying grounds used to be brick but with the advent of asphalt, some bright spark came to the conclusion that because black attracts the heat, drying would be quicker. I think wheelbarrows and shovels are the order of the day. Berries arrive from the grading process via water power and are collected in a trailer with a hole in the bottom. When the trailer is full, it is driven to the selected part of the drying ground, and as it moves along, the berries are deposited on the ground via that useful hole. Workers with rakes spread the beans out and turn them every fifteen minutes or so. There are furrows and raised areas, so they rake down the raised areas, creating new furrows and raised areas. The direction of the furrows is changed with each raking in order to take advantage of the direction of the sun so that the berries get maximum drying.

Then the berries are ready to continue their drying process in the machines, which allows the production crew more control over temperature and humidity. I think the next stage is getting rid of the dried husks, and then the resulting beans (as they are known once completely dried) are graded and bagged, ready for market. Unfortunately, we were a month too early to see everything in full swing. All was very quiet, but they managed to unearth an employee from somewhere to show us the collecting and winnowing processes. He has been working in coffee production for about fifty years, so he was a mine of information.

The history of the fazenda was quite interesting. The big coffee slump was in 1929, and apparently they were burning the coffee because they couldn't sell it. At that time, the owners sold out to a Japanese family who were part of the huge Mitsubishi group, so there was money there. Production has continued to this day, though many other fazendas in the region have long since given up. The main house certainly has Japanese overtones in the architecture, though I'm not sure whether that same family still has a finger in the business, or whether it is centrally owned by some coffee conglomerate.

Slaves were used originally to pick the coffee, and were housed in a long stone building with one low door called a *senzala*. It was a low door because if a man had to duck to come through the door, he was less likely to be able to attack whoever was on the outside. There were no windows in this building; it was just one long building split in two – one side for men, one side for women, though apparently there were separate quarters for married slaves. Apparently, fazenda owners practiced selective breeding, and only the strongest and fittest slaves were allowed to produce children, which makes one wonder if they actually bothered with marriage. Slavery was abolished in 1888 on May 13 at exactly 5.00 a.m. Immigrants were then encouraged to come to Brazil to take over where the slaves left off. The quarters were much improved with the addition of dividing walls and window and doors, but their living conditions were still fairly basic.

The Brazilian staple diet of rice and beans developed from slave cuisine. The barons, as the plantation owners were known, had the choice cuts of meat and the slaves were given the leftovers, such as pigs' ears, tails, feet, and so on, and these were used to give a bit of additional flavour to the ubiquitous pans of rice and beans. Pigs ears and tails and bits of skin and dear knows what else can still be bought in the market (including supermarkets) today, along with whole calves' heads. I don't think any bit of animal is wasted.

Because this was such a vast coffee producing region, some enterprising person decided to build a railway through the region to bring the coffee to the town. Our next trip that day was on said railway. There are several steam trains, which a group of enthusiasts have resurrected. It is almost entirely staffed by volunteers, and you pay your money for a trip pulled by a steam train. Our volunteer took time to explain how a steam train works – an explanation mainly aimed at children, which was quite fun. Right enough we went through some very nice countryside. Our trip lasted about one and a half hours. Passing through one farm, our guide told us that in the past, quite often, the owner of the fazenda would live on one side of the railway and the workers would live the other side. It was a pleasant day out, as well as interesting and informative.

The weather turned cold on the Friday - and wet. I had intended to take Kaye to look at the lizards in one of the parks, but as we left the flat, in the car, the heavens opened, so I decided to show her a couple of the churches instead. We went to one church which I would guess to be about 100 years old, very ornate, with pictures painted on every available surface. It was a bit gloomy inside. As Kaye commented, where any church in Britain would have heaters, this one had fans to cool you. They had an organ too, which is a rarity in Brazil. In contrast, I then took her to a modern church. It had a stained glass façade, and white marble interior giving it a very bright open feel inside. The backdrop behind the altar was also stained glass - from floor to ceiling - of the Virgin Mary. I found someone to turn the lights on behind Her so we could see Her in all Her splendour.

Kaye decided that it was definitely time to be going home! The weather had turned cold and she had finished the packet of proper coffee. Alan only drinks Nescafe and I don't drink coffee at all. I had bought a packet of *real* coffee for Alan Soutar, and Kaye had finished it.

Kaye's flight was on Saturday and we still had one call to make. This was to be an outdoor excursion, but Friday afternoon didn't seem too appealing. Saturday morning, bags packed, we went to visit Aparecido, one of Alan's employees, at his sítio. This was to be a whistle-stop tour, as Kaye had to get to the airport later that day. Aparecido has about two acres, on which he grows various types of oranges, coffee, maize, bananas, peanuts, soya beans, mandioca, and many other things besides. (He was the one who gave Alan about 80 bananas a few months ago.) He also has a pony (and trap) and donkey plus its year old foal.

He talks 'nineteen to the dozen', so I couldn't understand half of what he was saying (nor can many of his work mates!), but he is very enthusiastic about all his plants and happily chopped off the top of two banana trees to give us the bananas, then went on to pull up two mandioca plants to give us the roots; and as if that wasn't enough, he then proceeded to pick two large basins full of oranges. It was a wonderful sight, him in his straw hat, plucking oranges. He also pulled up some peanuts for Sarah to take home. The back of the car was laden with farm-fresh bounty. It is just as well that we were not going straight to the airport with a suitcase in the back.

I say he chopped the top off two banana trees; let me explain: Bananas grow on the leading shoot of a 'trunk' that is about ten to fifteen feet tall. A large pink waxy flower is produced in spring, which gradually bends downwards with the weight of the forming bananas. The trees look solid, but they are not. Instead, they are composed of layers of fleshy material, which is the result of leaves succeeding each other as the plant grows in height. The leaves are huge: four to six feet long and two feet wide would not be an exaggerated guess, so you can imagine the size of stem required to support that weight. There are usually four or five trunks growing up from the ground, which at that level are eight to ten inches diameter. Each trunk produces a flower, followed in late summer/autumn by bananas, growing in clusters on alternate sides of this shoot, with approximately six to a cluster and approximately six clusters per shoot.

Aparecido quite casually swung his machete at the trunk, and I was amazed when it went right through it. It takes about a year for the stem to grow up again. There I was, laden with a stem of bananas in each hand. Imagine the weight of about thirty-six bananas, then add the weight of the stem on to that!

Mandioca bushes grow about six to eight feet high and have leaves similar to chestnut, but they are more pointed and a darker green. The root system is shallow and pulled up quite easily. They are roughly cylindrical roots that can grow to eighteen inches long. 'Stop, stop!' we cried, as he enthusiastically hauled the second root system to my car. 'We don't know what to do with it...' I added, my voice trailing when I saw there was no way to dampen his enthusiasm. As it turned out, his wife told me what to do with it, so I am now quite good at producing mandioca chips, or you can just boil them or make soup.

It was the same with the oranges. 'Stop, stop!' we cried, as he sent his daughter to fetch another container. I say oranges, but these were more like tangerines. Maybe we were doing him a service by taking them off his hands, as he had quite a number of well-laden trees. He also gave me a few oranges of two other different varieties, so I could try them. There is a great variety of citrus type fruits here varying from small kumquat size to grapefruit size, and they are neither oranges, limes, nor lemons, but the flavour ranges somewhere along those lines.

Again, he happily hauled up a couple of peanut bushes so we could see the peanuts growing on the roots, and then he gave them to Sarah.

Some haul! We must have had about 150 oranges, 60 bananas, lots of mandioca, and guess what! Neither Alan nor Sarah eats bananas or oranges (though they will drink the juice of the latter). I had the dubious task of removing the bunches of bananas off the stems, which I achieved with a small sharp knife. I don't know how it is supposed to be done. The white sap does not wash off! Alan and Sarah may not eat bananas or oranges, but at least they eat mandioca chips! I spent the following week processing the mandioca for freezing, and bought an electric juice squeezer to process the oranges so that I could freeze the juice. I also gave away lots of bananas, oranges and mandioca.

If Kaye had not had a plane to catch, Aparecido would have had us there all day, such is his enthusiasm. He wanted us to stay for lunch, but we had to rush. Alan took Kaye to the airport, and Sarah and I stayed at home.

My cactus flowered about a month ago. It produced a bud that got bigger and bigger and bigger. Finally, after I watered it, it lifted the top petal, and then the other four petals followed suit and I had a large five-petalled purple *hairy* flower about four inches across. It looked wonderful on such a small cactus, but its 'delicate' perfume was something else. I knew there had to be a catch. It was stinking! Luckily, you had to have your nose close to the flower to discover its stench.

The other cactus, a squat prickly variety, has a crown of bright pink flowers at intervals. The third one, long and tall, just keeps getting taller and taller. It's great; for the most part I ignore them, and they seem to thrive.

I received a phone call a couple of weeks ago which, when I finally got the gist of what they were talking about, turned out to be a win in a draw. Sarah had won 100 reais worth of goods from the sports shop where we had bought her ballet stuff. Off we went – and it is not easy spending that amount when you have nothing specific in mind and are limited to what is in stock in the shop. (This amount is roughly equivalent to 100 pounds, if shopping in Belfast.) We chose some longer trousers for school, a leotard and ballet shoes of the right colour, all of which she needed, but not urgently. What next? They had some T-shirts with painted decorations on the front, so we chose a white one and a black one, and finally decided on a new bikini! With three reais left, we went for a couple of fancy hair elastics. To be quite honest, I hadn't realised that the customer satisfaction note we had filled in was going in to a draw, so it was a nice surprise all round.

On the subject of ballet, the mums were asked to come watch a class so we could all see what was going on. All very nice, but half way through the class, one of the budding ballerinas called out 'Toucano!' – and there on the windowsill was a toucan, peering in the window. Maybe he liked the music. When ten little ballerinas headed for the window, he fled and perched for awhile on the veranda of an apartment across the road, before disappearing. I didn't know that wild toucans ever ventured into an urban environment. Maybe he was an escapee from somewhere.

Whilst on the subject of wildlife, the other day Alan was coming out of the lift when something hit his leg. Having recovered from this surprise attack, he looked around our hallway and eventually discovered a small lizard on the wall. It was about three inches long and semi translucent, with black beady eyes. Had he been in the lift? Had he been on the outside of the lift? Had he climbed up the lift shaft? We will never know. We managed to catch him by putting a small bowl over him and sliding a piece of card underneath. Trying to catch him by hand would have been impossible, because they can move so fast. We put him out on the balcony. I felt sorry for him because it was cold (the temperature was lower than 20°). Maybe he had come inside looking for heat!

Balloon Competition and a Calango Andando

'Céu colorido' (Coloured sky) was the headline in the local paper this week, and the sky was definitely coloured – with hot air balloons. Every two years, Piracicaba hosts a balloon competition. There were twenty-six teams taking part. Not only does each balloon have a pilot (the less experienced ones have company on board), but there is also a rescue squad. Someone has to go and fetch the balloon when it has touched down somewhere distant.

There were balloons in all sorts of colours. Most of the balloons were sporting the logo of whoever was sponsoring them. There was a Nescafé balloon, which was dark brown with red bits, and a World Wildlife Fund balloon, white with a large panda on it.

Caterpillar was also represented, advertising the fact that it had been in Brazil for 50 years this year! I loved seeing the balloons floating about above the city like huge, coloured soap bubbles drifting gently wherever the breeze might take them. One afternoon, when I was talking to Alan on the phone, I startled him by saying, 'Good heavens, there's a balloon floating past the window!' That's how low in the sky they were drifting along. We are on the twelfth floor, and the bit I saw drifting past was the bulge of the balloon, so the basket at the bottom would have been even lower!

How do you compete in a balloon? According to the paper, there are five events. One, which sounds like fun, is called 'Hunt the Fox'. A balloon takes off, and after about ten minutes, the judges set two more balloons off to chase after it and try to follow it. I don't know if they actually have to catch it.

Other events are:

- The longest distance - Each balloonist flies for a predetermined length of time, then throws out a marker, which falls to the ground. Each marker is then measured from the starting point to determine which balloon went the furthest.
- The shortest distance - The same idea as above.
- Fly in - Each balloon takes off outside the competition area and tries to get as close to a predetermined target area as possible, at which point they throw out their marker.
- Elbow - as the name suggests, you have two 'legs' to this competition. The balloons take off, fly towards a target area, throw out a marker, then change direction and fly towards another target area and throw out a marker.
- To the line - The balloons have to fly to a designated area.
- Mast test - A key is put in a bag and tied to a mast or flagpole that is six to ten metres high. The balloons take off a minimum of three kilometres from this mast and have to try to get the key off the mast!

It all looked like such fun. The competition was based in one of the parks here - not a huge park - about one kilometre long and half a kilometre wide - with a lake taking up about a third of the space, as well as some trees, a small play area and a cycling test area. Not a lot of open space, and 26 balloons all had to take off from this area.

One balloon had a TV reporter on board, complete with camera - and she was hanging off the edge of the balloon to film the pilot!

We had wondered how they would cope with so many large hot air balloons in a limited space. We found all this out. It was really quite fascinating. The balloon is laid out on the ground with the basket on its side at the lower end of it. It is a huge piece of fabric when seen on the ground. The balloon is then attached to the basket section. The inflation of the balloon is started with a large fan. When the balloon is partially filled, the air from the fan is heated using the gas burners in the basket. I had imagined that the flames would rise up instead of going straight ahead. I guess the gas is coming out under such pressure that the flames go in the direction they are pointed. The heating of the air continues using the fire-breathing dragon in the basket, and eventually, the balloon starts to rise, bringing the basket upright. This heating of the air continues until the basket is almost off the ground. Then it is climb aboard, open the gas jets again and away you go.

It was great seeing the balloons all jostling together as they inflated. There is one here in Piracicaba that regularly flies on a Sunday morning. It takes off from close to our flat. The local dogs don't think much of the dragon noises overhead as it tries to gain height. We want to have a go, so we've put that on our list of things to do whilst living in Brazil.

A couple of weekends ago, we went on a nighttime calango andando. It was not a long walk this time, only about five kilometres, but it was well worth it. The aim was to climb a hill and watch the sunrise. It was the June solstice.

We started out at 1.30 a.m., and were bused to the bottom of the hill. There was a bit of confusion about buses, and it was about 3.00 a.m. or later by the time we actually started walking. There was a full moon, which was great. (There was an eclipse the night before, but I didn't get to see it because we have no windows that side of the flat and I didn't have the enthusiasm to get dressed at 2.00 a.m. and go outside!) The walk started along a track through newly planted sugar cane; nice flat walking. Then came the climb. Quite steep it was, too, through trees, and with fixed ropes in places to help you haul yourself up. Not rock climbing proper, just something to pull yourself up, hand over hand. That took time. There were ninety people in the group, but we eventually reached the top.

There was a clearing at the top, though well surrounded by trees. I had remembered to take my star book and a torch covered in red paper, but we couldn't see many stars. With most of the people being city folk, the torches were never off, so our eyes never got a chance to get accustomed to the dark. Even at the top while eating our various picnics (some had brought wine, and I heard a champagne cork popping), there were random sources of artificial light.

Sunrise was around 6.30 a.m., but it started getting light about an hour beforehand. As always at this latitude, sunrise was rapid. I reckon there were two minutes from the first gleam of sun, to seeing the whole disc.

It is obviously a fairly popular climb, as there were some shelters constructed from bits of wood and plastic, and a few pots and pans lying about the place. Various church groups seem to come. We had met about a dozen people coming down as we were going up, and they were from some church in the next city (this was at three o'clock in the morning!).

We were also overtaken by three people who can best be described as radical evangelists. They spent the time alternately praying and berating themselves at the tops of their voices. That didn't disturb us that much, because Brazilians don't know how to keep quiet anyway. Our lot were chatting away and shouting to each other.

After the sun came up, we came down, and then it was time for a bit of a rest.

View over countryside planted with young sugar cane

It was fun to have done it, but for us, the serenity of such a beautiful setting was slightly marred by the perpetual torches and the constant chatting and shouting - but that is the Brazilian way. They love talking, and there is no harm in that, and after we had returned to Piracicaba, we enjoyed breakfast at a local hotel!

Adventures in Ecotourism – Bonito and Pantanal

Off on our travels again, this time heading west. We visited a small town called Bonito in the state of Mato Grosso and then went a bit further north to the southern edge of the Pantanal – the world's largest wetland area. It measures approximately 800 by 200 kilometres.

We had to catch a plane in São Paulo, which meant a two-hour drive to start with, then a one-and-a-half-hour flight to Campo Grande, the capital of the state of Mato Grosso. This was followed by a four-hour drive to Bonito. Bonito is getting its own airport next year, as it is such a popular tourist destination. It is flat country there – cattle country – all those whitish Indian cattle with the hump on their shoulders (the Nelore ones). Campo Grande must be on a plateau, as after about two hours driving we fell off the edge; at least it felt that way! The road descends rather steeply via a series of sweeping bends (not hairpin turns). Bonito lies west and slightly south of Campo Grande. At one point, the road was blocked by cattle being driven by *vaqueros* (cowboys) on horses to other grazing lands. There didn't seem to be much driving going on; more milling around if anything. One vaquero had a wonderful woolly saddle blanket.

We also saw quite a number of rheas – the South American version of the ostrich. The farmers encourage them to stay on their property because they eat snakes.

Our destination was a hotel that consisted of a series of semi-detached chalets dotted around the main building, which is where the food and reception area was. There were lots of shady trees too, though shade is not so necessary at this time of year.

It was a cool night - which probably meant about 15°C if truth be known. Our trip in the morning was to the Grotto Azul, which is a large cave with a very blue lake in the bottom. It had a largish opening with a steep zigzagging path to the lake. The cave is filled with various stalactites and stalagmites, but because it is a fairly open cave, they were a bit weathered. The extreme blue colour of the lake is the result of particles of calcium carbonate suspended in the water, which reflect the blue component of the spectrum of light. Apparently, there are two dinosaur skeletons at the bottom of the lake lying in about 40 metres of water. The lake was said to be 80 metres deep at one point, but a subsequent survey put it at 200 metres!

For lunch we headed back to the town, which is so small that one could describe it as a 'one horse town'! There are about 17,000 inhabitants, and it has been around for about fifty years. There is a main asphalt road running through it, but all the other roads are dirt. It is full of tourist shops, but in spite of that, it has a very rural feel to it. There are shops a bit like McDowell's in Gleno, selling everything a farmer could want and more, and shops selling everything a cowboy/vaquero could want alongside the requisite souvenir shops. The veterinary supplies shop sells saddles as well. There are several tourist attractions in the area, but not in the sense of historic buildings and museums. Rather, the focus here is on ecotourism with the abundance of waterfalls, rivers and caves in this region.

There is a trip we really wanted to take called the Abismo Anhumas, which wasn't in our schedule unfortunately (we were on a package holiday), in which one abseils through a split in the ground, descending 72 metres to a floating platform in an underground lake. If you have scuba diving qualifications, you can go diving. Otherwise, you get taken to the dry section of the cave. Tourism is very controlled here.

Our afternoon trip was down a river in an inflatable rubber boat, negotiating four waterfalls along the way. The river was very flat in between the waterfalls. Our guide did a lot of paddling. Actually, he looked a lot like Francisco, our boatman in Amazonas. The biggest waterfall that we went over was about eight feet. It was very peaceful floating down the river between falls. We saw some toucans and various other birds, some monkeys and a large snake (yellow anaconda, I think) curled up at the edge of the river, partially immersed in it. I think he had recently eaten a fairly large meal. The bit of body we could see was about twelve inches in diameter, and resting lightly on it, the snake's head looked small in comparison.

It was my first experience of rafting. This was certainly easy stuff with flat calm most of the way, though the waterfalls were quite fun. Approaching them you get a sense of anticipation; will the boat go sailing over, flying in the air? Will it be a bumpy ride? And then at the very precipice you find yourself just sliding over and down them before you know it. Those sitting at the front got quite wet though, as the nose hit the water at the bottom.

We were accompanied by a chap making a film, and he sat right at the front of the boat, camera in a plastic bag, perched on his shoulder, filming us all. I admire his confidence. We all had to brace ourselves and adopt a more secure position when going over the falls. He, on the other hand, stayed sitting on the edge with his back to the direction of travel, not knowing when he would descend rapidly, and filming all the time. I guess he had done it before - lots of times!

There was an option to stop and swim, but it was too cold. The sun was behind the trees, so there was not a lot of direct solar heat. By the time we got to the end of the river run, our minibus driver was waiting for us, along with our dry clothes, at a place where they had a couple of macaws and a toucan for you to talk to.

The Macaw seemed to like doing the laundry ... but the toucan wasn't interested!

Bonito's main claim to fame is the crystal clear waters of the rivers (and there are lots of them), the clarity being attributed to the limestone in the area (or as the Indian legend goes, the blood of a fair damsel who died for pure love!).

The next day was a trip to the Estância Mimosa, which takes its name from the river Mimosa, to see seven waterfalls, with the opportunity to swim in the pools below them. We walked along a trail for about three kilometres hoping to see animals and birds, but they wouldn't play. We saw one frog! At one stage, the path climbed steeply for awhile (there are lots of wooden walkways and steps to make the ascent easier), and we arrived at the edge of a plateau area before descending again to the water's edge. The vegetation and trees at the top were markedly different to that along the edge of the river. Much sparser, drier and scrubbier – described as cerrado, and just like the scrubby trees we walked through with Roberto when we went to stay in Brasilia. Vegetation growing alongside the rivers is much more dense and lush, and is described as Mata Cílio, with *cílio* meaning eyelash. As the eyelash protects the eyes, so the forest protects the river!

We arrived at the first of the seven waterfalls, and some of us duly plunged into the pool. It was cold! Sarah and I swam, but Alan didn't. I stayed in for too long and got chilled because Sarah wanted to swim to the other side of the river and back (all of five metres!) after we had swum to the foot of the fall itself and scrambled in behind it.

We had a short boat trip to the next fall and then a short walk to the next one. One pool had a diving platform built six metres above it. Our guide and one other person were the only ones to take a plunge.

Another pool had a mini cave the far side of it and Sarah wanted to go to it. I was too cold to go in again, but our guide took her across even though I knew he was cold too.

Our guide today, whose name was Hellys, looked very German. His mother was pure German, and his father was half Polish, half Indian. I think they are quite proud of their mixed origins and happily recite the various nationalities in their backgrounds.

Not a lot of swimming was done in the seven pools. It was simply too cold. We arrived back at the Estância to a very welcome warming lunch.

The waterfalls here are growing, rather than receding, which is unique. I learnt in my geography lessons at school that waterfalls erode themselves backwards. These waterfalls, because of the high level of calcium carbonate in the water, are building themselves rather than eroding. Leaves and organic matter (in fact anything that falls into the river) get coated with limestone, and when enough of this builds up, a barrier is formed which eventually turns into a waterfall. They certainly looked different from any other waterfalls I have seen. They have a more rounded profile with large mushroom shaped slopes, and when we swam behind the falling water, we found mini caves with small, roughly formed stalactites.

After lunch, we lounged for a bit in the hammocks provided for guests (interestingly, these are made from strips of cowhide and not knotted mesh or canvas as we're used to) and then sat looking out over the lake. One of the cooks tried to entice Toni, a large jacaré (alligator – actually a *caiman* to be more precise) to come out of the water, but he wouldn't play. He didn't want any scraps of meat. He did come close to shore though. Of the seven jacaré in the lake, he was the largest at about two metres. The cook may not have enticed Toni out, but she did manage to provoke a brief skirmish amongst a couple of the other jacarés, which was quite interesting to watch. They can move extremely rapidly when they want to.

We saw an interesting sight on the way back to our hotel. I have seen many things being transported on motorbikes here, but this was the first time we had ever seen a bicycle strapped to the back of a motorbike!

Back at the hotel, the tree outside our chalet was full of green parrots all squawking away – what a noise – and I could not see one of them! It was as though the tree itself was alive and squawking. We also had a resident lizard (not inside the chalet, which would not be unusual) sitting quite still inside the housing of the wall light outside our door. We could see him silhouetted against the frosted glass. He must have been about four inches long. The light bulb is an energy saving variety, which means it does not get too hot, but it does attract insects, which get inside the lamp. What more could a lizard want – a convenient meal in a cosy, warm little house with no hunting required!

The next day we went to the Rio da Prata, which means River of Silver. It turned out to be a great day. It took only an hour's drive to get there, but mostly on a dirt road. It's a very dusty trip if you get stuck behind another vehicle – at least at this time of year. I gather that in the rainy season it is a different story. Again, I was struck by the sheer vastness of the country. We met perhaps two other vehicles and passed maybe four or five dwellings. The rest was just open grazing land dotted with trees and cows, surrounded by tree-clad hills.

The tourist agencies have a deal with the landowners on whose properties the tourist attractions lie. Only groups accompanied by guides are allowed, so that the number of tourists on the land at any given time is controlled and damage to the natural landscape is minimal.

On arrival at this attraction, we were issued with wetsuits, and then we walked about three kilometres (under the trees, I hasten to add). I had my wetsuit peeled down to my waist, but Alan and Sarah seemed happy totally zipped up. This particular landowner is eco-minded, and has set aside quite a large area of his fazenda for eco-tourism and preserving the natural environment. The trail was well looked after, with various trees labelled. We saw capuchin monkeys (macaco prego) and small wild pigs (quiexada) as well as various birds. We stopped at one tree trunk, and our guide said, "Look up," and it was in fact a huge cactus!

Our destination was a large pool at the head of a small river. There we were issued masks and snorkels and in we went. The water was fabulously clear.

Now I know what they mean by limpid pools: the verb 'to clean' in Portuguese is *limpar*! There are lots of fish in these pools, big fish at the bottom and little fish at the top – and none of them the least bit concerned by the wallowing 'whales' in wetsuits at the surface. After doing a circuit of the pool, we then drifted downstream. It was fantastic being carried along by the current with the wetsuit keeping us afloat. The river was the perfect width for us to drift abreast of one another – about three to four metres wide. Sarah's wetsuit unfortunately had a hole in the shoulder and she complained that her mask didn't fit despite trying three different ones. She didn't see much under the water, but floated down stream on my back or Alan's. I think the real problem was cold, and right enough she was shivering when we got out. This wee river is at a constant 24°C, but the main one further down was 20°C.

As we drifted along, I gradually began to notice that we were drifting a bit faster. At this point, there was a rope across the river, and our guide got us out. Good thing too, as the water was getting a bit turbulent. We were supposed to get back into the river a bit further on before being met by a boat where the river joined the main one, but Sarah was so cold that the decision was taken to walk.

We did stop at a point called Olho da Agua, or, Eye of the Water. It was at a bend in the river where water coming from underground (at the bottom of the river) joined the main current. It was fascinating seeing the sand at the bottom of the stream bubbling up quite violently in about half a dozen places.

A bit more walking and the boat met us and took us to the finish. At the landing stage we were met by masses of butterflies – white ones and yellow ones–all sitting on the ground or fluttering above it. I think they were drinking the water on the landing stage. Why the water here should be any better than elsewhere, I don't know, but they seemed to like it. All in all it was a brilliant trip, with so much to see, especially fish from one inch long to about thirty inches! There were black ones, yellow ones, stripey ones, friendly looking ones, sad looking ones – such an abundance of fish. Being so close to the natural environment, and drifting along as one with the fish, was wonderful.

Back at the reception area, lunch was waiting and there was time to thaw out, not that we were particularly cold. Sarah had warmed up by this stage.

We added an additional trip to our day out and went to visit the Buracodas Araras – or, Hole of the Macaws, and it certainly *was* a hole! A very big hole at that, with more or less sheer sides in an otherwise flat landscape.

It is about 126 metres deep and 150 metres in diameter with a green algae covered pond in the bottom with quite a number of trees growing around it. Apparently, two jacarés live in the pool, and no one is quite sure how they got there. About seventy pairs of red macaws nest there in holes in the cliff. It was brilliant seeing them flying across the gap and sitting in the trees around the edge. Another interesting note about macaws: they are always in pairs. They pair for life. These macaws had a deep red head and breast with blue wings and tail and a green back. The Amazon variety has yellow bits, and the red is more orange coloured.

As we drove back along the dirt road to return to base, the sun was sinking lower in the sky, silhouetting the palm trees dotted about the fields against an orange sky. It was a lovely end to a perfect day.

Next day was transfer to Refugio da Ilha, which is in the Pantanal proper, albeit only the edge. It was north of Bonito and west of Campo Grande. This trip involved a three-hour drive along 70 kilometres of dirt road. We crossed a range of hills called the Serra Bodequena. (Apparently, they shouldn't qualify for the title of Serra because they are less than 1000 metres, but I suppose the name stuck!) It made the drive more interesting having a bit of up and down thrown in.

The Refugio da Ilha (Island Refuge) lies ten kilometres off the main road, along a dirt road. The dirt road started out as a 'dual carriageway' but rapidly got narrower, and we had to open and close several gates along the way. It is a small family run business, with seven guest rooms, all situated in the house with the family. (The owner's son and his wife lived the other side of a small lake in front of the house.) The parents run the accommodation and food aspects of the business, and their son, his wife and one or two others work as guides. It is all on an island in the middle of the River Salobra, but there is so much wet ground that it is difficult to know what is river and what isn't – and this isn't even the rainy season. (That happens from December to March.)

They offered boat trips up the river, horse rides through the 'brush' and the *vazante* (i.e. the areas where the water drains from at this time of year; *vazio* in Portuguese means empty), walks through the trees and scrub, canoe trips on the river, all with the purpose of spotting animals and birds and appreciating the natural surroundings. We passed on the piranha fishing. We saw capybara (large semi-aquatic rodents), lots of jacarés, several howler monkeys, some capuchin monkeys, and several different species of birds (which is what the Pantanal is best known for).

Capybara ... and ... Southern Screamers

There are lots of birds around the house. Food is put out for them every day. There appear to be three resident blue macaws (those are the ones with turquoise bodies and a yellow tummy) and several green parrots – one of whom is fond of sugar and quite happily takes the top off the sugar bowl and helps himself. There are medium sized black birds with bright red rumps, small black birds with white tummies and red heads and creamy coloured birds with dark backs and a lumpy black top knot on their heads.

We were treated to a rare sight one morning: A pair of hyacinth macaws (dark blue all over) flew round the house several times. These are the largest macaws and are endangered. I can see why. If I wanted a macaw as a pet – that is the one I would choose. All the macaws are really very comical, the way they use their beaks as an extra claw, and quite happily slide down branches in a most undignified manner.

There was something very peaceful about the whole area. Maybe it is because they did not have the ubiquitous swimming pool and football pitch (with the accompanying noise that comes with both) that seem so necessary for the survival of the average Brazilian. Guests are free to swim in the river, as Sarah and others did, bearing in mind that this river is home to jacarés. In fact, I saw one trundling gently past her at one point, but it was on the other side of the river. Even travelling in a motorised boat seemed peaceful. We didn't spot very much, but the whole experience was very pleasant.

I enjoyed my horse ride because I had a responsive one that did what I asked. As our guide Mauricio said, that is rare in a 'tourist' horse. Mauricio was the son, and spoke English, having spent some time in London.

We rode along dirt roads and along muddy tracks. We splashed through wet bits, rode along grassy tracks and across open grassy areas. We saw rheas in the distance, but not anteaters! The mosquitoes in this last area were big, and they bit through my socks! This part of the Pantanal is not a malaria area, and received wisdom here in Brazil is that the prevention is worse than the cure anyway. Advice is to use repellent and wear long trousers and sleeves.

On our walk we were introduced to strangler figs in a big way. At first I thought they were just vines that selected a tree and climbed all over it, eventually killing it, but this is not the case. They seem to start out as vines, climbing up a tree, but eventually turn into trees in their own right, sometimes two or three vines combining to become one big tree. We also saw tapir footprints – large and three toed – but no tapirs. They are cousins of horses.

The aftermath of our walk was interesting. Mauricio had warned us to stick to the path to avoid ticks, which can attach themselves to you easily if you walk through brush or wooded areas. He also added that as he was first in line, he would get most of them anyway. He certainly did! We emerged out of the bushes at one point to see him unzipping and removing the lower half of the legs of his trousers (the sort that turn into shorts) and vigorously shaking them. He showed us masses of tiny ticks crawling all over them – and I mean tiny – little bigger than pinhead size and brown. We all duly inspected our trousers and pronounced ourselves tick free.

Later when we were all relaxing and waiting for lunch (we had a four-hour break in the middle of the day) I noticed four brown specks on the top of my foot that weren't there before. Ticks! I duly went to find Alan and Sarah and we all removed our trousers for a tick inspection. We found a fair number. Sarah had managed to pick up several bigger ones, the size I associate with sheep ticks, and Alan had gone one better and picked up a really big one that was more than a quarter inch across, which had already started burrowing by the time I tried to remove it. Ah, the joys of nature!

Evening excitement was feeding the jacarés in the pond in front of the house. Mauricio would stand by the pond with a huge bright torch, and several jacarés would crawl out. They have learnt to associate the torch with food – not that feeding them is the purpose for enticing them out of the water. They don't always get fed, and boy, can they can move very quickly when they want to. The family's Jack Russell terrier chases them back into the water when he decides the show is over.

We borrowed the torch later to do some bat spotting, and next thing we knew, the jacarés were crawling out of the water and coming towards us hoping for food. We hastily switched off the torch and retreated!

Pantanal is a bit like the Amazon in that it has an annual rise and fall of the water of about three metres (not the ten or more metres of the Amazon), but since the whole area of Pantanal is generally so flat and soggy, three metres make a considerable difference. There is the northern Pantanal, which drains into the Amazon, and the southern Pantanal, which drains into the Rio Paraguay, which in turn joins the Rio Parana, which joins the Rio de la Plata, which reaches the sea at Buenos Aires!

I was sorry to have to leave the natural paradise of the Pantanal and go back to reality. It was utterly peaceful there. The food was excellent, and even better, I didn't have to cook it! A three-hour drive to the airport in Campo Grande was not welcome, as it brought us closer to the noise and traffic that are part of life surrounded by too many people, but as Mauricio said, because we tourists come to see his verdant part of Brazil, he can live the sort of life he enjoys – at one with nature in the peaceful seclusion of the Pantanal.

Everyone says how wonderful Bonito is, and indeed, there were lots of nice things to do and see, but I preferred Refugio da Ilha for its serenity. Brazilians seem to have to be on the go the whole time, hence the football pitches everywhere. If they are not sightseeing, they are playing football! Refugio da Ilha was much simpler and so it suited us perfectly. The only swimming pool was the river, complete with jacarés and fish for swimming companions!

Towards the end of our flight home, we looked out the window and realised we were flying over sugar country. We could see at least twenty squarish fires burning – the definitive mark of the fields of sugar cane. That's when we knew we were back in our part of Brazil.

A Nature Walk and an Air Show

After spending some of July and August at home in Ireland, we are back to Brazil: back to work, back to school, back to Portuguese class and yoga class - and, wait for it - I've started going to an art class to fill the remaining few minutes of my spare time! Class is held just round the corner - well, two corners actually, which is very convenient. The instructor is a very nice little Japanese man, and he is determined that I should have a go at practically every medium you can think of. So far, I am working from a photograph using pastels, and he wants me to do about three pictures using this method, just to get drawing under control. Then we start on other things. Sarah wants to go too, so maybe in September I will start her in a class there. She doesn't want to continue with piano, so she can do painting instead if that is what she wants.

Alan's big lizard at work has reappeared. It is about six months since he last saw it, and he was getting a bit concerned about it. Someone might have eaten it - and I don't mean by another animal

We went for another long walk last weekend, this time about fifteen kilometres. There were seven of us in total, including Jose Ricardo, who is ten. Sarah opted out and went to play with Isadora. It was a very pleasant day for walking, not too hot. We took it in turns driving Alan's Volkswagen Beetle. At one point, we stopped at a location that seemed like stepping back in time: There was a wayside bar with a horse hitched outside, situated directly across the road from a church. The road changed from asphalt to dirt at this point, which added to the old-fashioned feel of the setting.

We partook of refreshments, then decided to take advantage of the facilities. The bar itself didn't have any toilets, but the proprietor handed us a key and sent us across the road to a lean-to (which was leaning against the church). Behind the padlocked gate lay a *boliche* court/pitch - well it wasn't a green. Bocche is Brazil's equivalent of bowls played on a long stretch of sand. It was all very ramshackle, with a gas ring, a couple of bare light bulbs and at the end a very basic toilet. What more does one need for a bocche championship! All very Brazilian! Basic is a word that springs to mind, but yet it is all perfectly adequate. What amused me was the fact that the bar owner happily handed us the key when we inquired about toilets. I guess the local bar is probably as good a place as any to keep the key!

We saw sugar cane being transported by lorry – one of the big ones with two trailers hitched behind it.

Farther up the road, a man with a horse and cart was also transporting sugar cane. I can't think of a better visual that captures the essence of Brazil, a land of contrasts.

We saw some kapok trees on this walk, and at this time of year they are casting their seeds. The trees are covered with fist-sized balls of fluff where the green seed pod has opened. The seed pod is about six inches long and shaped like a fat ellipse pointed at both ends. The fluffy bit that we call kapok is a carrier to catch the wind to transport a pea sized black seed. I don't know how many seeds a pod can hold, but you can find bits of fluff complete with seeds lying on the ground, and also hard dried segments of pod.

We finished our walk at another mini bar – this one on the edge of civilisation, where there was a bus stop. It was very pleasant with concrete seats and tables under trees.

As there were only seven of us, Alan suggested that we all squeeze into the Beetle instead of leaving two behind to wait for a bus. We managed it by squeezing three in the front and three plus Jose Ricardo in the back. It is just as well that Jose Ricardo is small! Once everyone had piled in, Alan put it in gear and the Beetle lurched into motion without a complaint. Apparently, there is a saying here in Brazil that V.W. Beetles are like the heart of a mother: There is always room for one more.

So it was a cosy ride back to base, and afterward unfolding ourselves and climbing out of the Beetle, we had lunch outside by the river. It was a very pleasant day.

On Sunday, we went to an air show at the local airfield here in Piracicaba. Every town of any size here in Brazil has a small airfield. We are not talking commercial planes here, but rather, small private ones. The highlight of the show was the Brazilian equivalent of the Red Arrows. They call themselves Esquadrila da Fumaça, which means Squadron of Smoke, and as you can guess, they left smoke trails behind them as they flew in formation. They were very good - the usual close formation flying and creating shapes in the air with their smoke while passing dangerously close to one another from opposite directions.

Esquadrila da Fumaça

However, it was their first stunt that impressed us most. They passed quite high overhead in a straight line, wing tip to wing tip, and each plane squirted out smoke at timed intervals. As the smoke drifted, it formed the numbers and word *236 anos* in the sky to celebrate Piracicaba's 236th birthday.

236 anos written in the sky

Thankfully, the airfield is within walking distance. Parking was a nightmare, and the cars were still inching their way in even after the Esquadrila da Fumaça had finished, and that was the highlight of the day. (Maybe there was a party afterwards that we didn't know about!)

I have been wandering about during the past couple of weeks photographing spring flowers, and anything that might be useful in my drawing class. The most spectacular flowers are on the trees!

The local name for this is Pata da Vaca, or Foot of the Cow because of the shape of the leaf.

Gorgeous Pink Ipe in full bloom

Bougainvillea, which comes in lots of brilliant colours

Holambra and a Wedding

Sarah's school had an *acampadentro* the first weekend in September, which means she spent the night at school with all her class. Apparently, they didn't go to sleep until about three o'clock, as is the way of these things, in spite of all efforts on the part of staff to suggest otherwise!

We had breakfast with her at school - theoretically at 8.00 a.m. the next morning, but they had a little presentation first about what they had been doing at school, which was researching their roots back to their grandparents, and saying where they had come from. There are a lot of Italian grandparents among the students, as well as many whose ancestors were Japanese, German, Spanish and Russian. Sarah added the English and Irish dimension.

Sarah had her first art class at 9.00 that same morning, and enjoyed it in spite of the lack of sleep. We picked her up from her class at 11.00, and as Alan wanted to locate the BMW club meeting, we went to where they were having lunch, the other side of Campinas - about an hour's drive away.

As we were in the area, we went on to spend the rest of the afternoon at what I can only describe as an annual event on the scale of the Balmoral Agricultural Show in Belfast, except this one is for flowers! Well, it wasn't quite as big as Balmoral, but it was in the same league. The Dutch settled in the area after the Second World War, and dedicated themselves to doing what they do best: Propagating plants. The town is called Holambra, and the buildings all have facades on the front to mimic the stepped roof outlines found in Holland. They have a huge export trade of their plants all over South America.

At the show, there was a large shed selling potted plants and another selling cut flowers, though cut flowers are not very popular here. (In a situation where we would take a bunch of flowers in Ireland, here you take a pot plant!) There were all sorts of stalls selling jewellery, fridge magnets, T-shirts, embroidered clothes and towels, and food of all sorts with an emphasis on Dutch cuisine, various eating establishments, a fun fair, themed gardens, and floral displays so elaborate that they make all the flower arrangements found in such displays in Ireland pale in comparison. They were wonderful, exuberant and exotic.

There were displays of Dutch folk dancing at intervals throughout the day, and a parade with various floats done by groups associated with the event.

At 5.00 p.m., the finale of the day was – no, not fireworks, as it wasn't dark, but rather, a shower of petals! They had a scaffolding tower about two to three stories high, at the top of which was a large blower. It was screened, so we couldn't actually see what was there. They blew rose petals out over the crowd as far as they could, and then it changed to tissue paper squares, which blew much further. It was lovely.

I thoroughly enjoyed the trip; Alan not quite so much, but there was a display of stunt motorcycling, which was just the thing for him. I'm not quite sure where that fits in with flowers; maybe someone thought of it as a way to keep the men entertained!

Saturday the 20th we attended a Brazilian wedding, and what a posh affair it was! An American chap here called Todd was marrying a local girl. He works with Caterpillar, and since few of his relatives were able to travel to Brazil for the wedding, he asked Alan and me to be his *padrinho* and *madrinha*. I think that roughly translates to something like god parents, but in this case, you function as witnesses. I think there were about five couples from each side. We had to sign a book, but it wasn't a large formal register like in a church. It seemed to be just a hard backed exercise book from the local stationary shop. The wedding was not in a church, but in a building designed for special events.

The event was due to start at 9.00 p.m.! Apparently, nearly all Brazilian weddings take place at night. (My guess is that it has to do with the climate – too hot to be enjoyable during the day.) Things actually got going by 9.50 – and that wasn't due to the bride arriving late. I guess she was due at 9.30, and certainly she sat outside in the car while everyone faffed around for quite awhile. Todd asked us to be there at 8.15, and people seemed to be trickling in from then on. Eventually all the padrinhos and madrinhas were asked to go and line up outside, in alternating order – one from the groom's side, one from the bride's side. After about ten minutes, during which Leila (the bride) was sitting in the car being filmed and photographed, Todd led the way with his mother, followed by his father with Leila's sister. We stood at the door and waited our turn. When the preceding couple had reached the table that served as an altar, we then walked, in a very dignified manner, first to the head of the aisle and then down the aisle. All us supporting cast stood in a semi circle behind the table (his on one side, hers on the other) while Leila made her way down the aisle with her father and was 'handed over' to Todd, who met them half way.

The marriage ceremony was much like any other ceremony, concluding with a prayer in which we all had to raise a hand (or both) in front of us. Then Todd and Leila turned round to face the cameras (two video and one still) which earlier had been milling around in front of us, behind the table, filming every breath that Todd and Leila took. The padrinhos and madrinhas (from alternate sides, of course) then had to go and hug the bride and groom (in Britain one would shake hands) and offer congratulations, turn and face the cameras and walk (still dignified – no drink taken at this stage) back down the aisle – being filmed of course.

Todd and Leila finally followed and then went out to what could be described as an arbour (but it was more contrived stonework than greenery) for the compulsory photo call. The supporting cast was allowed to sit down and then drinks and nibbles (posh nibbles – canapés in fact) were brought round.

Sarah was bored by this stage – and tired and hungry. First there was salad, a starter, and then more serious food followed in dribs and drabs. Sarah fell asleep with her head on my lap between the canapés and the main course.

The dress was formal. Given that we were part of the supporting cast, I thought that I had better look the part. I bought a dress, silver sandals and jewellery for the occasion, and did the same to kit Sarah out. Alan's suit was hired. It was like a morning suit, but without the tails. Hats don't feature at all.

Dancing followed at the same time as the pudding and wedding cake. There wasn't a huge cake cutting ceremony; instead, they were filmed cutting the cake while we all ate. While Todd and Leila were dancing, their wedding guests held hands forming a circle round them, which I thought was quite a nice touch.

Weddings in Brazil are done differently from what we're used to in Ireland. There was no 'top table' for the bridal party, just another round table, like all the rest. The wedding cake was not fruit, but sponge with a gooey filling with added strawberries. Alcohol doesn't play a large part at Brazilian weddings, either. We were offered glasses of water while hanging around waiting for things to happen, and at the meal, there was a choice of wine or beer, or water or soft drinks. Beer plays a very large part in Brazilian socialising.

Time was running out as the place was only booked until 2.00 a.m.! I don't suppose there was another event following, so there was no great rush. Mind you, it would not be beyond the bounds of possibility, knowing Brazilians, that there might be another event starting at 3.00 a.m!

As we were leaving, we were invited to sign the border of a partially framed photograph of Todd and Leila (a common practice for all sorts of events), and I was given some packaged sugared almonds. Forget the circles of fabric. This was a mini glass basket containing three sugared almonds, all wrapped in fine white netting silvered at the edge, and tied with a ribbon printed with the date and the names of the bride and groom.

Curitiba and a Trip on Its Railway

And the rains came – the first real rain we have had since February. Torrential with showers following in close succession so that one hadn't stopped before the other started. We have had a couple of wet days since February, but nothing like this. Also, it is the first thunder we have had since about Christmas. I think perhaps the rainy season has started. I can begin to appreciate what it must be like waiting for the rains to come so that your crops (and thus your vital food supply) will grow. Here in Brazil, though, there are so many rivers that lack of water for irrigation is generally not a problem, except in the northeast.

We went away for a long weekend recently. Alan had to go to Curitiba for the opening of a new factory (Perkins Engines); it was deemed to be in his interest to be there. Curitiba is southwest of us, in the state of Paraná. It's about an eight-hour trip depending on how fast you drive and how many stops you make along the way. We left early on the Thursday morning. The road became distinctly more interesting and scenic the closer we got to Paraná. We had to get down to a lower level than Piracicaba to reach the main road to Curitiba from São Paulo, which meant heading south to get off the plateau that comprises so much of Brazil. It was an interesting drive winding downwards with the road lined either side with Busy Lizzies – masses of them, in white, pink and deeper pink, though they look orange in the photo.

We had driven this road heading in the other direction in June of last year on our way back from our trip to the caves. Apparently it is called the Estrada das Bananas – the Road of Bananas because of the acres (or should I say hectares) of banana plantations either side of it on the lower reaches.

By the time we reached the main road, we were half way to Curitiba time wise, but not distance wise. The remainder of the trip was much faster going with a dual carriageway almost all the way to Curitiba. The bananas continued to line the road for quite awhile.

We had to cross a range of hills to get to Curitiba. This range is the divide between São Paulo state and Paraná state. It was definitely more scenic than endless miles of bananas. We left those behind when we started to climb. The road wound upwards through the hills, with the other carriageway frequently the other side of a valley rather than beside us, or perhaps the other side of a hill. There is a lot of lorry traffic, as everything is moved by lorry. Railways are very scarce in Brazil.

The weather changed abruptly the minute we entered Paraná. It started to rain – heavy rain, which made driving more interesting. We passed several hazards along the way, the most notable of which was a landslide that had happened so recently, that it was still blocking one lane of the road (there were three lanes at this stage), and no warning notices had yet been put up. The traffic police are usually fairly good about such things, but maybe they had to come from far away. Other hazards included lorries on their sides, having gone round the corner too fast. This is quite a common occurrence, and thankfully they do not usually block the road, but instead lie to the side of the carriageway. We passed three on the way to Curitiba and one on the way back, and there is frequent evidence along the side of the road of lorries not having made it round a bend.

Curitiba is supposed to be a model city, with lots of green areas and innovative ideas about how to move traffic around the city efficiently. The flow of traffic within the city may be very good, but if you don't know the system, it is a pain in the neck. They have various major one-way systems, with two carriageways going in the same direction and link roads at intervals between the two. They also have bus lanes in the middle of some roads. As I said – it is fine if you are familiar with the layout of the roads, but it really takes some getting used to if you don't. We found ourselves in the right-hand carriageway of a one-way street, wanting to turn left, and after we had managed to turn left we then found ourselves turning left again onto a street with three carriageways. Help! Which one to take? We went into the middle one and almost immediately realised that we were in the bus lane! After having rectified that little mistake and driving round in a few more circles, we eventually worked out how to get to the hotel. We knew where it was located, but our small map did not mark one-way street systems.

The hotel was very posh, but we stayed there only one night, paid for by Perkins Engines. Perkins held a reception in the hotel that night and all their guests were then trundled off to see the factory the next morning. Sarah and I did a bit of exploring in the morning while Alan went to the factory. It was cold. 12°C cold! We knew Curitiba was cooler than Piracicaba, so I had brought a light jumper and Alan and Sarah had fleeces, but it never occurred to me to bring shoes as opposed to sandals because we live so much of the year in sandals. I ended up buying a length of fleecy fabric, which I wrapped round Sarah's neck and then round her body, as we could not find a suitable warm coat or jumper. We also had to buy socks! Besides being cold, it was also drizzly. When we had left our house that morning, I knew that we were heading a good distance south of Piracicaba, but I did not expect such a different climate! I suppose it makes sense, though, considering that Curitiba is a mountainous region and closer in proximity to the sea than Piracicaba is.

The one place we got to know quite well was the shopping mall close to the hotel. When Alan came back from his trip to the factory, we moved to the more modest hotel we had booked, which was quite adequate without the soulless plush! Then we did a bit more exploring and bought our tickets for a train trip on the Sunday. Curitiba was settled mainly by Germans, Ukrainians and Japanese, and it certainly has a more Germanic feel about it.

The next day we took the tourist bus round the sights of Curitiba. It runs every half hour, and you can get off and on three times. Curitiba certainly has a lot of parks, which is very nice. Our first stop was the Botanic Gardens, which has a nice hot house in it. It was very welcome for us to get out of the cold and damp, but it was more a decorative feature with a pleasant array of plants than a true garden. On the whole, we were not impressed.

Botanic Gardens, Curitiba

We got back on the bus and went to the next stop, the *Opera Arame*, a small opera house in a lovely setting. The building itself seemed to be made from steel tubes, and it is set in what seems to be a now disused, flooded quarry. The effect is dramatic. They had a small coffee house there, which was serving some very welcome hot chocolate!

Opera Arame and its setting

We walked to the next tourist destination because it was reasonably close – the Parque Tanga. It is a big park, and makes excellent use of the cliff face in the area, with lots of grass, a lake and an artificial waterfall. We arrived at the top of the cliff, which seems to be the main entrance, but the weather was not conducive to spending much time there, so we didn't venture to the bottom of the cliff. Had the sun been shining, we most definitely would have explored further.

We got back on the bus again and soon were at the next stop, an old car museum. It was well laid out with lots of exhibits in good condition. (I'm sure Alan would have more to say on the subject, being a true car aficionado!)

We did think about walking to the Parque Tingi, which had a Ukrainian memorial in it, but we settled for gazing at the memorial from inside the bus, and then it was back to base. It was at this point that I decided to splash out and buy some socks. It wasn't quite so damp, so socks and sandals were a possibility.

We may not have gone to the Ukrainian Memorial, but we did have our tea in a Ukrainian restaurant – complete with waitresses in Ukrainian costume. They wore embroidered blouses, waistcoats, skirts and aprons, with red knee length boots and flowery hair bands. The food was good though nothing amazingly different. The service however was excellent. At one point, a waitress approached the table with a table-napkin on a plate. She then proceeded to lift the napkin from the plate with a pair of spoons and set it beside Alan. He hadn't even noticed that his own napkin had fallen on to the floor!

The toilets – apart from being spotless – provided practically everything a woman could want (I can't comment on the gents' toilet!), including a pair of tights in case you had ripped your own! To dry your hands there were individual towels - proper towels - which you then deposited in a basket beside the basin.

Other features of Curitiba are the modern architecture, the unique bus shelters, the taxis and the number of Oscar Neidemeyer buildings. Neidemeyer was the architect responsible for designing much of Brasilia in the 1960s. The bus shelters in the town centre are slightly elevated clear tube-like structures that you wait in, and when the bus arrives, a ramp the same height as the platform in the bus shelters extends outwards toward the bus so you can just walk across. It means the buses have to stop in exactly the right place, but they seem to have got that down to a fine art. The notable feature of the taxis was that they were all orange, as were the buses!

On Sunday, we took a train trip to a small town near the coast. The destination wasn't the highlight; it was the trip itself.

Trains are a rare feature in Brazil, mainly because of the terrain. This railway was built about 125 years ago but seemed to be in good condition. We passed through some amazing scenery, with sweeping vistas of tree-clad hills and steep sided valleys.

The sheer audacity of the engineers has to be marvelled at; that they would even contemplate putting a railway in such an area is admirable, but I guess it made economic sense to get goods to and from the coast.

Brunell's bridges in England would be on a par with some of these constructions, but he was putting up individual structures in reasonably accessible places. When you consider that mule power and manpower and ingenuity were all that was available to transport and construct these bridges/viaducts, you really get a sense of the challenges that had to be overcome. Now it is entirely a tourist attraction.

To quote the Guidebook:

> ...Constructed in 1885 to transport agricultural products from the interior of the state to the port of Paranagua, from where they were exported, the Curitiba-Paranagua railway is a daring work of engineering, on the hillsides of the Serra do Mar, in the middle of the Atlantic forest. It is 150 kilometres long, has 13 tunnels, and 67 viaducts, which came in pieces from Belgium, by boat.

One can only imagine building a railway through 150 kilometres of semi-mountainous terrain all overgrown and inaccessible. Some of the steel girders for the viaducts are quite large. I guess they started the railway at the coast, and as they laid tracks, they used them to transport construction materials further and further up as the railway got longer and longer.

... and we crossed that in the train!

The small town where the train stops mainly exists now because of the train, I think. It is primarily a tourist destination, with gift shops and restaurants. The shopkeepers and restaurateurs have the advantage of knowing when the train will bring all their customers, so they can probably have a lie in each morning until about 10 o'clock! The restaurants also know when the last train departs, so they have adapted their menus accordingly. The restaurant we ate in had a set menu with both fish and meat – specialties of the area, and it was all quite good.

Apart from the tourist shops, a mini highlight of our trip was meeting a snail nearly the size of Sarah's hand. Quite a bit of eating on that one, if they are suitable for eating!

We actually returned by bus along another scenic route that wound its way up from the coast, but low clouds impeded some of the views.

It was time to go home the next day, so we set off along the road, passed again through the mountains separating Parana state and São Paulo state, passed yet another lorry on its side...and then decided to take a slightly different route that entailed 35 kilometres of dirt road. As we got closer to it, the rain got heavier, and the first ten kilometres or so were a bit muddy and slippery. We began to wonder if we had made a wise decision. The surface improved as we started to climb, but it was a bit off putting to see signs saying that the road could be impassable in the rain. The road ran through a state park, and a sign at the entrance to the park suggested that one should check with the park police about road conditions before proceeding any further. We did this and they said that there shouldn't be a problem. It was no worse than what we had already come through. Thank goodness for that, as we were about halfway (or so we thought) and didn't fancy having to turn back. In fact, having left the flatter area, the road surface as we climbed was quite good, as there were no seas of mud to slide through.

The road was actually 46 kilometres of dirt before we hit tarmac again. The rain slackened off by the time we reached the tarmac (typical), but it was an interesting drive nonetheless, all through virgin forest that is probably full of monkeys and all sorts of exciting things. We met passed about four cars along the way.

Soon we were home again in sunny and warm Piracicaba. You should have seen the state of the car! The expression 'mud up the eyeballs' springs to mind. It looked like the lower half of the car had been plastered in red mud!

Family News and Updates

There are a couple of exchange students here, one, a German girl and the other a Canadian girl. They have the same Portuguese teacher that Alan and I go to and we offered to take them out for lunch one day. They are both very nice girls. The Canadian was delighted to be able to speak to someone in English rather than struggling with very limited Portuguese. The German girl's English is excellent, but she yearns to talk to someone in German. I couldn't manage that. Every time I tried to think of something in German, it came out in Portuguese. How do these multilingual people cope?

We took them for lunch by the river. It was very pleasant sitting there watching the world go by. After lunch, we went for a wander along the river and looked for cicadas, as the girls had never seen one. They make enough noise, but trying to spot them is not easy, in spite of them being over an inch long. We finally located one on a tree trunk and were admiring it when suddenly a fine jet of liquid came streaming out of its back end! What are the odds of find a peeing cicada? It took us all totally by surprise. Maybe it was marking its territory, a bit like tomcats are wont to do. It had quite a range!

Spring is doing what spring does, and Alan has a family of baby owls living at Caterpillar. He has been monitoring their progress over the last few weeks.

Burrowing owls seem to have their own 'patch', and our local one here in the town hasn't been seen on its usual lamppost recently, so maybe it has eggs or babies close by. Alan says there are two big lizards that live on the grounds at Caterpillar, which keep him entertained during boring meetings as he watches them through a large window in the conference room.

I had two pictures in an art exhibition recently and Sarah has two in an exhibition of young artists. Our art teacher stages the exhibitions. As I think I mentioned before, there seem to be art classes available on every corner here, and all the studios hold exhibitions, so there are exhibitions all over the place.

There also seem to be at least four schools of ballet here, all putting on Christmas shows. Sarah's performance of Cinderella went off very well. The costumes were magnificent with lots of sparkly bits on them, and there were all sorts of additional characters in the story so that all the little ballerinas could have a part. Sarah's class were all grey rats. The class below were all brown rats; another class was birds; another fairies; another butterflies and so on. All in all, it was quite professional looking – but what a lot of work on the part of the two teachers.

After the second performance, we asked Sarah if she would like to go out for a wee treat. She fancied the idea of an ice cream, so we went to an ice cream parlour even though it was eleven o'clock at night, with Sarah still dressed in her tutu, the ice cream parlour full of people – and no one turned a hair. One of Sarah's fellow rats also came in – still in her costume – and a 'bird' from the ballet too. That's Brazil for you. I had tamarind flavoured ice-cream (yum!) and also a sweet corn flavoured one.

We went to the dentist recently. That was an eye opener. I got to see my teeth on a TV screen – and he showed me (on screen) what problems he felt needed addressing, which was replacement fillings for the most part. Dentistry is a different world here. On arrival, a girl comes and offers you coffee or water. In the surgery, there are two assistants. You're given lip salve to put on your lips, and if there is going to be lots of water spraying about the place during your procedure, you are given safety glasses, and an assistant carefully mops your face. I had my teeth cleaned with ultra sound then a jet of water. Then he put a layer of fluoride on my teeth to protect them. He hasn't replaced the fillings yet. That is the next installment. If we were to win the lottery, I think I would opt for having my dental treatment in Brazil every six months!

It most certainly is the rainy season now. It has rained practically every day for the month of November, and we have seen very little sun. The river has much more water in it. It is certainly not cold however, but it is humid.

I went on another calango on Saturday, November 29th. This walk covered 24 kilometres, all along dirt roads. We were bussed to the start, about 25 kilometres north of Piracicaba. The countryside there is a lot hillier, and there are more cows and less sugar cane. The scenery was wonderful. We finished up at a *pescaria* (a fish farm for want of a better description) where you 'pays yer money and takes yer fish'. There was a river close by, and one of the attractions for those who didn't want to fish was to swim in the river and play in the waterfalls – which is what we did. It was great fun, and very refreshing after walking 24 kilometres!

Our proposed Christmas holiday this year is to Fernando de Noronha, a group of islands off the northeast tip of Brazil. Snorkelling and swimming are on the agenda plus lots more.

Fernando de Noronha

We arrived back from our holidays yesterday in need of another holiday to recover! We went to the municipal market to get some fruit and vegetables, and while we were there, the heavens opened. Torrential doesn't even begin to describe it! The market is roofed over, and having made our purchases, we headed for the door – only to be met by several people in one of the thoroughfares, trying to encourage a large puddle of water to go down a drain by sweeping it with brooms. Okay, we said, let's try another route. This one took us past a snack bar, where the employees were no longer serving customers, but instead were trying to hold up their plastic ceiling (again, with brooms) while water trickled down round the ends of the fluorescent lights. We joined the huddle of people at one of the exits and watched the raindrops for awhile, and then decided to make a run for it. The car was about ten yards away, and we made it, not too soaked.

We took a scenic route home to see the results of the deluge. There had been so much rain in such a brief period that spectacular 'rivers' were now running along the sides of the streets, fountaining round the wheels of parked cars and anything else in the way. The drains coped as well as they could, but water was fountaining over them as well and up through manholes. The best sight came when we were driving down a fairly steep hill, with manholes down the centre of the road. The volume of water running under those manholes was sufficient to dislodge them, and as we proceeded down the hill to the next manhole, there peering out from the edge of it was a rat! – a very wet rat. The phrase 'a drowned rat' takes on a new meaning when you see one as soaked as he was. I guess he too had nowhere else to go.

Yes, it is indeed the wet season.

New Year's Eve, as we witnessed two years ago, was predictably noisy with fireworks being set off all evening, rising to a peak at midnight. It would be much more spectacular (and noisy) if they could all wait until midnight. Living on the twelfth floor has its advantages in that we could see lots of fireworks – not organised displays, but individuals letting off their own fireworks.

But I need to back track and tell you about our holiday in Fernando de Noronha!

We decided to treat ourselves and stayed in our usual hotel (The Caesar Park) close to the airport in São Paulo the night before instead of getting up early to drive down the same day. We left home early Monday afternoon (the 22nd) because Alan wanted to look for a bike shop in São Paulo. I managed to navigate our way there with no side trips – not easy in São Paulo with all the one-way streets. There wasn't just one bike shop – there were hundreds of them, selling everything you could imagine that had anything to do with motorbikes! Alan was very taken with a yellow Gold wing. Obviously, this part of São Paulo is the bikers' quarter!

After that visit, we headed across town to the Eldorado shopping mall where we knew of a good Thai restaurant. The trip across town took us as long as the 150-kilometre drive from Piracicaba!

Somehow I managed to take us down the street where all the prostitutes hang out. I seem to do that each time we go to São Paulo! We noticed interesting variations of street names. In one area, all the streets were named after the countries of Europe (including Greenland and Turkey). This area had all the expensive car shops. Another area had streets named after people who had had something to do with electricity (James Joule, James Watt, Michael Faraday, etc.).

A tasty meal later, we took the ring road to the hotel. One advantage was that we could leave the car at the hotel and use their shuttle bus to get to the airport. We stayed at the hotel on the way back as well.

Next morning, we had a quick breakfast and we were off to the airport. I was using a small backpack, which was a free hand out from the company (complete with logo of course) with whom we had booked the holiday. We were wandering towards the check in area – and eyeing with some distaste the queue for checking in – when a young man approached us saying 'Ambiental', which was the name of the tour company. He took us to the group check in desk where there was no queue! I might just think twice before I object to wearing company logos!

The trend here is to book a packaged tour, and they are generally very well organised. We had everything arranged before we left – flights, transfers, accommodation and day trips. We knew that when we arrived, there would be someone to take us to our accommodation, and each day we would be picked up and taken somewhere, unless we decided to opt out.

A three and a bit hour flight took us to Recife, and then we had another one-and-a-half-hour flight to the island.

Yes, to get to the island we took a 50-seater plane with propellers! Fernando de Noronha is a group of islands about 300 kilometres off the North East tip of Brazil. It has one big island with about twenty small ones (more rocky pinnacles and islets than islands) surrounding it. They are mostly volcanic in origin. The airport takes up most of the centre of the island, but as most of the activities are sea based, no one was complaining.

The island is approximately seventeen by three kilometres and has lots of vehicles rushing about - small tourist buses, land rovers, open buggies. About five kilometres is paved road and the rest is dirt road. There are some stone paved streets in the small town. The island survives because of tourists. Throughout its history it has been variously owned by France, Holland and Portugal; it has been a military garrison, a penal colony and now a tourist trap. There are very few living on the island now who do not have something to do with tourism. It is a protected ecological area and a UNESCO cultural heritage site. The number of flights to the island per day is limited, and the numbers of people coming to the island are strictly controlled. We had to pay an environmental tax to be allowed to go on to the island - about £40 per person. Our accommodation was a pousada (a Bed & Breakfast), which was fairly simple in its amenities but scrupulously clean.

There is a rough and ready quality to the buildings here – and indeed in much of Brazil. With the typically warm climate, buildings don't have to be quite so weatherproof. If the rain gets in, the heat dries it out fairly soon.

There is an abundance of lizards here – and I guess not many predators. On one building we saw masses of lizards clustered in several groups on the wall. We took a closer look, trying to work out why they were grouped that way. As it turned out, they had a plan! It was not yet dark, but they were waiting under the lights. Why chase after flies if you can have them come to you simply by waiting patiently under the lights!

Food (for us) that evening was fish, barbecued in a banana leaf and seasoned with lime. The restaurant we chose had a set menu, which seems to be the norm for many of the eating establishments on the island. Very good it was too. There were also fresh salad vegetables and rice to go with it. I can recommend coleslaw with fresh coriander leaves added.

We were wandering up the road after our meal in the general direction of our pousada when a land rover stopped beside us and asked if we wanted to attend the lecture. Well yes, we did, but had been told that a bus would pass the pousada at 8.30, and it wasn't 8.30 yet. We got into the land rover anyway and went to a lecture on sea turtles. There is a research centre on the island that holds lectures six evenings a week on marine topics.

Unfortunately, we were just too early in the turtle season to see the babies clambering their way out of the nests on the beaches and struggling down to the water. December is the start of the egg-laying season when the turtles come ashore and dig holes in the sand to lay their eggs. After about 50 days' incubation, the babies hatch and have to dig their way to the surface, and then make their perilous journey to the sea, some 30 to 50 metres away; that is if lizards haven't raided the nest first and eaten the eggs. Not only are sea birds waiting for them on the shore, but crabs eat them as well, and once they get into the water, more predators await.

Another hazard for the hatchlings is that they head towards light, and if there is a lamp next to the beach, they will head for that instead of the water. Apparently, only one or two babies in every thousand make it to maturity. The females lay on average about 150 eggs. The sex of the babies is determined by the temperature of the nest during incubation. I think there are two species of turtle that nest here, the green turtle and (I think) the loggerhead turtle. (Interesting note: the name for the second species in Portuguese literally means comb turtle, meaning those whose shells were used for hair combs, and I'm not sure if loggerhead is the English translation.)

We only managed to see one turtle, and that was from the top of a cliff. The day we went snorkelling with the aim of swimming to the turtle area, Sarah had trouble with her mask, and we never got that far.

With the lecture over and the land rover having deposited us back at the pousada, I spent some quiet leisure time sitting out in the still of the night gazing at the stars. Being so far from urbanised land, the air is very clean here and the stars are fantastically clear. Orion was easily visible with Canis Major below him and the Pleiades not far above him. He is upside down here because Brazil is in the southern hemisphere. As usual, whenever I have the opportunity to see stars here, I don't have my star book in hand!

The next day, after a simple but delicious breakfast of fresh fruit, bread rolls and ham and cheese, we were picked up in a tourist bus and taken about five kilometres up a dirt road. Our destination was to a prime spot for watching the dolphins in Dolphin Bay. We spilled out of the bus, and after about a one-and-a-half kilometre walk along a narrow path passing through scrubby dry vegetation (we are in the dry season now), we arrived at the top of a cliff to watch the dolphins in the water below.

Dirt track trail along the cliff top to view ... Dolphin Bay

The dolphins come into this particular bay every morning at dawn and stay until about 2.00 p.m. They feed out at sea during the night and come into the bay during the day to rest, to mate, to give birth and to feed their young. There were over 500 dolphins in the bay, the two researchers told us. The most turbulent areas of water down below us were the areas where the males were busy chasing the females! All over the bay, you could see the dolphins surfacing, jumping and spinning (horizontally) before splashing back into the water. This behaviour is apparently a warning signal when they are out at sea, performed by the young males when they are on guard duty. This species are aptly called spinner dolphins.

The trees clinging precariously to the steep slopes down to the sea were full of gannets, brown ones and white ones. There were masses of them and various other birds as well. I think a variety of tern – completely white with very black eyes and beak. Literal translation of the Portuguese name for them is 'newlyweds'!

We met some of the island's feral goats on the way – black, white, brown – with floppy ears. Apparently, they are a variety specific to the island.

Our group this day consisted of six other people, plus the guide: A family of four with two adult daughters and an older couple from São Paulo. We went for a walk along the cliff top, stopping at intervals to admire the view. Along with sighting small lizards (six to eight inches), we saw several larger ones as well, some of them up to two feet long. They are shy creatures, and when they hear humans tramping along the path, they disappear into the undergrowth.

Sarah managed to find two mating lizards on the cliff top, much to the amusement of our guide and the professional interest and amazement of one of the dolphin researchers.

This photo is of one of the many lizards we saw that day.

There were also some marmoset type creatures among the rocks, but we couldn't get a photo of them.

The colour of the sea was fantastically blue, ranging from cobalt blue and deep turquoise, to a shimmery navy blue. The water here is crystal clear, which is why it is a haven for divers. Having admired the scenery from the cliff top, we then descended to the shore via two ladders set into a natural crack in the cliff.

Once you've made the arduous climb down, you are rewarded with one of the most beautiful, remote stretches of beach you've ever seen.

We swam on this beach (the water is not cold), and then scrambled over the rocks to the next beach. The rocks were covered in crabs: dark blue crabs up to six inches across, scuttling across the rocks to get out of our way.

We went to another beach that was mainly rocky, and there was a deep pool in one of the rocks. The water was fantastically clear, and the pool was teeming with small colourful fish, an abundance of tiny hermit crabs and coral. I could have stayed there for hours.

We stopped on the next beach for a snack and a drink. There are no shops along the beaches here (which is a standard part of beach life on mainland Brazil), but they had made an effort. Under a shelter roofed with palm leaves, someone was selling cold drinks from a polystyrene box full of ice, and he also had an assortment of basic snack foods. We picked up a friend here in the shape of a woolly black dog, and he accompanied us across the next couple of beaches to our pick up point, each beach as beautiful as the next – all golden sand with black basalt headlands in between.

After returning to the pousada, it was time for a shower followed by a stroll down to the town to replenish our water and snack supplies, and then out for something to eat. When our hostess heard what we were planning to do, she wouldn't have one bit of it! She was having a party, and would we please come and have something to eat with them. It was her husband's birthday and Christmas Eve besides. The food was the usual fare, salad and barbecued meat, but very tasty. We didn't like to intrude too long, so we took ourselves off for a walk. About 100 yards up the road, Sarah noticed a toad, and then we saw two other toads with him. They were big - at least six inches long, and solid looking too!

On Christmas day we went snorkelling - again. I seem to remember that we spent Christmas day last year snorkelling! The aim was to swim across to the other side of a bay to where the turtles feed, but as I said earlier, Sarah's mask didn't permit us to get that far, and I ended up towing her with her face above water. I realised that her face has grown and thus her mask was too small and was letting in water. I tried going back to look for turtles, having brought Sarah back to the beach to stay with Alan, but the rest of the group was coming back and I decided that snorkelling on my own was perhaps not such a good idea.

We then walked over a headland to another beach where turtles lay eggs. They lay their eggs at night, so we would not be interrupting them by going in the daytime. There were some fascinating pools along the side of the beach, which had been formed from lava flows that had cooled into flat pan shapes, and could be seen on the receding tide.

These were teeming with life, but we were not allowed to walk over these rocks to avoid damaging the coral that grows in these pools. We did stand at the edge, however, and gazed to our hearts' content. There was also plenty of free time for swimming, sunbathing and walking along the beach.

The lecture this evening was about Ihla de Trinidade, another remote Brazilian island located some 600 kilometres east of Espirito Santo, which is another State in Brazil a bit further south. Again, volcanic in origin, this island has some goats and a token military presence. There is a turtle beach there as well, where literally hundreds of turtles come ashore to lay their eggs.

The lectures take place in a research centre called the TAMAR/IBAMA centre. The TAMAR project is devoted entirely to working with turtles, and their focus is on convincing rural communities that it is more profitable to protect the turtles than it is to eat them and/or their eggs. IBAMA is a more wide reaching organisation that focuses on environmental issues.

The centre is a short bus ride, but longish walk from the main residential areas. There is no organised collection point where you can wait for the buses. The buses are large mini buses or land rovers, and the taxis tend to be open buggies. These seem to circulate round the residential areas calling out *'palestra'* ('lecture' in Portuguese) to anyone they pass, and pausing at restaurants. There was no lecture on Christmas Eve, but this evening, we were just finishing our meal (very good passion fruit mousse) when a bus drew up with the driver calling out 'palestra'. We, and several other diners, ate up, paid our bills and climbed aboard the bus. The driver seemed quite happy to wait.

Boxing Day was another walk and swim day, this time starting at the north end of the island and walking along part of the other side of the island. On one side of the island is the Mar de Dentro (the inside sea), and on the other side is the Mar de Fora (the outside sea). You can guess from the names where the sea is coming from and which side of the island is the most sheltered. Today we were on the more exposed side.

We had a 10.00 a.m. start to get the tide right, and were bussed to the petrol station by the harbour. Fuel prices are about double what we pay in Piracicaba. I think it is the only petrol station and it would make sense to have it by the harbour. There is also a wind turbine by the petrol station, the only large one on the island. I don't know whether there is some legislation that prevents them having more. It seems like a good solution to me. Maybe tourists might complain that they were an eyesore. Electricity is otherwise produced by two huge (Caterpillar) generators with two more for backup when maintenance is needed or one goes wrong. Electricity seems to go off regularly for short periods. Practically all water is heated by solar panels, though, but they are less obvious.

Our bus was full, so we were a group of about 20 this morning. We walked along a trail beside the beach, and then along the beach itself.

There is no sand on this beach, just rocks to scramble over. In the course of our walk along the shore (about two to three kilometres), we stopped and snorkelled in two natural pools, but both a bit different with similar rock formations to what we were not allowed to explore yesterday, but on a larger scale. (Sarah's mask trouble was sorted out by simply giving her my mask to wear!) The average depth of the pools is about two-and-a-half feet, but they are full of fish and coral and sea urchins, and there was even an octopus in the second pool! No sun cream and no flippers are permitted in the pools to protect the marine life.

A specialist guide came with us today, and he was a mine of information. He explained the reason for all the discarded crab shells laying about, complete with legs. Apparently the occupant had grown out of its shell and needed a bigger one, so he just oozed out backwards and waited until his new shell, already in place underneath the old one, hardened. There were lots of crabs scuttling over the rocks again, the same sort that we had seen previously, all dark blue with tiny white spots. They turn orange when mature. I don't know where the mature ones go because we didn't see any.

In the second pool, quite apart from picking up the sea urchins, our guide caught the octopus and let it wind its tentacles round his arm, and then he just hauled the poor thing out of the water. He offered it to Sarah but she said a very emphatic No! The octopus must have been about eighteen inches long, from top of head to tip of tentacles. It did squirt out its black inky cloud in protest, but to no avail. The humans weren't put off.

Apparently, of eighteen known varieties of coral, fifteen are found around the island. Certainly there was lots of yellow coral, which looks as much like rock as anything else. There was also deep pink coral covering rocks, and I saw brain coral, but beyond that, I think one would have to be a coral expert to be able to pick out more varieties.

Having exhausted the delights of the pools, we all liberally applied sun cream and set off along a path up the cliff behind us. We climbed for about ten minutes. The landscape at the top of the cliff was much bleaker than the other side of the island. No one lives here, for a start, and it was strewn with black boulders and exfoliating rocks. (These rocks were splitting apart because of the heat rather than freeze thaw, which is what I learnt in geography lessons pertaining to rocks in cold climates.)

The bleakness reminded me very much of Connemara except that the rocks are a different colour. The vegetation was sparse, dry and scrubby, but that also might be because it is currently the dry season here. March to August is the wet season. In Piracicaba, it is the other way round!

We walked to the other side of this headland, and looked down from the cliff to another incredible pool teeming with sea life, but it is practically inaccessible unless one is keen on abseiling. The water was a wonderful deep aquamarine colour.

We walked on, descending through increasingly lush, verdant vegetation to a sandy beach. Once there, we discovered another large natural pool. This one was very different in character with its sandy bottom, but it too had coral growing in it. It also had an octopus, which I almost missed because it was sitting in a hole in the bottom of the pool with just the top of its head sticking out.

We stayed there quite awhile snorkelling and exploring the beach. I found some vaguely hexagonal rock formations, but nothing as dramatic as the Giant's Causeway. As the island is of volcanic origin, I was keeping an eye out for such things. There were lots of crabs crawling over everything, jumping from rock to rock and climbing the rocks behind us.

When it was time to go, as we walked across the beach a different species of crab came scuttling across the sand. He wasn't trying to jump from rock to rock; instead, he was just hoping to avoid the unwanted feet on *his* beach. He could shift quite rapidly too, causing squeaks from some of the group.

It rained just as we were leaving the beach, and we were a group of very soggy people with muddy feet as we climbed on to the waiting bus. I felt sorry for the bus driver, or whoever had the unpleasant job of cleaning the bus after we had thoroughly muddied it!

Food tonight was along the same lines as the first night: another restaurant with a self-service salad bar, and a man who comes round with a selection of barbecued fish. The *sucos* (fruit juice drinks) offered were wonderful: tamarind, cupuaçu (which is a relative of the cocoa plant), caju (which is the fruit the cashew nut grows on) to name some of them. I had never had a tamarind suco before. Delicious! We can't get it in Piracicaba. These fruits are native to the North of Brazil, and thus are more easily available here than further south. I have had suco de cocoa - the fruit from which chocolate comes, but it is fairly tasteless. Chocolate comes from the seeds that are surrounded by this fruit pulp. The bill for our meal was written out on a paper napkin.

Most of these casual restaurants have outdoor seating only. Some have fairly solid palm leaf roofs, and some just have tarpaulin stretched over very ramshackle looking supports, but it was all quite adequate. We passed on the lecture tonight because of an early start in the morning.

On December 27th we had a 4.30 a.m. start for a 5.00 a.m. pickup to watch the dolphins coming in to the bay where we had seen them before. It started raining as soon as we climbed into the land rover. Ah, well; at least it wasn't cold. We also picked up the two researchers. These are two girls in their twenties, and they start each workday at the same time, six days a week. We walked along the trail we had trekked earlier in the week. The rain had stopped, but the ground was muddy. We slogged our way along with a torch at the front of the group, a torch at the back and about ten people in between.

We arrived at the cliff top, and as it grew lighter, I could pick out groups of dolphins coming into the bay. They come in groups of about seventy, all following one after another. It is amazing to watch them surface as they enter the bay. The two researchers counted 670 this morning (using binoculars). I don't know how they count them, but they are obviously happy that they've come up with a reasonably accurate count. It wasn't wildly exciting, but it was nice seeing the dolphins again. We also provided a dawn snack for the various biting insects in the area. It seems that I'm always very tasty.

Back to base for breakfast, and then we had the morning off. We decided to visit the TAMAR centre and look at the various exhibits, so we walked to it, only to discover that the centre itself was closed until January 5, and only the lecture bit was open. We sampled the local bus service on the way back. It was a large minibus size, which runs back and forth between the airport and the harbour every half hour. No worries about whether we had got on the right bus. We went back to the pousada and lounged about in the hammocks until our next trip.

Our afternoon entertainment was a boat trip. There are several smallish boats available that carry about twenty-five people each. As we headed out of the harbour, we were immediately surrounded by dolphins leaving the bay. It was much more fun seeing them up close than from far away!

Spinner dolphins up close

These apparently are the young males doing their guard duty bit, keeping an eye on the boat while the rest of the group pass underneath. It was fascinating watching them.

We went out towards a couple of the offshore islands. The volcanic ones are the rocky pinnacles, and the flatter islands are calcareous. Some of them are riddled with small caves. Whatever their origin, they seem to shelve steeply and the boat was able to go in quite close.

We then headed along the side of the island, looking at the shore. We were in the Mar de Dentro side so it was reasonably calm. At the end of the island there is a large hole in the narrow spit of rock through which you can see the sea at the other side. At one point, the hole looks like the shape of Brazil.

We turned back then, following along the shore and saw these distinctly columnar formations in the cliffs. We stopped and anchored in a sandy bay so that whoever wanted to could swim and snorkel. The water is superbly clear, and you can easily see the bottom some 30 feet below. At first there was not much to see, but when we went to the rocky outcrops at the sides of the bay, there were lots of fish. It was a very pleasant afternoon, just sitting in a boat in the sunshine.

We had tea that evening with the family in our group with the two adult daughters. The parents were celebrating their 25th wedding anniversary, and their daughters had come with them to share the experience. We went to a restaurant that offered seven different types of soup, all very thick and filling: prawn soup, vegetable soup, onion soup, meat soup, ray (as in rays that swim in the sea) soup, and sururu soup. Sururu is a type of shellfish. I had a taste of nearly all and half a bowl of two sorts, and I was stuffed!

The palestra bus came past twice, and the third time round we all got on and went to the lecture. This time the topic was two tiny islands in the Atlantic called São Pedro and São Paulo. Sarah fell asleep on my knee, so I took a taxi (one of those open buggies) back and Alan came back later on the bus.

Sunday was our final day and we had another earlyish start, with a 7.20 a.m. pick-up to go diving. Alan and Sarah planned to dive under the waves. I thought that I would be quite happy staying on top of the waves, especially because once I hit a depth of about six feet, my ears complain. They assured me that this was normal and the instructors would sort that all out, but I decided not to go. I've lost interest. Fifteen years ago, I was quite keen, but now... it just seemed like more effort than fun!

The diving excursion was not part of the package, but an extra which we had arranged for ourselves. We had to miss the historic tour of the town because the dive operators don't operate on Sunday afternoons. In fact, very little happens on a Sunday afternoon, as it is the only time that those working on the island have any time off. Quite a number of the restaurants are closed, or else they close early. It must be a rather thankless task entertaining tourists day after day after day, every day of the year. Christmas Day was business as usual.

There seemed to be masses of people all going for a 'taster' of sub-aqua, but there were various boats and we ended up with another family of four plus an instructor (or, assistant instructor as he turned out to be) and a boatman. We set off for the appointed spot, and along the way, another chap joined us from another boat. He was the instructor. There was momentary panic when they discovered that we were not Brazilian, but we assured them that we spoke enough Portuguese to understand what they were saying.

The instructor gave basic instructions on the way, and we soon anchored in a bay off a small island. Alan and Sarah went first. It was a ratio of one instructor per person! They got Alan kitted out and into the water, then they tried to put the cylinder on Sarah but she wasn't tall enough to put it on in the boat, so the instructor laid the cylinder and supporting jacket on the water and she had to lie on top of it while he strapped her in. We had hired a wet suit for her, which was enormous on her, but they assured us that this was not a problem, because she wouldn't have to do anything, and she was a lightweight so the instructor would have no bother towing her along if necessary.

They disappeared in a cloud of bubbles, and I took myself off to visit the fish closer to the shore. I am enthralled by the exuberant colours of the fish. There are so many colours! If you can imagine any colour, you will probably find a fish to match it somewhere in these waters. After living most of my life in a region with fairly dull-coloured fish, it was incredible to see their brilliance: purple and yellow; black and yellow stripes; black with royal blue fins and tail; black with neon blue stripes where the fins join the body; green with deep pink outlines to the scales; yellow and silver stripes; deep blue with yellow spots. The fish come in all shapes and sizes. I was quite happy looking at these delights from the surface.

I arrived back at the boat just as Alan and Sarah were surfacing, two happy children! Sarah saw three large rays and an octopus. Getting her out of the gear was a reverse process of getting her in to it, laying her out on the water while the instructor unstrapped her. She enjoyed it, but I don't think she is addicted ... yet. Diving is too expensive for one thing. That is what put me off fifteen years ago when I did a 'taster' in Carrickfergus swimming pool. I couldn't afford the club fees. Sarah's 'taster' was a lot more interesting than mine was!

With Alan and Sarah back on board, the instructors went down with the next two. As with yesterday, it was pleasant just being out in a boat in the sunshine with nothing to do. The sea is *so* incredibly blue, and so calming and blissful.

While we were waiting for the last lot to come up, other boats from the same company appeared and anchored nearby waiting for us to finish. With the last of our lot on board, we prepared to go back to the harbour. Sarah's instructor meanwhile gathered his stuff together and swam across to another boat holding his dry stuff above his head. While we headed off, I noticed that on the other boat, Sarah's instructor was preparing to go into the water again with another child. Maybe he is the only one qualified to take children. Sarah had to say she was ten as that is their minimum age limit. (Her tenth birthday is in two weeks' time, so we weren't stretching the truth too much!) We were back on shore by eleven o'clock.

We were delivered back to our pousada, where we showered and changed, and then decided to go back to the harbour as we hadn't had time to explore there. The harbour is very small. There were a few snack places but little else.

We followed a sign labelled 'shark museum', which took us about 500 yards to the other side of the island (this is on a spit of land at the north end of the island) where there were two more eating places, a small Japanese restaurant, and the shark museum, which was also an eating place! It had up to a dozen boards, each with a set of shark's teeth and information about that particular type of shark. It also sold shark related souvenirs (Sarah now has a necklace with a shark's tooth on it), and many of the snacks were made from shark meat. We ordered some *bolinhos detuberão*, which were small deep fried balls of shark meat and mandioca. They were quite tasty, too.

Then we took a brief explore of the area. The coast looks very much like the north Antrim coast, which stands to reason as both are volcanic in origin.

We then returned to the harbour where Sarah and I had a brief swim. It has a nice beach and is very clean. This is the beach where the locals come to swim.

We sampled the taxi service, and came back in the evening to eat at the Japanese restaurant. I wanted lime in my drink, but the waitress explained very apologetically that the island had run out of limes, and the next ship was not due in the harbour for a couple of days. The meal was quite good - the best we had on the island, in spite of the fact that the meat could have been better. Alan ordered a meat based dish and came to the conclusion that one should stick to fish. It is an island, after all, with an abundance of fish. The locals have permission to fish within the park area and that is where many of the restaurant owners get their raw ingredients.

The next morning I decided to go for a walk before breakfast - it was about 6.00 a.m., but just as I reached the gate, the heavens opened. I decided I didn't want to be packing wet clothes for the trip home so I opted to watch the raindrops from the comfort of a hammock on the verandah. The rain was torrential but short-lived, and my hammock was very comfortable, as I watched rivers run down the road and people negotiating the worst of the water. The tourist traffic soon started, with a constant stream of tourist buses, land rovers, buggies, etc., all coming to pick people up for whatever activity they had booked that day. Our bus was due at 11.00 to take us to the airport, so we had a leisurely breakfast and then lounged on the hammocks after packing our things.

It is a delight to go to such a small airport with none of the frenetic activity of the big ones. It had two tourist shops, each about six feet square, a snack bar and two check-in desks, only one of which was being used. It seems the airport employees all multitask, having at least two jobs, if not more. Here is another benefit of flying out from a small airport: We only had to wait fifteen minutes from the time the incoming flight arrived to when our flight departed!

The River Paranense

Alan still had a few days holiday after our trip to Fernando de Noronha, and we had vaguely planned to visit one of the state parks in São Paulo State, staying over one night. I had picked out some possibilities. We finally opted for the one furthest away in the west of the state, threw some things in a bag and set off. We spent eight hours driving, and stopped overnight in a town near the park where we had an excellent Chinese meal. The salad dressing was especially good, and as much as I persisted, they wouldn't give me the recipe for it! Must be a trade secret worth keeping. The next day, we drove another 100 kilometres to the park. It was a pleasant enough park on the banks of the River Paranense, but the promised visitor centre was closed (probably due to the holidays) and there were no guides available. We took a walk along one of the trails, which took us to the banks of the river with a 'hide' from which to watch birds.

We did see, close to the visitor centre, some jack fruit growing. It is very large, and hangs from the trunk of the tree. The taste is sort of perfumy but with little flavour. We also saw the nests of some sort of weaverbird.

We then walked down the track leading to the entrance of the visitor centre and came across some butterflies feeding intently on I don't know what, but it must have been either very tasty or very necessary in their diet.

One trail described in the guidebook was barred by a locked gate, but we resorted to the same tactics as the locals and squeezed through a gap in the fence. It was worth the effort. The track wound steeply up to the top of the highest point in the area and there was a wonderful view.

Brazil – all the way to the horizon!

After that we headed back to the car for a 200-kilometre drive to another city in the north of Paraná state, and the following day we drove all the way back home again. It was a crazy thing to do. The park was not worth the effort, but it was interesting to see a different area. Again, we were struck by the sheer vastness of Brazil, and how one can drive through endless countryside seeing nothing but huge areas of grassland, dotted with cattle and little evidence of habitation. Living in such country would certainly require one to be self-sufficient.

Not only did we pass through cattle country, we also passed through vast areas of arable land, given over mainly to soya beans. We saw crops of sugar cane and some coffee, but it was mainly soya –vast acreages of it. A farmer couldn't plan on ploughing those fields before lunch! It probably takes weeks, and the mind boggles at the logistics of harvesting. We took a different route for the trip back home, so all in all we got to see quite a bit of the country.

Rio and the Carnaval Parade of Champions

We're into February now. Carnaval is looming and every evening we can hear drums as various schools practice for the parade. Alan located a practice ground – by dint of going out on the bike and listening. We all went up later. It is noisy. Lots of people with lots of drums of different shapes and sizes. Each different drum has a different rhythm to beat out, but they all integrate into a wonderful pulsing sound. It is very difficult to stand still and listen. You just want to be moving. There were also people practicing their dance steps for the parade.

Carnaval at last. Piracicaba was scheduled to have a parade of three Samba schools on Saturday the 21st and another on the Monday of three more Samba schools. We went down on Saturday night in anticipation of a colourful parade only to find it had been cancelled because of a bit of rain. The papers said that short of a disaster, the parade would go ahead, rain or no rain. There were a few people like us about, looking for a (damp) parade, and some disconsolate food vendors packing up, having set up their stalls by the road, to feed the hungry crowds. One vendor was reported in the paper the next day as saying he had reckoned to make 2000 reais (£400 - £500) that evening. That is a lot of money for one night's work when you consider that 200 reais is the minimum wage – for a month.

Monday night and all the schools did parade. We watched the first one go past and then went to the collecting point to see the next one set off. Each "school" consists of several hundred people, parading and dancing in blocks of different coloured costumes. Costumes were wonderful, from full dresses with swirly skirts to skimpy sequin bikinis with a few added feathers.

It is all very colourful. Age is no bar. The older ones, even the grandmothers, swirled in their long dresses, and there were a couple of three-to-four-year olds, albeit a bit bewildered, parading with Mummy (wearing the same costume as Mummy, no less). There was also a block of children – I guess six-to-ten-year olds – and they were the best dancers of the lot.

I can only say that the floats are contrivances of ingenuity. They were not motorised, just pushed along, but all of them had on average four people jiggling about on top and it all looked a bit precarious. Colourful, noisy, a bit disorganised, but everyone was enjoying themselves. This being a small local affair was more tangible. You were at the same level as the parades and many of the dancers were breaking away from their group to greet friends in the crowd. The crowd was not as big as I had expected, but then we went down early – it started at 8.00 p.m., and each school was scheduled to take an hour from one end of the route to the other, all of 600 yards or thereabouts. It wasn't so much that the parading took an hour, but there was only one "sound" lorry, equipped with huge banks of speakers. The singers paraded in front of the lorry, with microphones wired to the front of the lorry. This lorry had to discharge one lot of singers, drive back to the start via another route, get the next lot of musicians, and so on. We watched one school parade, then went to watch the next school organising itself, and setting off. Then we went home. It was after 10.00 p.m. by this time.

For some reason, I woke up during the night at about 3.00 a.m., and when I heard the blast of loud music, I knew what had startled me awake. Curiosity got the better of me, so I went out on the veranda to investigate. The music was coming from the parade route about a mile away. It must have been the last school reaching the end of the route. *Only in Brazil*, I thought, and tried as best I could to get back to sleep.

On Friday, the 27th of February, we set off on another expedition, this time to Rio to see the parade of the champions of the Carnaval Parades that had been held the previous weekend. We went by bus, which was a marathon in itself. It was a mini package trip. First, we caught a bus to São Paulo. That took two hours, and then we had to find our way to another bus terminal. We used the metro and found it to be very efficient. The buses for the next leg of our journey arrived bit by bit. There were 20 buses on this excursion, and we were eighth in line – and the buses didn't arrive in numerical order. It all seemed a bit chaotic, but given that they were trying to marshal about a thousand people in a limited space, they did very well. Our bus left São Paulo at about 11.30 p.m.

We arrived in Rio de Janeiro at 7.00 a.m. or thereabouts, had breakfast in a small hotel and then there was the option of going to see a couple of tourist sites (Cristo and Pão de Açúcar, which we had already seen), or hanging around waiting for our hotel to be ready to take us in. We went to our hotel and checked in without any bother despite being told that our rooms probably wouldn't be ready until about 11.00 a.m. We slept for awhile then went out exploring, first along a small cobbled street behind the hotel and then we found a place to grab some lunch before going to the modern art museum.

Street at the back of the hotel... and one of many nice old buildings in Rio

It was soon time to get a snack and head back to the hotel for a 7.30 p.m. departure for the *sambódromo*, which is the purpose built carnival parade setting. We were all issued with yellow T-shirts without which we would not be allowed to get on the bus to take us back to the hotel at the end of the night. We didn't have to wear them; we just had to be able to produce one each. Wearing them, however, makes it easier for the various guides to locate their tour group.

And off we went. The bus left us as close to the sambódromo as possible given the traffic chaos, after which we were directed to the entrance. We found our seats and settled in to wait. We had also been issued with small cushions made of PVC-covered squares of foam with the tour company logo printed on them, a necessity for sitting on the concrete tiers of the viewing area. They were ours to keep. We had hardly sat down when fireworks started at the far end.

We were a bit beyond the half way mark of the route. The first was a mini parade more to get people settled and ready for the parades proper. The first group was a small but colourful one promoting some Italian self-help society, which had been started in the early 1900s when masses of Italian immigrants arrived.

There was a pause while the next lot got assembled, more fireworks, and they were off. Each samba school chooses a theme for their parade each year. The first group was promoting sugar cane and the fact that Brazil is going to export a lot of sugar alcohol to Japan for car fuel, the inference being that this was going to be the way of the future, with Brazil exporting more and more fuel alcohol.

The second school's theme was the colour red. There must have been at least a thousand people in each school and about half a dozen floats. Each school must have at least five floats but no more than eight.

As shown in the photos here, each float was towing a generator, dressed in the same manner as the float. One float had go-karts driving round on it.

There were lots of colourful and glitzy costumes covered in sequins and sparkle, and masses of feathers. (I think there must be a lot of naked birds in Brazil come carnival time!)

One of the most notable aspects of a Brazilian carnival parade is the noise, and this one was no exception. Each school had its theme tune, which it blared out for the entire hour and twenty minutes of parading from one end of the sambódromo to the other, a length of about 600 yards. The music is not pre-recorded. Musicians and singers perform live – all greatly amplified of course. There were blocks of dancers, each block wearing a different costume, all relating to the theme of the school.

It was not as well coordinated as I had expected. Anybody can go to one of the schools and for a fee, hire a costume and parade with the school. This accounted for some of the chaos, but they were all having fun.

We watched three schools parade. By this time it was 1.30 a.m., and there were still two or three more schools to go. Sarah was wilting fast, so we decided to take a taxi back to the hotel. We didn't see the winning school, but as someone said to us later, in all honesty, once you have seen one, the rest are very similar, the only difference being the costumes and a float pertaining to whatever is the theme of the school.

We didn't actually spend much time sitting on our cushions. There was about twenty minutes between the end of one school passing and the next one arriving close to our location. As the school approached, everyone got to their feet – including the three of us! – to samba along with the music and wave their arms in the air and generally have a good time. The words of the theme song of each school were in the programme so everyone was singing along too.

Something that amused us was the gang of sweepers that came behind each school, a neat, horizontal line of them, all frantically sweeping the debris of confetti and streamers and no doubt bits of lost costume, and these were followed by about three vacuum cars picking up what the sweepers had missed.

After the third school, one of the sweepers seemed to be lagging behind, out on his own. He turned out to be part of the entertainment, and would sweep a bit, then do a typical samba style dance using his broom and dustpan as a dance partner, produce a Brazilian flag out of the top of his broom handle, and then continue on his way. It was a bit of light comic relief.

Throughout the evening, there were vendors threading their way amongst the crowds with large boxes on their shoulders containing drinks, ice creams or beef burgers. Quite an impressive feat to balance such a heavy weight whilst climbing up and down concrete tiers littered with stray cushions, bags and assorted paraphernalia, not to mention the waving arms and dancing feet of so many people!

Those that stuck the pace got back to the hotel by 6.00 a.m. We were back by 2.00 a.m. The taxi drivers were trying to cash in on gullible tourists. The first taxi driver wanted 20 R$ to take us to the hotel. The next one we asked was looking for 40 R$. The next one wanted 25 R$, but finally agreed to 20 R$. Our guide on the bus had said that 15 – 20 R$ was about the right price.

Our bus was due to leave Rio at 1.30 p.m. the next day. We went to bed, slept 'til about ten o'clock, had breakfast, and sampled the delights of the hotel. It was a smart hotel with two swimming pools, a few beauty salons, fitness rooms, a sauna and a spa complete with massage services. Rio is full of such hotels, being a major tourist destination. We swam, and then made sure we were ready well ahead of time so that when the bus arrived we could claim the few coveted seats with plenty of legroom.

Then it was back to São Paulo. The bus left us off close to the terminal where we would catch yet another bus for the final leg of the journey back to Piracicaba. We finally arrived home about midnight. It was a long weekend with lots of time spent on buses, but it was worth it just to see what all the fuss is about when everyone says that Carnival in Rio is one of those things you *must* do whilst living in Brazil.

Brazilian Living

When the cat is away, the mice will play. While Alan was away in Ireland, end of March/ beginning of April, I invited the choir to come to lunch on Sunday, bringing a contribution towards the festivities. It was a good party. It seems if people bring something they feel more a part of things and don't politely wait to be offered food, drinks and so on, but get stuck in and just sort themselves out. It suits me because it makes everyone feel more 'at home'. I had lots of help organising the meal, setting out the plates and washing up. It also helped that this group all knew each other so there was no breaking the ice. All in all it was a great idea, and a good time was had by all.

Sarah's school had a trip to the observatory as part of their schoolwork. I was impressed to see that children in Brazil learn basic astronomy in primary schools, something you don't see everywhere. I trailed along too. Practically every town of any size has an observatory, and the one here is open to the public every Saturday evening and by appointment at other times. It is run by the town council's department of education, and they have two astronomers on staff who man the observatory when required. The local paper publishes interesting updates in the astronomical world, such as when Mars was at its closest point to earth, which wouldn't happen again for hundreds of years. The observatory opened that day specially and it was bunged, with people queuing on the hard shoulder of the dual carriageway to get in. In fact, they were open the following day as well, such was the demand.

With the school, we learned about sundials, and how the pointer has to be at the angle of your latitude for a sundial to work properly. We learned a bit about telescopes. We watched the rotation of the earth by fixing the big main telescope in the dome so that it stayed still, and the sun was projected onto a piece of paper so that we could watch it set as it moved across the paper with the movement of the earth. Normally the telescope has a device that makes it ignore the earth's rotation and stay focused on whatever you are looking at so that it doesn't go out of your field of vision as the earth turns.

As it got darker, we looked at Venus. Later after a brief talk, we looked at the moon and Jupiter plus three of its moons, and Saturn and its rings. As well as the big telescope in the dome, the observatory has a variety of smaller telescopes in a hut with a sliding roof.

Tuesday night we had the best thunderstorm yet. It went on for about two hours and the rain was torrential. Apparently, a skip parked on a hill was washed down the hill and did considerable damage to a building at the bottom. Reports say that as much rain fell in 50 minutes as would normally fall in a month in the wet season! Meanwhile, Alan hopes for another drought so there will be a demand for generators because there won't be enough water in the reservoirs to generate sufficient electricity for the country. The paper the next day carried all sorts of stories of flooding, as well as a story about three children who had gone missing as a result of the rain. The news media described it as a mini cyclone.

When living in a climate that is prone to torrential downpours, you certainly see how damaging water can be. The small holes in our road suddenly became mini craters overnight, and gullies have appeared in the pavements, particularly the ones made from a mosaic of small stones.

Speaking of torrential downpours, a few months ago Alan and I went out on the bike at about 10.30 at night. He was wearing shorts and a T-shirt, and I had a sleeveless top on, and that was comfortable as it was still fairly warm then. We came back about half an hour later and were soaked - the heavens opened when we were about half way home! But at least it was less than a ten-minute drive. The warm evenings, I think, are the reason why there is such a hiving nightlife in Brazil. It is very pleasant to sit and sip your drink outside and watch the world go by.

Our destination that particular evening was a garage to meet a friend of Alan's. Garages are a focus of nightlife too. Some of them close the pumps about 10.00 p.m. and let the social trade take over. They all have beer and soft drinks. Many of them provide tables and chairs, and you just turn up with your friends, open the car doors with the stereo at full volume and chat with your mates.

Another interesting aspect of nightlife in Brazil is how late it gets started and what time things finally wind down and everyone goes home! Recently, Alan was invited to a birthday party at a nightclub. Nightclubs tend to start thinking about opening at around 11.00 p.m. at the earliest, so Alan left the house at midnight to go to this party thinking surely he wouldn't be the first to arrive. When he got there, he was told that he was too early! That is the norm here. Coming home at 4.00 or 5.00 in the morning after a night out at weekends is average or even early to be arriving home. They like their nightlife, but for much of the year it is not cold at night, and so they give no thought to running around in skimpy party clothes at night.

In mid April, Alan and I went away for a weekend on the bikes, which was fun. We went to a very scenic touristy area about 200 kilometres away. Amongst other things, we found a town whose claim to fame was selling knitted goods at cheap prices (but all machine knit I hasten to add). I bought a lightweight jumper with buttons all up one sleeve, which continued up into the collar. The collar with the buttons done up would be a polo neck, but with the buttons undone, it forms an attractive asymmetric collar. The cost was the equivalent of about £8. We bought Sarah a light polo neck jumper in a market where they were selling three items for about £2. We only wanted one so we paid £1 for her jumper. Can't complain about prices that good! The weather wasn't quite as warm as we would have liked, but it was fun to get away on the bikes. We tried to stick to smaller paved roads as much as possible, which in this area was easy to do. Generally, one has the big main roads and then the dirt roads off them. I guess we clocked up about 400 kilometres in total on this little weekend trip.

A Canadian friend came to stay for a long weekend at the end of April. We packed in as much as we could in the few days she was here: a walk in the university grounds; a party in Campinas; a trip to a coffee fazenda; a trip to Pedreira (the town I described earlier where they sell inexpensive crockery and semi-precious stone items).

She got a taste of sugar cane juice; we bought fruit and vegetables in the big market; ate sweet corn ice cream; visited the shopping mall; walked along the river and through the engenho, (the old sugar mill complex) and explored the town centre. We ate pizza, which is a fun experience here – the waiters come round with different pizzas and you can have a slice of as many different types as you can eat, including banana and cinnamon, and they have a chocolate pizza!

We accomplished all this in three and a half days! It was busy, but so much fun. The morning she left, we got up at 4.00 a.m. to take her to Campinas to get a bus, which would take her direct to the airport in time for her flight to Cordoba in Argentina.

It seems she brought the cold weather with her; well, to us it seems cold now that we've been in this subtropical climate for some time! I suppose it felt warm to her coming from Canada, though Vancouver Island does have the sea to temper its climate more than most parts of Canada.

Daytime temperatures are around 20° -23°C (68° – 73°F) falling at night to as low as 11°C (50°F). 'That's not low!' I can hear you say! It is warm enough out in the sun (when it shines), but inside it is distinctly cold, and few houses have any means of heating. You have to go out and buy an electric heater if you want to heat your house. When we feel too cold in the flat, we retreat into the kitchen, shut the doors (all three of them leading to the kitchen) and light the oven leaving the oven door open. That heats the kitchen fairly rapidly. Alan came home one morning with a colleague from work to find Sarah seated in front of the cooker wrapped in her dressing gown warming up after her swimming lesson. The water temperature was about 25° (77°F) but the air temperature was 12°C (54°F).

I still have in my mind that you put on a coat when you go out to keep warm, and then you take it off when you reach your destination – be it someone's house, a restaurant or wherever you're headed, because you will be inside upon your arrival and thus you'll be warm. That would be standard practice in Ireland, but is not the case here. The houses, restaurants and shops are equally cold. You have to decide what you are going to wear bearing in mind that you may be eating a meal dressed in your over coat or a thick warm jumper. The architecture in Brazil is designed for hot weather. Most eating establishments are open air (with a roof overhead), and they have plastic screens they pull down when it gets a bit draughty, but it is not the same as a solid wall protecting you from the cold outdoor air!

Since going out in the evening is such a way of life here, especially from Thursday to Sunday nights, the cold weather doesn't stop many people from doing so. The more adventurous sit out drinking and chatting with their mates as usual, but instead of wearing lightweight clothing, they just bundle up in overcoats and woolly hats!

I am told that usually these cold spells last about a week. This one has lasted at least a month. Even the dogs have little overcoats! Mostly the smaller ones, but I did see a Labrador sized dog in a pink velvet coat!

The several colder mornings we had (11°-12 °C, or 50°-53°F) brought fog from the river. Mostly it stayed over the river, but some days it spread inland as far as our flat, cutting off our only source of heat. The sun shines obliquely in through our balcony windows from 7.00 to about 9.00 in the mornings when it shines at all. That is not a lot of heating, though we get sun in the kitchen in the afternoons.

Not only has it been cold, it has been unseasonably wet, raining two or three times each week, at a time of year when it is supposed to be drying up. And I mean heavy rain, not just a passing shower. During our first year here (in 2002) it rained briefly at the end of March, and then didn't rain again until July, when there was damp drizzle for two days just as I was trying to get clothes dried so that I could pack them for our trip home to Ireland!

This wet weather has meant a delay in the sugar cane harvest because the foliage is too damp to be burnt, and the ground is too soft to allow the machines on to it. Quite a lot is cut by hand still, but machines do most of the work now. Because of this delay, a bonus for us is that we aren't getting the regular 'black snow' of charred sugar foliage as the cane is burnt before cutting. I'm sure they will make up for it later when everything will be permanently black for weeks. Also, with the excess of water in the ground, the cane that is mature and ready for cutting will lose some of its sweetness, and presumably will produce less of whatever it is supposed to produce for whatever process, be it sugar or alcohol.

Last weekend, (which was also the last weekend in May) we went on another calango andando – this time the walk was about 23 kilometres. Alan walked too. Sarah stayed with Isadora. The day after (Sunday), Alan and I followed part of the same route and a bit beyond on the motorbikes, which took us all through sugar fields. Part of the walk took us past a sugar cane processing plant. Even though much of the harvest is delayed, that factory was in full swing, so the cane is coming in from somewhere.

On both days, we were passed by sugar cane lorries going in both directions, empty in one direction and full in the other. You wouldn't want to be in front of one of those going downhill on a dirt road.

Someone mentioned that they carry 35 tons of cane, which represents about 30 square metres (or 100 square feet) of crop space in the field. Many have two large trailers in addition to the trailer attached to the cab. Having so many lorries on the road made for some challenging motorcycling, especially when approaching a corner or a summit. The cane is planted along the contour of the hills, and at intervals also following the contour, there is a higher ridge. This was all very noticeable where the cane had been harvested and replanted. It is to stop the fields turning into rivers in the wet season, and having all the soil ending up at the bottom of the hill with great gullies down the slope.

You can see Piracicaba beyond the perfectly contoured sugar cane fields.

At the other end of the factory process, there is a residue left, and this is taken in lorries and dumped in the fields ready to be used as fertilizer for the next crop. There is also some sort of effluent, which, in the setup we passed, was pumped to what I can only describe as a slurry pit, some distance away from the factory. I'd rather have the smell of slurry! It was stinking! It is called *vinhaça*, which is translated as wine according to a handout from one of the factories! Okay, so wine is *vinho*, but it conjures a strange image to the foreign reader, that of wine being sprayed over the fields!

As it is now the month of May, we had the annual Festa das Nacões - a fund raising event in which the various charities participating choose a country or a region of Brazil, and produce food typical of their chosen nation/area. This can be anything from snacks to three course meals. This Festa lasts for five days! - though on the first three days, Wednesday to Friday, it operates evenings only. At the weekend, they start about 11.00 a.m. We had a French main course (fondue), Sarah had an Italian pudding (deep fried ice cream) and I went to look for a Cuban pudding (bananas with caramelized peanuts), but didn't find what I wanted.

There are also various other stands plying their wares, as well as musical bands, singing and dancing. Each nation has a queen and an ambassador, both of whom have to parade. Scotland was represented, but they didn't have haggis! They had managed to find a piper - a Brazilian student studying in São Paulo I think. I can't think that there would be much demand for a bagpipe teacher in Brazil, but he obviously found one. He was kitted out in full highland rig too - though not evening dress. The Brazilians love to get together and eat and talk, so this is a perfect fund raising event for the charities, most of which help the underprivileged members of the community, especially the children, but retirement homes and handicapped benefit as well.

The elderly are very well respected in Brazil. Sunday is a great family day and the restaurants are full of families taking granny out for lunch – and grandpa. On the bus coming back from the calango (we usually get the local bus back – heaven knows what the regular users think of this hoard of noisy sweaty walkers invading their bus), if an elderly person gets on the bus, a seat is immediately vacated – and usually by a young person. You also see young people sitting keeping elderly relatives company, outside the houses. It puts Britain to shame.

Just a short note here about the attention of waiters in Brazilian restaurants. I think I have mentioned before that waiting at table here is very much a profession, rather than being something you do as a student to earn a bit of spending money. When we were out for lunch last Sunday (replacing all those calories burnt up on the calango), a waiter put our drinks on the table and away he went. About five minutes later, another waiter noticed in passing that Sarah's straw was facing the wrong way, so he reached over and quickly moved the straw so that it was pointing towards her! Is that service, or what?

A couple came to our house for dinner last October, and she couldn't take her eyes off the quilt I have hanging on the wall. Eventually she asked if I would teach patchwork to a therapy group in the Caterpillar Centre for the Promotion of Health. There were twenty-two students on the list, but three didn't turn up. It was fun. In preparation, we made up cushion kits: eight squares and sixteen triangles in four colours of fabric, and we also cut the papers too. Given that there were only four classes, we felt we had to start half way through the process. The results were wonderful, and it was a joy to teach a class with such creative pupils. One girl turned hers into a bag. A couple of others added other patches and made bigger cushions, whilst others added borders, edgings and appliqué pictures in some squares. Now they want me to teach a Patchwork 2 class. I enjoyed it, even if I didn't find it tranquil as some of them described it. I feel like I am giving something back, having spent the last couple of years taking.

We finally found the monkeys in the university grounds; not caged ones. These are wild monkeys, but not big ones – they're more like the little tamarind types, and they will come and take food from you. They are wee sweeties. You can hear them calling to each other in the trees, but as it is a high-pitched noise, it sounds like birds until you learn the slight difference:

the monkeys' sound is more a drawn out whistle rather than the more abrupt notes of the birds.

There are also feral cats, which means lots of kittens about, one of which came and lay down on the rug beside us hoping for food. Lying on the grass must be tickly on its tummy - and it was a bit skinny. We were very tempted to bring it home, but common sense prevailed.

We have discovered the answer to a puzzle, which has been niggling at us since we arrived here: Why are house numbers not consecutive? As you're driving along looking for a particular street number, you might see 383 next to 373, which then jumps to yet another set of numbers. The answer is so simple and logical. The number of the house is the distance in metres that the house is from the end of the road. I'm not sure what happens in rural areas. They probably don't have numbers because the locals (and the postman) all know who lives where. Motorway exits are similarly treated. They are not consecutive either, but are numbered according to the number of kilometres from the city where the motorway started.

Sarah's swimming is progressing well. She is now concentrating on building up stamina, and I think is up to nearly 1000 metres in a lesson. That is the distance I swim when I go to the swimming pool at the sports club: 40 lengths of a 25-metre pool. We now go to the teacher's house as her pool is smaller and easier to heat than the one here, and there are two other (younger) girls taking lessons at the same time, which is more fun for Sarah.

A Trip to Minas Gerais

In June we went to visit the 'cradle of European Brazilian civilization' with Sarah's friend Isadora's family. Brazil was discovered by the Portuguese in 1500, and by the 1700s had discovered gold and diamonds in the state that today is called Minas Gerais - which actually means General Mines. There is a group of towns in that state dating from this period full of old buildings and cobbled streets. We visited São Joao del Rei, Tiradentes, Ouro Preto, Mariana and Congonhas, but there are more.

It was a fairly hectic weekend, but we started on the Wednesday in order to have plenty of time to explore the area, since it takes an eight-and-a half-hour drive to get to there. We arrived at our B & B at 10.30 at night. We passed through what must have been a lovely mountainous region, but it was dark by then so we really couldn't take in the scenery. At one point, a lorry towing a caravan passed us. Caravans are rare in Brazil so that was unusual. A bit further on we passed a pickup truck towing something. In the glare of our headlights, we saw another very unusual sight. The truck was towing a cage, and in the cage was a tiger! We decided that a circus must have been on the move.

Along the way we found a small restaurant in an equally small town called Minduri, somewhere in the dark in Minas Gerais. It was empty apart from one person with a bottle of beer. There was a small selection of hot dishes (the ubiquitous rice and beans and a couple of others) on a wood fuelled stove typical of Minas Gerais, a selection of salads, and the good lady offered to cook whatever meat we wanted. The price, including our drinks was ridiculously cheap. When Alan asked what we owed her, she said ten reais. He gave her ten and she tried to give him two reais change. Translated into pounds, the meal for us all cost less than two pounds, and she wanted to give us money back!

Otherwise, it was an uneventful journey until we reached São João Del Rei, when we couldn't find our way out of the town onto the road that would take us to our B & B. We did about two laps of the town - all very scenic and historic, but after a long day of driving, we were in no mood to appreciate it, and so we stopped and asked directions at a garage.

When we finally arrived, the B & B owner (or part owner) was waiting for us, a very voluble Brazilian girl with a French husband. We weren't the last to arrive. This weekend had been planned by Isadora's family, and they weren't arriving until about 2.00 a.m., and our hostess happily sat up and waited for them. I like her life style. Her French husband is a ski instructor. They spend five months in France during the ski season and seven months in Brazil, which means they enjoy the winter seasons in both places. Her brother manages the B & B. in the Brazilian summer (which in the northern hemisphere would be the winter months) and works on the Côte d'Azur in France during the European summer months. I think I could cope with a lifestyle like that!

After a good breakfast, we were on the road again by 9.30 the next morning (Thursday). Fernando, Isadora's father, got all their family out of bed. We had a guided tour of São João Del Rei – Fernando picked up a guide along the way who showed us all the local attractions.

In the afternoon we took a steam train ride to Tiradentes, where we saw more churches and historic buildings. Tiradentes was the nickname of one of Brazil's historic figures. He was one of twelve men who were prosecuted for an uprising against the Portuguese crown. They were fed up with Portugal taking all the wealth from Brazil, along with various other grievances. Tiradentes was hanged, drawn and quartered, and the others were deported either to Portugal or to Portuguese dependencies in Africa. He was a dentist, as denoted by his name Tiradentes, which means to pull (tira) teeth (dentes).

Friday, for me, started about 7.30ish with a walk along the road outside the B & B in the mist while everyone else was still sleeping. We were about four kilometres outside the town, so it was fairly rural and hilly. At the end of the road was a thermal spa with mineral filled pools of natural warm water (only 27°C – about 78°F) steaming gently in the cool morning air. There were also drinking fountains of the water, with a list of the minerals contained in the water posted alongside and a description of the ailments that drinking it would supposedly cure. I drank and continued on my way up the tarmac road until it stopped. There was a gap in the fence at the end of the road and a trail winding upwards – just waiting to be explored. My intention had been to go to the gates of the thermal park and return to the B & B by 9.00 a.m. when we planned to depart for the day's outing.

The trail was too inviting. Up I went, up, up, up, quite steeply. It was a well-defined trail, and looked as though it may have been a major path through the mountains at one time, as it was semi paved with large flat slabs of stone in places. I climbed up into the sunshine and looked down to the mist still lying in the valleys. It was serene, sublime, peaceful - utterly magical. I wished that I had brought the camera.

I continued climbing, telling myself, *I'll just go to the next bend- and the next - and the next.* The track passed over a saddle between two hills and started to descend. At this point, I knew it was definitely time to go back. I went down the other side just far enough to get a better view. Grassy slopes with lots of scrubby trees and the trail going down into the valley the other side and onwards, following a rocky path. There was no sign of habitation of any sort for miles. The pressure of time prevailed, and I decided that if I went any further I would just keep going, and I didn't have any water or food with me for sustenance - and of course we were supposed to be leaving at 9.30. Reluctantly, I knew it was time to turn back. When I got back to the B & B, I asked where the trail went: all the way to Tiradentes! If we hadn't been leaving at a set time that morning, guess what I would like to have done!

Now that I was back at base, I joined everyone for breakfast, and then we packed our luggage and hit the road. First stop was a small town called Resende Costa where the local industry is hand weaving. This is a very small village where every other house is a small shop selling handwoven items: scarves, shawls, bedspreads, throws for your sofa, place mats, table runners, rugs and mats of all shapes and sizes, and all quite inexpensive.

The whole region is serra after serra after serra, range after range of small mountains is the best way to describe the terrain. How on earth the early explorers (they were called *bandeirantes*) managed to penetrate such difficult terrain 400 years ago, let alone find gold, is mind boggling. What's interesting is that they were actually looking for silver.

Our next stop was a town called Congonhas, which is the name of an herb that grows prolifically in the region. The attraction here was a church with lots of sculptures by another of Brazil's famous sons. He was called Alejedinho - which is a nickname that means 'little cripple'. He had leprosy, and the story goes that towards the end of his life he would get someone to tie his tools to his wrists so he could finish whatever he was working on. His trademark was figures with pointed noses, curling hair and moustaches starting from the nostrils! Outside the church at Congonhas, there are statues of twelve prophets, carved in soapstone, and each one is supposed to be a representation of one of the twelve ringleaders of the uprising.

Church at Congonhas

On the hill below the church were more of Alejedinho's works. There were some half dozen mini chapels, each containing life size figures depicting scenes from the life of Christ. All I can say is that his output was prolific. Ouro Preto has works by him as well. Many of the figures in these chapels were in the process of being restored during the time that we visited, so one was gazing through the doors of these chapels at restorers as well as statues.

Next stop, when we were nearly at the next B & B where we would be staying, was an old gold mine. The open cart down into the mine on the end of a steam-driven cable was the most exciting part. The mine consisted of dark galleries disappearing into the distance along either side, and a lighted gallery where you could see miniscule seams of gold in the rocks and the pillars of rock left behind to support the roof. There was a lake flooding the lower galleries, which was quite attractive.

This is a gold mine ... and this is how you get in and out of it!

Our B & B was in a small town called Mariana, which at one time had been the capital of Brazil, as was Ouro Preto and São Joao del Rei and many other towns! Lots of towns claim to have been the capital at one time. More recently, Rio de Janeiro was the capital until 1960, and now it is Brasilia – purpose built for the job.

The town of Mariana is similar to the other small towns we had already visited on this trip, filled with churches, cobbled streets and old buildings. Two of the churches were built right beside each other, and there is story behind their proximity: Two of the barons of old were competing to show off their wealth, and so they both built ostentatious churches.

We spent Saturday touring around Ouro Preto, which is full of overly ornate baroque churches, old houses and cobbled streets – and I mean original style cobbles made from available stones, not the 'newer' squared off stones one usually thinks of as cobbling.

Ouro Preto, the best preserved of the towns, is built on a hill and has lots of steep narrow streets all crying out to be explored, but unfortunately time did not permit.

It also has lots of tourists! We visited two churches – one whose claim to fame is that more than 40 kilos of gold were used in the original decoration.

We decided we had seen more than enough churches for the weekend. We ate lunch next then decided to tour through a couple of museums.

The first was, for want of a better description, a decorative arts museum, but Brazil isn't museum orientated enough to make that distinction. It was a collection of old/historic objects from the area, such as woodcarvings, paintings, beds, a couple of sedan chairs, and so on, displayed in different rooms in a large old building. There really was no particular theme to it.

Decorative arts museum in the main square of Ouro Preto, and a view of the surrounding countryside

The next one was the museum of mineralogy, which, quite apart from depicting mining, has a wonderful collection of crystals and gemstones in their raw and cut states. One room is filled with the finest specimens of the collection beautifully presented, which was fantastic, and then another room contains all the leftovers: masses of them laid out row after row in those old, wood framed glass display cases found in practically every old museum.

We had time for coffee and hot chocolate before returning to our B & B. As we walked to our cars, we saw that someone had laid out some jewellery items for sale on the bonnet of their car parked outside the coffee shop, and I succumbed to a pendant with green and pink tourmaline set in silver. Ouro Preto is full of shops selling all sorts of jewelley at all sorts of prices, and there are plenty of street traders like the one we bought from. Lots of it is very nice, but I don't use jewellery that much, so I was able to restrain myself from spending too much.

Back to the B & B, time for a shower and out for a wander round Mariana in the dark, with some leisure time for sitting and enjoying drinks and a nibble. We passed the two churches that had been built side by side. One was closed, but the other had a wedding almost in progress. The guests were arriving all dressed up to the nines, and it only remained for the bride to arrive. We found a small bar just down the street from the church, and sat and chatted while the girls (Sarah, Isadora and her sister Anna) migrated between us and the front of the church, waiting for the bride to arrive. Arrive she did, and according to the girls, she was wonderful.

The next morning I went for a walk before breakfast. It was Sunday and the place was deserted. Saturday morning, I had also gone for a short wander before breakfast, and the place was hiving with activity. Sunday was a marked contrast. I walked to yet another church perched on a hilltop overlooking the town, which is reputed to have more gold than the one in Ouro Preto, but I didn't get to see it. It was closed at 8.00 a.m. The early morning mass was taking place at a church in the centre of town.

For our trip home, we had planned to take the same route back again so we could see the scenery in the daylight, but unfortunately, we missed our turn in the mist, and ended up going home the whole way by motorway, which was longer in distance but probably a bit quicker in time.

Towards the end of that motorway is a strawberry growing region, and there are a lot of strawberry stalls at the side of the road. We stopped with the idea of buying bulk because usually the cost at these roadside stalls is cheaper than the prices in the shops in Piracicaba. To our surprise, they weren't cheaper! They were the same price we're used to paying, and the third stall we stopped at was dearer, but we bargained the seller down to two thirds of the price. We bought eight punnets with the idea of making jam and ice cream.

Somewhat less exciting was the traffic jam about an hour out from São Paulo where all the holiday traffic (it was a long weekend) had to filter into a contra-flow system because of road works.

Home again finally, with just enough time to get something to eat and then fall into bed. It had been a long drive and a busy weekend in places that warrant much more time and exploration, but we had a glimpse, if nothing else, of Brazil's beginnings.

July and the Festa do Divino

Recently we hosted a meeting of The Auld Lang Syne Fellowship – a group formed by this (retired) Portuguese American because he wants to talk English and his Brazilian wife doesn't speak much English. I had asked one of our fellow calango walkers – the boss in fact – whether he would be prepared to give us a talk in English. He had done the Santiago Compostela walk across the north of Spain two years ago, and I had been to one of his talks about it (given in Portuguese.) He likes a challenge, so he agreed to do it. All went very well. Once you have been accustomed to talking to someone in Portuguese, it seems a bit strange to talk to them in English. I had to actually remember to talk to those people in English, which made me feel that I had progressed very well in learning Portuguese!

More recently, we went to see the recent Harry Potter film in Campinas (about one hour away) because they didn't have a subtitled version here in Piracicaba, only dubbed. (It means we don't have to concentrate if we don't have to listen to the dialogue in Portuguese.) The film was terrible. We get all the big films here in English with subtitles. When the film is aimed at a younger audience, it is dubbed.

Returning from Campinas at about 10.30 p.m., we found ourselves stuck in traffic again, about one kilometre from our turn to Piracicaba, which was very frustrating. The outside lane was moving but we wanted to turn off, so we had to put up with it. Bad idea! It transpired that everyone seemed to want to turn off at the same place. Why? There were cars and buses full of people in high spirits, many of them wearing cowboy hats. 'What is going on?' we asked ourselves. We had seen signs in this area saying 'Festa de Peão', which means 'Cowboy Festival'. So we put two and two together and nearly made four. They weren't coming *from* the Festa at this time of night, but going to it! There was obviously going to be the party of the century (or rather, this being Brazil, the party of the week) taking place at this Festa, and all the world and his wife were going. Being little more than an hour out of São Paulo (until you reach the traffic jam), I would guess that a lot of people had come from that city for the party.

Having seen the chaos at our turn off, we decided that if we were going to arrive home before 3.00 a.m. we would have to take another route. Not so easy in this country, where you have main roads between cities, which are well lit, paved and sign posted, and then dirt roads (which would be the equivalent of back roads in Ireland) which have no lighting, or sign posts, and aren't marked on the map. We stayed on the paved road and went on up the motor way for another half hour to the next city where we knew there was a direct route to Piracicaba. It seemed as though it took forever, but we got home again eventually. Sarah had gone to sleep in the back of the car. We carried her upstairs (well, up in the lift actually) laid her on the bed, removed her shoes and trousers, covered her, and left it at that. All I can say is that it must have been some party!

Last weekend, the 26th of June, we did another calango. We were told that the walk was going to be 20 kilometres. Alan decided to do it because it wasn't too long. Sarah was going to stay the night at Isadora's house along with a gaggle of other girls, so that was sorted out. At 11.30 p.m. on the Friday night, an urgent email came through. For some reason, our walking group wouldn't be able to use the ferry on the proposed route, so we would have to make a detour, which would add another four to five kilometres.

We arrived at the starting point at 5.45 the next morning, to be greeted with the information that the buses to take us the first 10 kilometres to the starting point of the walk weren't coming for some reason, and we were going to walk the whole route – all 34 kilometres! There were a couple of points within reasonable reach of a bus route, so you could slope off if you wanted. We did the lot – and I'll admit that I was quite happy to reach the end. So was Alan – in fact, I think everybody was glad to see beer and lunch looming ahead.

Not many people sloped off, so there were 80 or 90 of us sitting down to lunch. Brazil is full of small ramshackle looking wee bars. Lunch had been arranged in an up market version of one of these. It was more than just a lean to. Numbers had been phone ahead, so there was rice, beans, salad and meat waiting for us when we arrived. Carlos maintains that the only reason he does the calangos is that the beer at the end always tastes so good! He sloped off early, much to our surprise, but he was there at the end with the car, so we were offered a lift home, which was great. I did not relish the idea of having to walk to the bus stop, and then having to walk from wherever the bus left us in Piracicaba to home.

Overall, it was good walk – a very scenic route, after the first ten kilometres, which was all urban. After that, it was dirt roads with some (very small) hills, which caused some consternation amongst the walkers. (They are not used to hills here!) Also, the walk was mostly off the main dirt roads, so we didn't have to watch out for sugar cane lorries lumbering along, though we did pass one being filled, and the same field being prepared for the next crop. Sugar cane farmers can get two crops a year if they organise the crop production efficiently. There has been the normal amount of rain for June – in other words, almost none, so cane harvesting is very definitely in full swing. Every evening we can see fires from the fields being burnt prior to cutting. It is incredible; when we look out our windows into the distance at night, we can see squares of land burning brightly and then all of a sudden, the fire disappears – it stops completely, and the burning squares disappear into black nothingness. They burn the square of cane from the outside inwards, and it gets to a point where there is nothing left to burn and the fire just goes out. We are not close enough to see the smouldering remains.

At 5.00 p.m. the same day as our calango, we were invited out to tea by my patchwork teaching partner. Her husband works with Alan. She had a wonderful spread of breads, cheese, cake, jam, small biscuits and a gooey strawberry tart to round things off. They live on the seventeenth floor, and while we were there, a square of cane quite close to the city was being burnt so we had a good view from that height. It was really quite dramatic. The fallout from the fire was quite dramatic too. When we came out to the car a bit later, it was covered with strips of charred black foliage up to two inches long and a about a quarter inch or more wide. Our flat thankfully was fairly clear of this 'black snow' in spite of being closer to the source. I guess that the heat sends this charred stuff high up (it is extremely light) and it travels a bit before coming down again. We were obviously near enough the source to miss most of it.

It is June again, so lots of Festas Juninhas – any excuse for a party – with food, drink and dancing in the street! As always, Sarah's school had one – as do most of the schools and many areas of the city. The more up market venues (such as sports clubs) have a fireworks display as well. We went to the Festa at our local sports club and then to Caterpillar Club Festa to see the fireworks there.

At the Caterpillar Club Festa, there was a stall selling food typical of the north of Brazil. We tried tapioca, which is nothing to do with school milk puddings, and Alan tried something called acarajé. The acarajé was a deep fried ball of dough – probably made from mandioca, split through the middle and filled with a hot sauce and prawns still in their shells. You eat them, shells and all! I think the Brazilian version of tapioca is made from dried grated mandioca. To cook it, they smooth a couple of spoonfuls of a paste of it onto a hot griddle, and this makes it all stick together. You then choose a filling to put in the centre of this flattened 'pancake' and the tapioca is folded over the filling omelette style. I chose cheese, and Sarah chose coconut with condensed milk. Hers was the better choice. Mine was definitely rubbery, but Sarah's had sufficient filling to offset the rubbery texture. I would like to have gone back for a banana and cinnamon tapioca, but I was still quite full from the first one I'd eaten, and time did not permit. Perhaps another time!

Alan went to the big Festa Juninha in Tupi again this year, and this time he stayed to see the embers of the bonfires being raked out, and people walking across them. He said it was a bit of a con because the embers were spread very thin on the ground at the edge of the fire.

I mentioned Quentão before, which is a drink typical at these Festas. I said that it is made from pinga, the local sugar cane hooch. I have since learnt that it is supposed to be made from pulverized ginger in caramelised sugar and *water*, with a nip of pinga! I might like it better if I could find any made that way instead of the rocket-fuel type stuff made from 90% pinga!

We finally got to see the start of the Festa do Divino. It happens every year at the beginning of July, and in the past two years we have either forgotten about it or been on our way to Ireland. It is a religious festival (as are most of them), but this one involves masses and blessings. It starts with a mass in a building close to the river, and then two boats (about twelve feet long) are carried down to the river about 100 yards away: one by a group of women and the other by men. It is a procession headed by a padre and a banner. Then come the boats, and then the band.

When the boats are launched, people throw flowers and leaves into them or into the river itself. Meanwhile, the padre is standing on a floating platform saying prayers, which are punctuated by the people shouting 'viva!' (meaning, to live). He finally gets around to the blessing and liberally splashes holy water over the boats and anyone nearby. The whole procession is punctuated by firecrackers going off at intervals - huge rockets that make a lot of noise but offer no visual display - and at the crucial point after the blessing, a battery of firecrackers is set off. I noticed people tying knots in the ribbons attached to the banner. I can only assume that this has the same significance as lighting candles in churches.

It is a short, simple and moving ceremony that originated in Portugal in the thirteenth century popularised by Queen 'Santa' Isabel in *'Honour and glory* (I'm translating word for word from the local paper) *to the third person of the most holy Trinity, the Holy Spirit'.* I think it is connected with giving thanks for survival in times of suffering and disease. It probably started after one of the plague epidemics in Europe arrived in São Paulo in the seventeenth century. This tradition was adapted to the local situation where malaria was rife in the riverside communities of the Rio Tietê (which runs through São

Paulo) *'where they lacked everything and survived suffering, principally fevers',* according to the account in the newspaper.

After the boats are launched in Piracicaba, there follows a re-enactment of when the remedy for the disease was first brought to the community. All the participants are dressed in red and white.

This ceremony has been performed in Piracicaba for 178 years. The Festa do Divino continues with a mass each day in different houses alongside the river, then the following weekend they have a parade and food and dancing on both Saturday and Sunday.

Our First Balloon Trip!

When our friends Johny and Crispie came to visit, we decided there was no better time than to fulfill a dream we've had since coming to Brazil two years ago, which is to take a trip in a hot-air balloon, and so we did. This trip had originally been planned for Sunday at 7.00 a.m., which was the day after J & C arrived. Nothing like throwing them in at the deep end! However, weather did not permit and it was postponed until further notice – which happened to be the following Thursday afternoon. Just as well, because we wouldn't have been able to do it any later with our various other commitments.

The launch pad is an area of grass beside a pond in front of one of the university buildings nearby, so it was within walking distance for us. I have mentioned this balloon earlier. We see it frequently on Sunday mornings. They had got the basket off the trailer, attached the balloon to it, and had nearly blown it up completely by the time we arrived. All we had to do was wait until everything was nearly buoyant and clamber in.

A few more roars from the gas bottle dragon in the middle of the basket and we were off, ascending steadily to avoid the various hazards around us, such as trees, electricity wires and apartment blocks.

There wasn't that much wind, so we had time to gain height. In fact, we went up fairly high looking for a bit more wind. (Alan tells me we went up to about 800 metres above the ground.) It was very pleasant; I won't say peaceful, because the dragon in the middle kept roaring at intervals. Cold it was not. The late afternoon sun was quite warm, and the heat from the flame was quite hot as well.

It is always fun trying to pick out landmarks from the air, and there is sugar cane as far as the eye could see, from tilled fields ready for planting, to fields with lorries in them waiting to be loaded with the harvested cane.

Oh, sugar! Lots and lots of it.

Our driver/pilot had all the mod cons: satellite navigation, radio, bottles of water, bits of string to pull. He was in constant touch with the ground crew, telling them which direction we were going and where he thought we would end up. There is limited direction control. One is that you go up and down until you find a stream of air going in the direction you want. The other is that you can open flaps in the side of the balloon which lets out a jet of air and pushes you round a bit, but that would be more in the line of fine-tuning rather than directional flying.

He gave us instructions for the landing drill in the event that it was a bit windy on landing and the basket might tip over. This entailed crouching down in the bottom of the basket whenever he said so. We ended up landing at one of Piracicaba's other universities (there are four campuses in Piracicaba) having travelled less than ten kilometres in the hour we were in the air.

The only casualty was my water bottle. I had taken a half-litre bottle of water with me and drunk the lot while in the air. The bottle I brought out of the basket was well distorted from its original shape due to the change in air pressure as we came down!

The ground crew were waiting at the selected landing spot, by the swimming pool, but when we didn't drop down low enough in time for that spot, they then had to race through the university complex on foot at top speed to the next proposed landing site the other side of the buildings! This time we *were* low enough, with the basket almost touching the rooftops below us. We were within shouting distance by this time and instructions were duly issued. It was time to anchor us to the ground, so the pilot threw out an umbilical in the form of a stout strap. Those on the ground grabbed the end and started hauling for all they were worth, in the direction where they wanted us to touch down.

It was interesting. The dragon roared at intervals to keep us off the rooftops. The crew on the ground were hauling us in the direction of the clear space to land. This also exerted a downward pull. The security men at the university and various bystanders joined in this tug-o-war, which added to the excitement.

Once clear of the building, the pilot opened the flap at the top of the balloon and we gently came down the last few metres to touch the ground.

No emergency landing procedure was needed. Having come down to earth on the grass, they then decided to 'fly' us onto the trailer. So the dragon roared again and we rose up a couple of feet and were pushed and pulled in the direction of the trailer. This is certainly much easier than having to lift the basket onto the trailer afterwards. Once there was sufficient air out of the balloon so that it wouldn't immediately take off again when we abandoned ship, we were allowed to climb out. By this time, somebody had hold of a sturdy rope attached to the top of the balloon, pulling it in the direction in which they wanted it to lie down.

Meanwhile, a plastic table was taken out of the back of the truck and set up on the lawn. A plastic 'lace' tablecloth was set on top and the refreshments appeared: sandwiches, cake, fruit juice, iced tea and champagne! The champagne is apparently a tradition that started in France. You *always* have a glass of champagne after your first balloon flight! Sarah had her share too.

It was brilliant. I shall feel jealous every weekend now when I watch the balloon going up from the university.

Next day we were all up bright and early again for a 5.00 a.m. start to drive to Rio de Janeiro. We took a scenic route, stopping along the way, so our trip that day took us about thirteen hours. Alan had already alerted our host that food and bed would probably be the order of the day when we arrived. One of our stops was at the TAMAR Project in Ubatuba (we had been here before and also learned more about the project when we were on holiday at Fernando de Noronha. It seeks to promote awareness of the plight of marine turtles, and how they can be helped). They have several tanks of the various species of the turtles, so you can see them close up. The tanks are all far too small given the distances those creatures are known to swim, but it is a temporary measure for research purposes and to let people see them, which is how the TAMAR Project gains much needed funds (from the entry fees). Turtles tagged in Brazil have been found off the coast of Africa!

We arrived on the outskirts of Rio in time for the Friday evening rush hour, but with maps and a little hazy prior knowledge, having stayed at Omar's house before, we muddled our way through the traffic chaos and arrived at our destination with only one wrong turn, which was easily rectified. Omar was amazed. He had been expecting us to phone when we got to Rio and he would come and guide us. Did we have satellite navigation, he wondered? No, just me with some maps and a vague sense of the destination we were aiming for, and Alan's ability to remember roads.

Barbecue and bed! His wife was not in - she had been called out to do an emergency operation on a turtle - not the big sea going ones, but one of the small freshwater cousins. I have mentioned earlier that she is a vet, and works for the zoo.

The weather that weekend was not good. We went up Pão de Açucar in the mist and rain and didn't see much of the view. To fill some time, we also went to a shopping mall. Saturday night, Johny, Crispie and I went to a glitzy show based on Brazilian folklore; The 'Plataforma Samba show'. Expensive, yes.

Fun, yes. It is one of those 'must do' things in Rio. Alan and Omar had been before, and children under the age of twelve were not permitted. There were lots of sparkly 'over the top' costumes, not to mention the under dressed, minimal sparkly bikinis. One highlight was a capoeira troupe, which is basically a combination of a martial art with gymnastics, and very popular in Brazil. The accuracy, speed and timing of their performance was stunning. One out of sync move, and someone would have had someone else's foot or hand connecting very hard and painfully with another part of their anatomy. There is lots of dancing and noise, of course, and one act was showing off various traditional instruments – mainly drums, but it was all extremely well done. The whole show was very professional. It was very much a tourist show, but J & C thought it was brilliant. We then went to an Irish pub, had some good food there, and returned to Omar's home.

Sunday's weather was not much better. We headed out with the intention of visiting Cristo on his lofty perch over the city, but as we reached the centre of town, the heavens opened, and we couldn't see Cristo. It is miserable up on the hill with Cristo in the rain. You can see nothing and it is freezing cold with the perpetual wind up there. We went instead to a market that claimed to promote items from the North East of Brazil, but it was mainly foodstuffs, though there were a number of craft type stalls. Crispie managed to get the promised football jerseys there. The sports shop in the mall only had the official football jerseys at an extortionate price, but we knew there were copies available somewhere. Sure enough, the market had them.

We went from the market to lunch, dodging the raindrops. The weather did not let up – so what to do in Rio on a wet Sunday afternoon? Alan knew that Peter Waugh (who lives in Whitehead and works in F.G. Wilson) had a brother living in Rio, whom Johny had met. They phoned directory inquiries and managed to get his number. The rest as they say is history. He thought it was a wind up at first, but it turned out he lived within a 25-minute walk from the bar in which we were sitting, and he duly arrived. Meanwhile, Luciana (Omar's wife) and I took our daughters to a small shopping mall across the road for a wander round, rather than try to entertain them in the restaurant/bar while the others talked. Not wildly exciting, but it passed the time.

We finally gathered ourselves together about 5.00 p.m., and as we were leaving the bar, we could see Cristo looming above us. We decided to go for it. We piled into the cars and headed up the hill (steep) to see Cristo. We got there just as it was beginning to get dark, but J & C were delighted to have made it even if they only saw the city in the (nearly) dark.

At one point in our peregrinations around the city, we had to pass through a toll. Omar has a sensor on his car which, as he approaches the toll, is scanned and the fee automatically debited from his account, thus signalling the barrier to lift. We were in two cars, so as we came closer to the toll, Omar phoned Alan and said that we had to stay about three feet off his bumper so that we could squeeze through right behind him. Yes, you've guessed. With us tailgating, there was sufficient time for Omar and us to get past the barrier before it dropped, and so we went through the toll without paying. We haven't received any fines through the post, so I think we got away with it! Alan was not too happy about driving so close behind Omar, but it worked!

We returned home to Piracicaba the next day. It rained the whole way, all eight hours of that long drive. We did stop at the Finnish village where we had stayed when Kaye was here, but that was the only 'touristy' stop we made the entire way home. The next day, Sarah and I were on the plane to Ireland.

We are back to Brazil after a summer holiday in Ireland, and it's hard to believe this is the start of our fourth year living here. The time has flown, and now it seems more like coming home when we return here than when we go 'home' to Ireland.

We finally arrived back in Piracicaba after waiting to meet friends from Belfast at the airport in São Paulo. They had flown in from Rio de Janeiro. I do not recommend arriving the same day as guests after you have had a long flight, but they were very understanding. I threw their sheets and towels at them and they had to make their own bed!

They were only staying three nights before moving on to explore other parts of Brazil. They had a whistle-stop tour of Piracicaba one day, and another day they went round Caterpillar (Jerry works for F.G. Wilson in Larne). I took them to the coffee fazenda, which makes it my third visit there. I'm becoming quite an expert on coffee production!

Carlos completed his MBA in June along with about thirty others from Caterpillar, and they had their graduation ceremony in August, in São Paulo. I thought that their group was one of many such groups and all were going to meet in S.P. for the graduation. We all dressed up to the nearly nines and in mid afternoon, got on a bus organised from Caterpillar to go to São Paulo for a 7.30 start to the ceremony. As it turned out, it was just us lot. No other groups – so why did we all have to go to São Paulo? Anyway, it was a night out, and we sat and watched thirty people receiving their certificates, and then we had champagne and nibbles. At least we didn't have to sit through hundreds of people we didn't know receiving their diplomas and shaking hands!

The weather has heated up sufficiently to make the swimming pool pleasant again. From our 12th floor eyrie we can see the cityscape gradually greening as the trees grow new spring leaves. Also, splashes of colour appear here and there and stay for several days then fade as trees come into bloom. We are keeping an eye on a pair of burrowing owls in the hopes that soon the babies will make an appearance – all grey and fluffy.

Our most recent excitement was the parade in the town centre celebrating the declaration of independence on the 7th of September. It was a public holiday. It seemed that every organisation in the city had a group parading. No fancy floats or sparkly costumes, but lots of flags and bands – mostly consisting of drums.

It started with the national anthem, then the parade. The parade was headed by two army veterans being driven in jeeps, and this was followed by a detachment of army. One thing I did notice was that the ropes cordoning off the pavement from the street were green and yellow – the Brazilian colours!

It started punctually at 9.00 a.m., which must be a record. Things in Brazil tend to start late! It was scheduled to continue until mid-day. We left at about 10.00 a.m. and people were still arriving to watch it. (Maybe they were certain the parade would get off to a late start!) The better prepared came with drinks and nibbles, though there were street vendors providing such things.

There are going to be local council elections here in October, and candidates have had posters out since we arrived back in August. I don't know how many council members there are, but there seem to be an awful lot of candidates. There are people standing at traffic lights waving large flags emblazoned with the names and numbers of their preferred candidate on them. Last Sunday as we were enjoying a drink of Garapa (sugar cane juice) from our friendly vendor, a truck came past plastered with posters, blaring music and with a group of (probably students) doing some sort of song and dance routine in the back, all to advertise a candidate. Another candidate had four or five students doing a circus act at traffic lights to promote himself. Never a dull moment, but to have to keep up the pace for two months must be hard going. I saw an article in the paper about candidates and their personal trainers who advise them on keeping fit and eating the right sort of diet. Can you imagine Ian Paisley with a personal trainer going to the sports centre for a daily workout?!

I learned something else this week! The leaves of the cinnamon tree are just as aromatic as the bark! – but it is the bark only that is used to make the spice we know! Sarah's swimming teacher has a cinnamon tree in her garden, and when she feels a sore throat coming on she makes a tea out of cinnamon leaves! They have much the same texture as bay leaves.

I ran away for the weekend of September 18 and left Alan and Sarah to fend for themselves! I went to a yoga seminar in São Paulo. The seminar was part of a teacher-training course, and this particular weekend they had a speaker from India. For this reason, it was open to anyone who wanted to go. My yoga teacher was going, so that made it an easy decision to go along too. We got the bus from Piracicaba at 5.30 a.m., to arrive in time for an 8.00 a.m. start! Breakfast and lunch were awfully far apart that day!

Never mind the teacher-training course; what was as much fun was that it was based in an area of São Paulo called Liberdade, which was settled by the Japanese. The street lights were pseudo Japanese lanterns, and there were shops full of strange looking food and others full of tacky Japanese souvenirs, and others full of some very nice Japanese giftware in the form of tea sets, sushi sets, rice bowls, tea cups (without handles), saki sets, fancy chopsticks, and much more. We didn't have very much time for poking round the shops, but that part of the city is worth another visit with Alan and Sarah, and without a yoga course to tie up my free time.

Another excitement in Piracicaba, was visiting the gemstone lady. She's not an ornament, but someone who deals in precious and semi-precious stones. Carlos took us. A friend of his from the U.S. wanted to buy some stones. Apparently Americans buy a lot of stones. We arrived at a block of flats, not a shop, and went to this woman's flat. There in her living room on the table she had set out for us, about a dozen small glass topped cases of semi precious stones. It is small business, which she runs from her home. I assume she has a very secure safe somewhere. We didn't see that bit. The stones were lovely. Lots of amethyst and citrine and something called amethystine, which is half citrine, half amethyst. Tourmaline does the same thing, and she had stones that were half red and half green. She also had topaz, peridot, garnet, smoky quartz, beryl, and precious stones. She showed us emeralds, aquamarine and ruby, all beautifully cut and nestling in their cases. It made me wish I used more jewellery!

Discovering Peru

We have set a departure date for mid December but there is a lot to do before then. We will be returning home to Ireland for the holidays, but before that we are planning a 'look-see' trip to India, as Alan is considering transferring there with Caterpillar. On another note, as I said to Alan recently, we can't live in South America for three years without taking a trip to Peru to experience the magnificence of Machu Picchu. He agreed, and so it was settled. October would be the month for making this journey!

It was an eight-day whistle-stop tour, taking in the major tourist spots, and so it was fairly hectic. We left Piracicaba on a Wednesday night to drive to São Paulo. We had to be at the airport at 7.00 a.m., so we decided to stay in the city for the night, as we've done before to avoid having to drive down early in the morning. São Paulo never stops. The ring road follows along the River Tietê, which encircles the city almost completely. There is a big project on at the moment to dredge it and tidy up the banks to stop it flooding so much. It seems the work goes on 24 hours a day. When we were driving along the ring road at about 10.00 p.m., we saw a long queue of lorries waiting to be loaded with all the stuff that had been dredged out of the river during the day.

Bright and early the next morning we were met at the airport by the tour company rep with our final tour details and three more travel bags. We now have quite a collection of shoulder bags and small backpacks. Check in, hang around, explore the airport a bit – the usual sort of thing – but the flight left on time, and after about four hours, we were landing in Lima, Peru. From the air you can really appreciate how vast and empty the country is. There is no sign of human habitation for miles, but there are signs that humans have been there. Brazil has a reddish soil, which gradually became more yellow as we approached Peru.

Then the hills started. Settlements were in valleys with a patchwork of fields in the valley bottoms. Peru had a dry landscape – as seen from the sky, rivers were a narrow line meandering in a much wider bed. They probably fill up during the wet season. Higher up the hills, the settlements were surrounded by a patchwork of brown fields, and on the slopes there seemed to be almost the memory of cultivation. The shape of fields was still there but they were a bit indistinct. It was an arid looking landscape. As we continued on, valleys became deeper. To the right of the plane (north) were jagged snowy mountains. To the left – endless brown hills/mountains cut by deep valleys.

We flew over a vast lake. I think it was probably Lake Titicaca, as there isn't any other sizeable body of water in that region. We flew over more dramatic deep valleys and jagged peaks, some with a dusting of snow. Then we saw a large city surrounded by a patchwork of green fields. Other than oases of cultivated green here and there, it was a dry, brown landscape. I wish I had had a topographical map with me at the time so that I could determine where we were by matching the landscape seen below. I think we must have flown west from São Paulo and then turned north to follow up the Peruvian coast for quite awhile – a coastline of more nothingness.

And so to terra firma, and there was someone to meet us and take us to our hotel. Next day was a city tour. Lima is an unprepossessing sort of place. When we were there the weather was grey with practically no sun. We learned that it is almost permanently shrouded in mist in the winter months, and it *never* rains.

Coastline at Lima, Peru

The cold-water Humboldt current that comes up from the south is responsible for the mist, which I gather is a feature of much of the west coast of South America. Lima is built on top of cliffs approximately 150 metres high, which are comprised of fist sized rounded stones embedded in a greyish-brown soil. The beaches reflect this topography and are not very appealing in the way that one usually thinks a beach should be.

The temperature was not particularly warm (about 18 to 20° C). The surfers, all in wet suits, enjoyed the waves, though. Apart from them, there was little beach activity. There is no palm-fringed paradise here. I'm sure it's a different scene in the summertime, though. Maybe when the mist clears, the beaches fill up. Paragliders take advantage of the up draught from the cliffs. There is a pervasive grey/brown dust over everything, no doubt blown from the cliffs by this same up draught.

About eleven percent of the country is coastal strip, roughly 60 percent is mountainous and the rest is Amazon jungle. Statistics didn't say how much was desert. Lima has 50 percent unemployment. There was a huge migration of the rural population to the cities some fifteen years back because of terrorism, but some of those are drifting back to the country again now that the terrorist leaders have been imprisoned.

Those of Spanish descent, the Criollos, tend to hold themselves aloof from the indigenous population. In truth, Peru has two flags. One is the official flag with its red and white vertical stripes with a coat of arms in the middle, which is recognised by the Criollos and internationally. The other has the seven colours of the rainbow in horizontal stripes, which are the colours of the Quechua peoples who consider themselves descendants of the Incas. (Inca simply means King!)

Lima has some attractive old buildings from the colonial period, but not much else to offer.

The Spanish took over around the year 1500, wrecking the Inca civilisation and stealing all their gold. There are Moorish influences in some of the architecture and decoration from Spain's Moorish period. Spain seems to have brought a much stronger religious influence than Portugal brought to Brazil, but then I haven't done the same sort of tourist trip to Brazil and been shown all the churches in the capital. Trouble is Brazil's capital kept changing!

We visited a well-preserved church that was formerly a monastery, and which had been built over the original cemetery of Lima. It had a seventeenth century library with huge leather bound hand scribed books and numerous other small (leather bound) volumes.

There were lovely Moorish tiles in the cloister and that intricate geometric Moorish woodwork in the cupola (made of Panamanian cedar). In the catacombs under the church, they had arranged all the bones from the cemetery on shelves and in a couple of large holes! It was all very neat and tidy.

After our city tour, we were taken to the Museu de Oro – the Gold Museum. Right enough there was a vast array of Inca and other gold bits and pieces: plates, jewellery, drinking vessels, some textile items, pottery, bone, but the museum was also home to an enormous collection of weapons and uniforms from all over the world, not to mention saddles and stirrups and spurs as well. It was too much to take in.

After that we were taken to the Parque de Amor – the park of love, a small Gaudi-esque (like Barcelona) style park with a huge sculpture of a couple kissing. The sculpture is appropriately titled 'The Longest Kiss in the World'. The park is situated on the cliff top overlooking the sea.

Parque de Amor, Lima, Peru

Car horns are used liberally in Lima. This is in stark contrast to Brazil, where car horns are seldom used and then mostly as an appreciation of the girls walking along the pavement! We got a bit fed up with the tooting taxis. We were obviously tourists, and the taxis cruising round the place would slow down and toot their horns as if to say, 'Do you want a taxi?'

Buses seemed to be large minibuses, with their destinations painted on the front and along the sides, but there seemed to be few official bus stops. As far as we could make out, you get on and off the bus wherever it suits you!

Most of the houses in the poorer sections of town are unfinished. Many have no roofs; they build as and when they can afford to and add another story or a roof. As it doesn't rain, lack of a roof would not be a big problem.

We found a small street market selling Peruvian crafts – lots of alpaca (and other) woollies, stalls with jewellery, leather, decorated gourds, and all reasonably priced. We decided it was worth another visit on our way back from Machu Picchu before returning to Brazil. No point carrying more stuff all round Peru!

Our next stop was the city of Cusco. We had a 7.30 a.m. pick up from our hotel in Lima to go to the airport for our flight departing at around 9.20 or thereabouts. Lima airport was hiving with people - mostly tourists, I think, and all seemed to be trying to get to Cusco. There seemed to be a flight every 20 minutes to Cusco! I think it was just a morning phenomenon, with all the package tours getting their tourists to Cusco in time to do a city tour in the afternoon. It was a 55-minute flight, going from about 200 feet to about 12,000 feet in that short space of time. We landed in brilliant sunshine, a marked contrast to the gloomy mist of Lima. We were taken to a very nice hotel and welcomed with a cup of coca tea - coca being the leaf that the Indians chew for energy. It is supposed to help with altitude sickness. It didn't taste of anything much to me, but Alan thought it was revolting.

Cusco is very much a tourist town, with hotels and gift shops all over the place. And yes, we did have a city tour scheduled for the afternoon. Knowledge of Inca history seems to date from 1500, which was when the Spanish arrived. They seem to have stripped all the gold and silver items from everywhere, brought Christianity with them and built their own churches, which, come the big earthquake in 1650 - did not survive. They neglected to look at local building techniques that had been used long before they got here. With local building techniques, apart from having no mortar and the stones fitting tightly together, everything is built to lean inwards, supporting itself on itself. Doorways do not have vertical sides, but lean inwards. It is unique and ingenious, no doubt brought about by years of experience with the vagaries of the region.

Inca architecture - note the unique sloping design of the doorway and the niches cut into the walls.

The Quechua people consider themselves to be direct descendants of the Incas. Our guide was Quechua and full of interesting snippets of information. He seemed to speak a multitude of languages. We heard him speaking Spanish, English, French, and Italian, as well as Quechua, of course, but I didn't hear him speaking German.

After looking at churches and old streets in Cusco, we then went to some ruins close to Machu Picchu. How on earth did those builders work the stones so that they fitted so closely together? I say stones, but they are actually more like mammoth blocks, cut to whatever shape was required - cut to go round corners, cut to accommodate a doorway on the corner, and of course, cut to fit on top of the stone underneath. Current thinking is that they used the stone available on site so to speak, rather than hauling it from some distant place. No matter the explanation, it evokes tremendous admiration for the work involved.

At every tourist stop, we were besieged by the local populace selling anything from sweets and paintings to shawls and rugs. There were also children in traditional dress clutching lambs or young llamas or alpacas, and for a small fee you could photograph them. Women in traditional dress doing some traditional craft would also pose for us.

At one point our bus stopped a little further down the hill from the usual tourist stop (so that we could admire the view), and within seconds, a group of Indians came running down the hill to pose for us. I noticed that they were all female, and our guide, in response to my question as to why this was so, said the men and boys were out in the fields working.

One thing that I did notice was how clear the air was; clear and cool. There are wonderful vistas of distant mountains. I was also aware of the reduced oxygen content too, being at a higher altitude (about 7,000 feet).

The next day we headed to the focal point of our trip to Peru: Machu Picchu! We had an early start. The train left at 6.15 a.m., and the journey took four hours. The train had to zigzag to get out of the hole that the city of Cusco lies in.

Cusco in a hole!

We trundled along for awhile, and then the train stopped. We trundled along in the other direction for a bit and the train stopped again. Then we trundled the other way again, and so on, climbing higher with each change of direction. There are no fences, walls or barriers of any kind separating the railway from the rest of the world. Anyone and anything can wander onto the tracks.

Once out of the city 'basin', the train then trundles along the bottom of a fairly wide valley, one that is well cultivated and surrounded by hills rather than mountains. I use the word trundled because we were not gliding along at high speed on a super modern train, though if you take the posh scenic train with see-through roof, you might glide a bit more smoothly – but that of course costs a lot more. We were on the 'backpacker' train, not the 'smart suitcase' train.

I saw potatoes, oats, barley, maize and onions being cultivated, and other crops that I couldn't identify, and there were cows, sheep, pigs and chickens wandering about freely. The houses are made of mud bricks and have tiled roofs. Nearly all the houses also had a small cross flanked either side by two ceramic bulls (for protection, presumably). We rattled through a couple of villages and a more sizeable town. In one, a fruit and vegetable market was just setting up with produce spread out on the ground and the stallholders squatting beside it. The railway shared the valley with a good road and an ever-expanding river. We were going gradually downhill. Every bit of flat land was cultivated, and there men and women working the fields, the women in the traditional dress of skirts, cardigan and bowler, with their hair in two plaits down their backs. We saw no tractors being used to work the fields. Ploughing is done by hand or with cows.

As the valley narrowed, the mountains became higher and craggy with snow on their tops. At one point the train had to do another zig and zag to get a bit lower. As we dropped down, the vegetation changed: it became more luxuriant, with more trees. The valley sides were steeper, and there was little valley bottom.

The mountains were the soaring crags one expects in the Andes.

The end of our rail journey brought us to Aguas Calientes – which translates as 'hot water', so I guess there must be some thermal springs in the region, but that is not what we were here for. Aguas Calientes is another tourist town, but much more ramshackle than Cusco. We clambered down off the train and walked along beside the tracks (no platforms) past all sorts of stalls selling tourist tack. At the level crossing there were lots of buses waiting. We did have a guide – she had identified herself to us on the train and we were to meet her again outside Machu Picchu. The bus journey up to it was quite dramatic – about 20 to 25 minutes of hairpins up what seemed like a cliff face! Well, it wasn't quite that steep, but there were a lot of hairpin bends. Hiram Bingham would never have found the place in 1911 if some local shepherd boy hadn't taken him there!

Always plenty of tourists at the entrance to Machu Picchu

Our guide guided us in past the ticket booth and then promised to produce an English-speaking guide for those in the group who wanted English. The buses deposited us beside a restaurant outside the ticket booth, and at first, we just stood there wondering where the ruins were! Eventually we learned that if we followed a path round the edge of the mountain, it would take us directly there. We did exactly that, and as you round the bend – the amazing vista unfolds in front of you, and you are looking at Machu Picchu.

It is perched on the top of a pinnacle in the midst of towering mountains and steep sided gorges. Most photos you see of Machu Picchu show the ruins, but they do not give any hint of the dramatic setting. I would go as far as to say that it is awesome.

We had time to stand and admire the view and wonder whether we were going to get soaked as it was trying to rain. To add to the atmosphere, while we were waiting for our guide to appear, there were a couple of thunderclaps, which echoed round the mountains. (Thankfully, the sun came out soon thereafter, and it quickly became quite hot.) There were lots of terraces, complete with llamas and alpacas that live there…

...and a vast array of ruined buildings. As it was with the ruins around Cusco, the construction design seemed to follow the earthquake rules. Apparently, the quality of the stonework of each building varied with the economic status of the occupant, as is so often the case.

It seems that at one time there were a number of priests and a lot of serving people, and presumably others of different status in between. It is solstice oriented, with a sun temple, and elsewhere a huge 'energy' stone, which you could touch to recharge your energy. I couldn't feel anything while touching it, but I *was* aware of strong energy whilst approaching it.

The Incas used a triptych design to symbolise the three worlds: The top level, the spirit world, is represented by a condor; the earth level, the living world, is represented by a puma; and the world of the dead is represented by a serpent. This shape turns up all over the place, especially as pendants and earrings for tourists!

Servants' quarters and a solstice stone with windows aligned in the walls. Note the gorge far below.

If we'd had the time, I would have liked to visit the temple of the moon perched on a pinnacle high above. I also would have liked to have lingered in order to appreciate the surroundings more fully, but lunch was waiting for us in a hotel at the bottom and we had to be at the train station at three o'clock.

We headed back to a bus and boarded it, and soon we were winding down the mountainside to our lunch, which had been organised for us at a hotel in Aguas Calientes. With lunch consumed it was time to head for the train. There was a uniformed official waiting at the railway tracks to direct us to a gathering/ ticket inspection point. The route to this took us through an absolute warren of souvenir stalls. Prices were actually quite reasonable given that they had a captive market, but I guess they know that they have to compete with Cusco even if it is a four-hour train ride away. We did spend some money, and then it was back on to the train to trundle and rattle the long route back to Cusco in the gathering dusk.

A bus met us at the station and tried to take us back to the hotel, but when we arrived at the road our hotel was located on, we found it closed to traffic. We told the bus driver it was no problem; we would get out and walk because we could see the hotel from where he had stopped, and off we went. There was a religious festival about to start. People were making pictures on the road – literally *on* the road, large pictures, spreading half way across the road (if not more) using coloured sawdust and flowers. Various businesses along the street (including our hotel) were responsible for the pictures, and most had erected an altar on the pavement with a figure of the Virgin Mary and other religious accoutrements all decorated with flowers and ribbons to match the colours used in the picture on the road.

As I mentioned, our hotel was very nice, and we arrived each evening to find the light in our room switched on, the bedding turned back and a sweet waiting on the pillow! We noticed something quite interesting. In hotels, one sees signs saying, 'In case of fire, do not use lift'. They go a step further here: 'In case of fire and earthquake, do not use lift'! Another thing I noticed all round the town is that you can find Internet access everywhere. Entrepreneurs are cashing in on all these tourists wanting to keep in touch with the world and their families back home.

Next day, we had another early start. We took a bus from Cusco to Puno on the shores of Lake Titicaca. It was supposed to leave at 7.30, but it was after 8.00 a.m. when we left. This was a tourist bus – air-conditioned and very comfortable seats – and full of tourists, most of them Italian. It was a nine-hour trip, but with stops on the way to look at various sites and to have lunch. We were driving alongside a river – and we were assured that this river went on to join the Amazon.

The valley bottom was cultivated, and we saw some ploughing being done by ox-drawn ploughs. Both men and women were working in the fields, breaking up the soil with a mattock, which is similar to a pickaxe. Herds of cows and sheep were being minded, usually by women. There was evidence of old terracing and fields on the lower slopes. The women work in their traditional dress of skirts, peasant-style blouses and bowler hats – and usually sandals or bare feet. Quite often, they have a bundle in a shawl on their backs. Our next stop was to see more ruins, Inca in origin. There was a temple, housing and a storage area. Much of the building was done with mud bricks reinforced with straw and cactus juice, of all things! To preserve their food supplies, the Incas used an herb called muña, which repels insects because they cannot stand the smell of it. Our guide dispatched a local in search of some of this herb so that we could smell it. I found it a fairly pleasant smell, reminiscent of mint. It was used in the preservation of mummies as well.

Temple ruins and dwellings associated with the temple

The women minding the tourist stalls outside the ruins wore an all black costume embroidered with flowers, with flat black hats perched atop their heads so precariously that the slightest puff of wind would send their hats flying. A woman was weaving, with her loom pegged out on the ground. Another woman was spinning using a drop spindle.

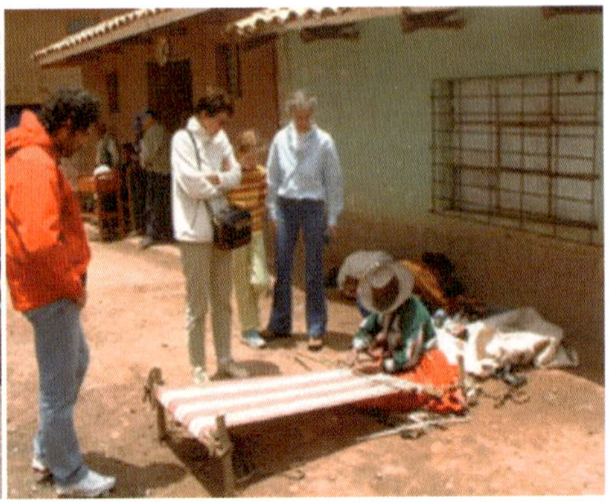

Moving on a bit in the bus, we saw people washing llama/alpaca pelts in the river and laying them out to dry on the bank. Another group were washing their woven goods, presumably getting them ready to sell. Another thing we noticed from the bus was that a lot of the roofs are made of what appeared to be galvanised tin. Whatever it is, it glitters silver in the sun.

Next stop – another enterprising family business where you could interact with tame baby llamas, alpaca and a vicuña, and in a shed, some guinea pigs! There were also lots of stalls selling things. The 'boss' did his bit by blowing his 'horn', which was a conch shell (quite noisy). Sarah purchased a small 'patchwork' rug made from scraps of very soft llama and alpaca skin, designed to depict a llama.

Vicuñas at the back, Llamas in front ... and guinea pigs!

Our lunch stop was specially organised, not at a restaurant, but by a caterer contracted by the tour company to produce lunch every day, and very nice it was: hearty and delicious salad, rice and chicken stew, with coca tea if we wanted it. The pudding was a very sweet rice pudding made with caramelised condensed milk.

Once we were all back on the bus, we headed to our next stop, which was also the highest point of our journey at about 4,300 metres, which is somewhere in the region of 13,000 feet. All the buses stop there for the thriving market of tourist goods, and this benefits the local population, too, as they depend on this income.

Market on the roof of the world

This is the start of the *altiplano*. At last, I know what they mean by altiplano, other than its being a flat area high up in the Andes. The Andes divide at this point into two ridges, and the altiplano is that section enclosed between the ridges. We had climbed (in the bus of course) 800 metres in about half an hour to reach this point. The landscape is very different. No trees, just flat rough grassland where very little will grow. Night time temperatures can drop to -15°C. Quinoa grows. The seeds are edible and used much like rice. Otherwise, the main activity is herding llamas, alpacas, cows, sheep, and anything that can be herded. There is no sign of any irrigation as there is in the lower region nearer Cusco, but if little grows, there is no point.

It is a bleak landscape. Flat and bare with a harsh climate - very hot during the day and very cold at night, yet people live here. They chew coca leaf for energy and endurance and drink alcohol for warmth - at least that is what our guide told us.

The houses are mud brick with straw roofs. There is no electricity and no form of heating as there is very little to burn. The houses are grouped in clusters, usually near water. There are quite a number of small lakes (with ducks) up here. We saw many groups of animals munching their way across the landscape, each group with a minder – again, usually a woman. There are pumas (amongst other things) in the mountains, so the animals need a protector. They are driven home again in the evening into an enclosure of some sort.

A railway runs a regular service across the altiplano from Cusco to Puno, mainly because of the number of tourists visiting this region. The rail service from Puno to Ariqueipa (further west) runs intermittently, depending on when there are enough goods to take in that direction

We eventually arrived in Puno; elevation 3,800 metres. (Our guide was determined that we should know what height we were at!) We dropped down rapidly after passing through a fairly ramshackle town called Juliaca, and Lake Titicaca came into view. Water everywhere, as far as you can see.

Lake Titicaca

Then we headed down into Puno, the town where our hotel was located. We were beginning to wonder what our hotel would be like, as the town is filled with the same half-finished houses we had seen in Lima and Juliaca, but as it turned out, the Hotel Sonesta Posada del Inca was very posh and right on the shores of the lake – an oasis of wealth and affluence in an otherwise bleak area. It felt wrong to be tucked away in this luxury hotel surrounded by such poverty. I almost felt guilty staying there having come through country which must have one of the harshest lifestyles on the planet.

We took advantage of the luxury, and showered and had dinner in the hotel. It was on the lakeshore and had an old ship, which we could visit, moored at the end of the pier. There was a tourist stall (of course) at the end of the dining area attended by two ladies in full costume complete with bowler hats. The hats always look too small and seem to be perched on top of their heads. Their skirts had six layers, starting short and getting longer to just below knee length.

Our reason for coming to Puno was to visit the Indians who live on floating islands in the lake. The lake is the highest navigable lake in the world with an area of 8000 square kilometres. Two-thirds of the lake is in Peru, and the other third is in Bolivia.

This duck looks like a coot, and this one is an Andean blue-billed duck.

We were sitting outside the front door of the hotel the next morning, waiting for our guide to pick us up for our trip out to the islands. She surprised us by appearing from inside the hotel! She had come by boat, and it was waiting for us at the pier. So much the better; we were being given a private tour, just us. The islands were only about 20 minutes away by boat (and this was a chug-chug boat, not a speedboat.) These islands are the most touristy, being closest to the town.

There are other islands further out, some of which you can stay overnight on. You can do what they call a 'home stay' and spend the night with a local family. It's a B & B sort of arrangement with dinner in the evening, so you can get some idea of what life is like for them. We stopped at what I would describe as 'the tourist island' where one can look at the reed huts, buy souvenirs (which we did) and learn about the reed, called *totora*, that is so vital to the locals' way of life.

They make floating islands out of this reed starting with clumps that have the roots still attached and then piling layers of reed on top. A fresh layer of reed has to be added twice a week, and an island lasts for about five years before a new one has to be built, starting from scratch all over again. They make their boats out of it as well, and the boats used to be made entirely of reed, which had to be replaced every seven months – until they discovered plastic bottles.

Now they use plastic bottles as an inner core for buoyancy and the reeds serve as an outer layer. The boats now last about two years before they have to be replaced. For a fee you can take a trip in a reed boat; this was more or less expected, though you could refuse, of course.

We were taken to another island by a reed boat that was rowed, or perhaps sculled is a better term, by a solid lass complete with petticoats and hat.

The boats have one large oar out the back to propel and steer. Hard work I would say. We saw other small conventional rowing boats. They row them standing up facing the direction of travel – quite a contrast to our sitting down with our backs facing the direction we're heading. Our chug-chug boat and guide followed a bit later.

This larger island had a school and a church as well as houses, and lots more souvenirs. The church would have held about four people kneeling down, but I guess services are mainly open air. It is certainly warm enough to do so at this time of year. The school was two large huts, more substantial than reeds, and the children were well turned out in their school uniforms. They were oblivious to the tourists snapping away. Each school day the children come from all the neighbouring islands, and the teachers come from Puno.

We passed a hospital on a separate island close by. The previous president of Peru did a lot for the Indians, providing the hospital with solar panels so they have electric light. However, it is still not an easy life, so the tourists provide a welcome source of income.

They domesticate ducks and cormorants. The cormorants serve a unique purpose: They are used to 'cure' epilepsy. Apparently, people come from miles around for the remedy, which involves drinking the blood of these cormorants.

They eat the reed, or at least the base of it. We tried some and it was very juicy - not unlike cucumber, but chewier. It is full of calcium and iodine, and certainly they all have very good teeth.

When we were ready to leave, our boat took us back to shore. Normally it would have taken us back to the hotel, but we asked to be taken to the town. It saved us taking a taxi to the town later on, even if it did mean carrying our souvenirs with us. Puno is a small town with a cathedral, a town square, and a 'tourist street' full of restaurants and souvenir shops.

We chose a restaurant and ordered our meal. Guinea pig was on the menu! We learned that Guinea pig is typically served on special occasions, such as birthdays or when guests come. Tourists are considered guests, and so most restaurants serve it. We ordered half a roast guinea pig. Sarah ate most of it. Unfortunately, it looked like - well - a guinea pig, complete with ears and teeth. Alan couldn't bring himself to eat it, but Sarah has never known guinea pigs as pets. As far as I could see there wasn't much eating on it. There seemed to be an awful lot of bone. I ordered vegetable soup with quinoa.

With lunch over, there was not much else to draw our attention, so we decided to make our way back to the hotel on foot - a walk of about three kilometres. It was interesting, getting away from the tourist bit and passing various street markets selling all sorts of things. There were bicycle taxis and three wheeled motorbike taxis, which all slowed down and offered us a ride.

We saw in the distance someone herding their sheep on a bit of grass amongst the houses. Old habits die hard I guess.

We knew that the railway passed the front of the hotel – it literally crosses the road in front of the gate – so when we found the railway, we did what the locals do and followed along the tracks. The service is infrequent, at best, so there was no danger. There were people herding their animals along the track, and at one point we saw someone herding a sow and half a dozen piglets!

One of the shepherds seemed to be a teenager just out of school, still wearing his school uniform and with homework in hand. Schools seem to finish at lunchtime, maybe to allow the children to go home and help out with whatever their families do. All were well turned out in smart uniforms. What a land of contrasts, with our luxury hotel in the midst of all this.

Literally outside the gates of the hotel were people herding animals, washing clothes and drying them on stones, and someone washing her hair, all at a water spout close to the hotel. A big contrast!

We didn't have the enthusiasm to go back into town to look for a cheaper evening meal, and so we ate at the hotel again. The hotel was putting on a 'floor show' for entertainment this evening. It consisted of a group of musicians and several dancers showing various folk costumes and dances.

The next day was our last day at the hotel, so we had free time to do as we pleased, which was quite pleasant, as up until now our time had more or less been scheduled doing this trip or that trip. We lounged in the sun for awhile. The air temperature is cool, but the sun is strong at this elevation, especially this time of year. We then visited the boat moored at the end of the hotel jetty. The boat had been made in England (sometime around 1890), sailed to the nearest seaport on the Pacific coast, dismantled and brought up the Andes in pieces using mules, or for large pieces, slaves. Some undertaking! An interesting note is that they weren't allowed to bring the guns up. Now there is a restoration project afoot masterminded by – who else? – an Englishwoman! The hotel also has a letter from Prince Philip giving his support for the idea. They plan to use it as a pleasure boat for giving tours around the lake.

We decided to go for a walk along the road outside the hotel to photograph the contrast between rich and poor in Puno. We also found several small restaurants close by where we could have eaten last night instead of paying an arm and a leg at the hotel. Guess where we had our lunch!

A large bus picked us up after lunch and took us to Juliaca, which is where the airport is that we would be flying out of on our journey homeward. (We had passed through here on the way to Puno.) Juliaca's reason for being such a thriving centre on the edge of an area of subsistence survival is that it is a commercial centre for goods coming from Bolivia, such as fruits and vegetables, which are then shipped by plane, train or lorry to the rest of Peru.

Driving along the road towards Juliaca, we saw schoolchildren in their neat uniforms, going home, walking or cycling. On the outskirts of Juliaca we saw people herding their animals just as they must always have done even though they had migrated to the city. We had to take a detour in the city because of road works. This took us through a more commercial area than we would otherwise have seen, which was much more interesting. As I said, the bus was large, far too large when there were just the three of us. It was interesting trying to drive through some of the streets. Again, I felt a bit uncomfortable. The bus shouted louder than words that here were more of those wealthy tourists.

There were masses of the three-wheeled-cycle taxis – rickshaws for want of a better description. Our guide told us there were about 8000 of them in this relatively small city. One reason is that the terrain is completely flat. We passed along one street where the fruit and vegetables were stacked on stalls on the pavement, and people had to walk in the road. It was also teeming with people. It would have been interesting to stop and poke around in some of the shops – but alas no, we were foreign tourists, cocooned from the realities of Peruvian life by a big air-conditioned bus.

Ah well. We had chosen a package tour because of the limited time we had available. Our guide saw us check in at the airport to make sure all went smoothly and then left us to watch the world go by. There was a market of tourist goods the other side of the parking area, which we visited. The Juliaca Airport is not a very busy airport, which always makes departures easier. There were two flights on the departure board while we were there. We had a drink and smiled to ourselves about the 'Safe area in case of earthquake' sign, and it was soon time to board the plane. It was a routine flight, and our original guide in Lima met us at the airport there and took us back to the same hotel as before. We had a snack round the corner from the hotel that night, as none of us were particularly hungry.

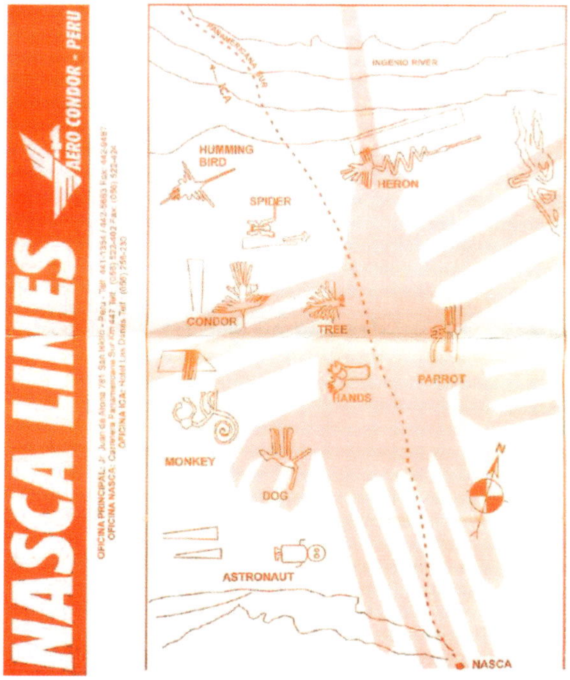

We had an early start again the next day to see the Nazca lines. The Nazcas were yet another ancient people who lived in the area in times long past. They made drawings in the desert – or rather outlines – of animals and other shapes, which can only be seen from the air. How did they do it? There are all sorts of theories, which include visits from extra-terrestrial beings, but no one has an answer yet.

An old Dakota type aircraft took us, along with about forty Japanese tourists, from Lima to Ica. There, we landed at what turned out to be a private airstrip, and after about half an hour, we were directed on to a couple of fifteen-seater planes for the flight over the outlines. It took about 40 minutes flying time to get there, 20 minutes flying over the outlines, and 40 minutes back again. We approached at a high level and had to wait for clearance from the control tower at Nazca. Other tourist flights operate out of that town.

Clearance obtained, we descended to viewing level and circled over the various outlines. The pilot circled first one way, then the other so that everyone on the plane could take photographs from their window without having to peer over someone's head. He also kept up a running commentary (in three languages) about what we were going to see and when and where to look. It was fascinating. It is a brown arid landscape with large triangular areas cleared on the desert floor with etchings of these line drawings. Unfortunately, the photos we took aren't great, but I have included a copy of the tourist handout showing the different figures.

Cutting through the middle of all this, straight, as far as the eye could see, was the Pan-American highway – totally devoid of any traffic.

Back to the airport at Ica, we wandered round the mini zoo to meet Pepe, a large condor, and then returned to a bus to be taken to a hotel for lunch and afterwards a brief city tour with a stop at a museum and a visit to an oasis.

This whole thing is obviously somebody's private enterprise. The airline is called Air Condor, and it seems to consist of one Dakota, two fifteen-seater aircraft and a couple of smaller aircraft. The pilots were all properly turned out in black trousers, white shirts and gold trimmed epaulettes – even for the small craft. Our pilot spoke not only Spanish and English, but also Japanese! That shows just how many Japanese tourists they get.

It was interesting to see the oasis, having never seen such a thing before. It is now set up as a tourist resort, but there it was, a pool of water surrounded by high sand dunes.

Back to the airstrip, back on to the Dakota, back to Lima where our trusty guide was waiting to take us back to the hotel. It is about a 45-minute trip from the centre of Lima to the airport, and it would have made more sense for us to stay closer to the airport as our activities for the couple of days centred round the airport, so to speak. Maybe the tour company considers there to be nothing suitable for tourists in that area.

We took advantage of the fact that we were in the same hotel and went back to the market we had found at the beginning of our Peruvian journey, and this time we made a few purchases. We ate a Chinese meal at a restaurant nearby, which we couldn't finish, and took the remainder with us with the intention of giving it to one of the beggars in the street. Murphy's Law prevailed, however. We didn't pass any on the way to the hotel, but I saw a family a bit further down the street – a woman and two small children – who looked as though they needed a good meal. Alan took the food to them and said they were delighted to have it.

We went back to the airport the next day for our return flight to Brazil. Our guide told us that the airline Lan Peru, which we had flown with to Cusco and from Juliaca, had collapsed the previous day – which was the day after we had come back from Juliaca. Were we lucky or what!? There were lots of stranded tourists, and thankfully, we weren't among them. Our guide said that his company were having a meeting later that day to decide whether to charter a plane to rescue the tourists on their books. The airport was quiet compared to our previous visits, but whether that was because of the collapsed airline or because it was later in the day, I don't know. There were lots of Lan Peru staff about, most seemingly busy, but some standing in groups talking, no doubt concerned about future employment.

It was a four-hour flight back to São Paulo, but with the time difference, we arrived six hours after taking off. We spent the night in São Paulo again, and the next day visited the Japanese quarter so Alan and Sarah could see it. And finally, we were along the road to home.

It was a hectic trip. I would have liked to spend more time in each place without a guide breathing down my neck, but we had booked a guided tour and so we had to go through with it, but at least I got to see Machu Picchu! For anyone going there, I would advise spending a night in the village at the foot of the mountain rather than doing the train trip there and back the same day. That way you can linger amongst the ruins that day or go back up at your leisure the next day if you want. There were also a couple of trails in the mountains, which would have been fun to explore.

So now we're back home, but only for six days and then we're off on our travels again – to India! But that is yet another story. I don't know when I will tell it. Life is getting a bit hectic here with so much packing to do and French lessons for Sarah (she'll be attending a French school in India), on top of all our usual activities – and lots of rain!

Our Life in Brazil Comes to a Close

We are starting to wrap things up here in Brazil in more than one sense of the word. I finished my 'magnus opus' at my art class. I have been painting a picture of the Engenho – the disused sugar mill which is such a feature of Piracicaba. (I've only been at it for the last six months.) We have seen quite a number of paintings of it and wanted one for ourselves, but never quite found the right one, so I painted one at my art class! I went about it 'tijolo por tijolo', as my teacher put it, which means 'brick by brick'.

It will be displayed as part of the Christmas exhibition in a couple of weeks' time along with the abstract I have been doing in acrylics. I chose acrylics because I wanted the experience of using them and because I needed a medium that would dry quickly enough to be packed up in December, and oils wouldn't do – even in this climate!

We finally managed to get a picture of sugar cane being burnt. This was taken from our balcony. Needless to say, we had a sprinkling of 'black snow' shortly afterwards as all the charred bits floated our way. I suppose we had to experience one last snowfall before departing Brazil!

We did another calango, one that we had done before, but it was one of my favourites, as the scenery is more varied: less sugar cane and more ups and downs. It also took us through/alongside what one might describe as smallholdings rather than huge farms with endless acres of sugar, which gives one a delightful glimpse of rural life.

It was fun talking to the cows and pigs, but we eventually found our way out into the ubiquitous sugar cane. It really does dominate the landscape. I had to take a photo of our last calango andando. We've had a lot of good times and interesting conversations on these walks.

As our time in Piracicaba draws to a close, there seems to be so much to do and less than a month to do it in. Time is just flying, and everything is blurring together.

We are starting on the round of farewells. Bill, the president of the Caterpillar plant here, is leaving too, going back to the United States to take up a post further up the corporate ladder. It seems like an offer he couldn't refuse. I know that, like us, he would prefer to stay on here in Piracicaba. A dinner had been organised for him at a fancy restaurant in a small town nearby, and we were among the selected guests. He was presented with a large aerial photo of the Caterpillar plant.

Alan had a farewell party organised for him at the Caterpillar Club, and a good time was had by all. We are planning our own farewell at the Cat Club, with George doing the barbecue. Never mind the meat; he does the most delicious barbecued bananas with syrup and ice cream.

Sarah had another ballet performance at the local theatre. It was created by her teachers to accommodate all the classes. Her class were costumed as Spanish dolls. As before, it was a superb performance, given the age of the dancers. We didn't go out for ice cream afterwards like last year. There is just too much to do and not enough time to do it, or so it seems, and we were ready for bed after the performance.

My choir will be singing at the school's graduation ceremony again. It is an annual event, and dress is what I would term formal though they just call it 'social dress' here. I remember the girls all looking stunning kitted out in their formal dresses last year, and I'm certain it will be no different this year. This time I am going to wear the semi sparkly backless number I bought a year ago because I just love the styles of the evening dresses here. If I don't wear it now, I don't know when I will wear it at home in Ireland!

I have wanted to capture as many memories of Piracicaba as possible before we leave, but there just doesn't seem to be enough time or film to do so. But one shot I've wanted to capture is this one. Let me explain: There is a local sculptor here who makes *bonécas*, which translates as dolls. He makes figures out of anything he can lay his hands on and lines the riverbank with them. He usually salvages his raw material from the river. It is his statement against pollution. So far, they have survived the rise in the river, which has been quite dramatic with all the rain we've had recently. When I first saw the bonécas, it was from a distance and I wondered what all these people were doing lining the riverbank.

Another photo I just had to take is of a mural/relief that adorns the recreation area of our apartment block. It is about ten feet wide and was designed based on a photo taken from an aeroplane flying over the Andes.

For ages I thought it was just an abstract mural, but then someone told me that whoever took the photo could see the face of Christ formed by the snow on the mountains, which is why he took the picture. I looked and looked and couldn't make it out, but eventually I 'saw the light' so to speak. Now I see the face of Christ whenever I look at it and wonder why I never saw it before! I think it might be easier to see the details in a small photo as opposed to glancing at a large mural as you pass by. Can you see the face?

Below is another photo I've been meaning to take for ages but never had the camera with me at the right time when the water lilies were in bloom! I've been carrying the camera with me everywhere now to get pictures of scenes I want to paint one day.

And now it is time to say goodbye to this beautiful corner of Brazil that we have called home for three years.

Epilogue

We left Brazil in time to spend Christmas at home before moving on to India. Packing up was chaos - trying to decide what was being shipped direct to India and what was going back to Ireland to be stored until we eventually came home. Alan had planned to ship home his car – the trusty VW Beetle – and our two motorbikes, but at the last minute we were told this was not possible (in spite of having been assured earlier that there would be no problem). He had a week to find buyers for them, which he managed, and didn't get too bad a price either.

We were very impressed with the efficiency of the removals firm we hired to get all our things packed and ready to go. They wrapped and boxed everything, and transformed our chaos into neat stacks of boxes. They wrapped our furniture very professionally.

Complete transformation, from chaos to order!

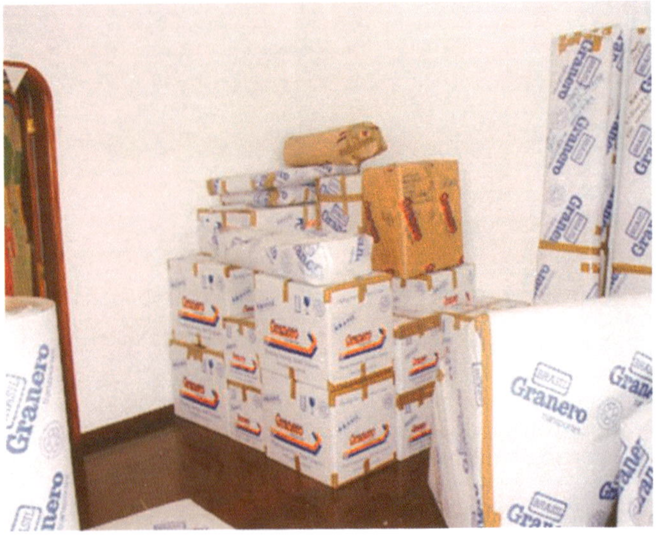

All we had to do was fill several suitcases with our personal belongings, but it seemed to take forever. We had left Sarah at a friend's house, as she would have been bored in the midst of all the packing. It was very time consuming trying to get everything fitted in. It was nine at night, time to pick her up, and we still weren't packed. We shoved everything in the car, picked up Sarah and drove to the hotel where we were to spend the night, looking like refugees with carrier bags and boxes along with our various suitcases. It did all fit into the cases, eventually.

Next morning, the new owner of our car collected his purchase. The driver from Caterpillar picked us up and we were on our way to the airport in São Paulo. Twenty-four hours later, we were back in Ireland, tired, cold and ready for a traditional family Christmas instead of spending it in yet another hotel in an exotic location. Brazil was now history - a series of happy memories and photographs. We would have loved to stay on, but the Brazilian government ruling is that you can only renew your two-year visa once. Our four years were nearly up and it was time to move on. India was beckoning. A small Caterpillar concern out there needed a new manager, and Alan was the man chosen for the job. We were on our way, via Ireland.

Much to Sarah's delight, we woke up to snow on Christmas day. Not a lot, but it was something we hadn't seen in a long time - white snow, that is!

She said the snow was her best Christmas present.

10976246R00158

Made in the USA
Charleston, SC
20 January 2012